Praise for Repa

"It's heartening to see the rise in pop   ss
communities gathering to collective.   ......, share technical
skills, honor value, and celebrate creativity. I hope communities can
use this book to continue building support for a repair revolution."
— **Katrina Rodabaugh,** author of *Mending Matters*

"Fixing something is one of life's great pleasures. *Repair Revolution* is
an inspirational yet practical primer on how to build and strengthen
communities, one reclaimed, repaired, or restored object at a time."
— **David Malki !,** author of *Wondermark*

"The impulse to repair is present in every part of our lives. This book
tells the important story of the people leading the repair movement."
— **Kyle Wiens,** CEO of iFixit

"A gold mine of inspiring stories, full of fascinating information and
insights — the what, who, how, where, and, crucially, why of the growing repair movement. If you want to kick-start the repair revolution in
your community, this book is a must-read."
— **Catherine Weetman,** host of the *Circular Economy* podcast
and cofounder of Rethink Global

"This book delivers good news at two important levels. It chronicles
the growing worldwide repair movement (sibling to the Maker movement) in abundant, inviting detail. And it inspires and instructs the
actual fixing of things in your life."
— **Stewart Brand,** creator of the *Whole Earth Catalog*
and author of the forthcoming book *Maintenance*

"Encountering a chair on the street one day that just needed a bit of
glue, my fixing self said, 'Someone has to do something about this!'
Taking a look around, I discovered an upwelling of energized engagement in repair in every quarter — folks organizing to help neighbors with fixes, academics conceptualizing maintenance and repair,

thought leaders rearticulating the shape of the economy, activists rattling the cage in the political arena — and it was happening across the globe. Well-researched, articulate, readable, comprehensive, and compelling, *Repair Revolution* is a very important contribution to the international repair movement and offers extensive resources for taking action."

— **Vita Wells,** founder of the Culture of Repair Project

"*Repair Revolution* appears at a critical time, as the USA must reconsider its commitment to recycling. Repair and reuse are the highest forms of recycling, as they retain the embodied energy, labor, and materials of valuable finished goods rather than raw materials. Repair and reuse enterprises provide well-paying jobs to formerly unskilled workers, reduce the waste stream, and provide good merchandise to low-income communities. *Repair Revolution* presents the what, why, and how-to of bringing repair and reuse to every town in the USA. It describes the origins, motivation, culture, and decentralized structure of this sector, whose emergence today is as important as the initial recycling revolution of the late 1960s."

— **Neil Seldman,** president of the Institute for Local Self-Reliance

REPAIR
REVOLUTION

REPAIR
REVOLUTION

HOW FIXERS ARE TRANSFORMING
OUR THROWAWAY CULTURE

JOHN WACKMAN & ELIZABETH KNIGHT

New World Library
Novato, California

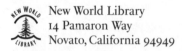

New World Library
14 Pamaron Way
Novato, California 94949

Text design by Tona Pearce Myers

Right to Repair fist logo on cover and interior courtesy of iFixit, the free repair guide. ifixit.com

Credits for photographs and illustrations can be found on pages 285–87.

Library of Congress Cataloging-in-Publication Data

Names: Wackman, John, date, author. | Knight, Elizabeth, date, author.
Title: Repair revolution : how fixers are transforming our throwaway culture / John Wackman & Elizabeth Knight.
Description: Novato, California : New World Library, 2020. | Includes bibliograph-ical references and index. | Summary: "Repair Revolution chronicles the rise of repair cafés: non-profit, volunteer organizations devoted to repairing electron-ics and household items for free. After outlining the philosophy of repair cafés, the book discusses practical details such as online repair resources, fixes for common product malfunctions, and tips for founding new repair cafés."--Provided by publisher.
Identifiers: LCCN 2019058720 (print) | LCCN 2019058721 (ebook) | ISBN 9781608686605 (paperback) | ISBN 9781608686612 (epub)
Subjects: LCSH: Repairing. | Sustainability. | Repairing--History.
Classification: LCC TT151 .W23 2020 (print) | LCC TT151 (ebook) | DDC 643/.7--dc23
LC record available at https://lccn.loc.gov/2019058720
LC ebook record available at https://lccn.loc.gov/2019058721

First printing, October 2020
ISBN 978-1-60868-660-5
Ebook ISBN 978-1-60868-661-2

Printed in Canada on 100% postconsumer-waste recycled paper

New World Library is proud to be a Gold Certified Environmentally Responsible Publisher. Publisher certification awarded by Green Press Initiative.

10   9   8   7   6   5   4   3   2   1

Contents

Experiments in Repair Culture

Let us raise a standard to which the Wise and Honest can repair.

— George Washington, 1787

U sed to be, every town had its repair shops. Everyone knew where to go when they needed something fixed. That know-how was often close at hand, practiced by parents, grandparents, aunts, uncles, neighbors, or a local "fix-it man." We can call this a remnant of the Great Depression, of course, but its roots stretch back to Benjamin Franklin's Poor Richard and the tradition of Yankee thrift.

How has our society changed? The immediate answer, almost always, is that we no longer get things repaired because ours has become a throwaway culture. The economic explanation for this is that since World War II, the world has embraced the materials economy, that is to say, a wasteful, rather than regenerative, use of precious resources.

1

As the axiom coined by Twitter cofounder Evan Williams puts it, "Convenience decides everything." The argument can't be made that this is sustainable.

But if there is a Repair Cafe or Fixit Clinic or Tool Library in your town, you have a different answer. The place to get something fixed is at the library or a church or your town hall or community center. The concept couldn't be simpler: whatever you call it, wherever it is held, a community repair event invites you to bring a beloved but broken item to be repaired for free, by an expert who is also your neighbor.

There's one catch. This is not a drop-off service. You bring your item and stay with it during the repair process. You sit down and describe what it's not doing that it's supposed to be doing, when it stopped working, and where you think the defect might be. This is not a monetary transaction — it's an interpersonal transaction.

The consumer economy is powerful. The growing repair culture is a countervailing force: community initiatives that are creative, socially vibrant platforms for building awareness about the larger challenges facing our planet.

There is something about the act of repairing that motivates and satisfies deeply felt parts of our nature. We can trace this insight back to Aristotle: one of the greatest sources of human enjoyment is being able to *enact* one's knowledge, to share what you know. The act of repairing involves "troubleshooting," which to many people is an irresistible proposition.

Repairing in Community Is Powerful

All over the world, people are pooling their resources, sharing information, and learning how to be more than just consumers. They are learning to be fixers. And they are starting to fix their world.

— Northeast Recycling Council

Repair culture is about these things: Extending the life of stuff that you care about or rely on. Feeding your curiosity about the way things work.

Using tools and using your hands. Honoring, preserving, and passing on repair know-how. Sitting elbow-to-elbow at a worktable with your neighbor. Sharing skills. Reducing waste. Making friends.

You might think that the most common comment people offer about their experience at a repair event is something like "I'm so glad they fixed it" or "It was free." But the words people use more than any other, hands down, to describe their Repair Cafe experience are "It was fun."

Almost every item people bring has meaning to them. Every item comes with a story. Laughter and tears are common. Some of the comments our customers leave are straightforward description: "Pants mended." "Clock fixed." "Toddler bike now roadworthy." "$200 printer back in service after the company said, 'Buy a new one.'" Others are more effusive: "I can't begin to tell you what an absolutely lovely and wonderful experience this has been." "There is a strong beam of hope and light coming from this space."

Every repair event is locally organized. Partners include libraries, congregations, town boards, environmental and conservation groups, Rotary Clubs, climate activists, and at least one County Emergency Communications Association. Librarians say they love repair events because they offer hands-on, intergenerational learning. Faith communities embrace the theological aspect: this is caring for creation. County waste management or resource recovery agencies recognize the value of any grassroots initiative that will help slow down the pace of waste reaching their landfills. Clubs from technical colleges and school districts bring their team spirit, and high school and college students commonly volunteer to get community service credit. Not surprisingly, the kids often end up behind the digital worktable — or with their hands on a sewing machine, some for the first time.

When journalist Harry Smith brought the *NBC Nightly News* crew to our Repair Cafe in New Paltz, New York, he beautifully interpreted what he found: "The idea is exquisitely simple: neighbor helping neighbor. They fix a lot of stuff. Things left in attics and garages. Things that just stopped working. And what we marveled at was the care, the meticulous, painstaking care that goes into every repair."

WHY WE DO IT

- To transform our throwaway culture, one beloved item at a time
- To reduce how much stuff goes into the waste stream
- To preserve repair know-how and skills, and pass them on (re-skilling!)
- To show the people who have this knowledge that they are valued
- To feed our curiosity about the way things work, be creative, and have fun!
- To build community resilience

An Idea from Amsterdam

Weggooien? Mooi niet! ["Toss it? I don't think so!"]
— The motto of the Repair Café International Foundation

By 2009, Amsterdam journalist Martine Postma had reported extensively on sustainability and the plight of our planet. She hoped that her stories had helped change minds and attitudes, but after the birth of her second child, she wanted to do something more. "In Europe, we throw out so many things," she reflected in a 2012 interview with the *New York Times*. "It's a shame, because the things we throw away are usually not that broken. There are more and more people in the world, and we can't keep handling things the way we do. But how do you try to do this as a normal person in your daily life?"

Inspired by a local design exhibition that focused on repair and creative reuse, Martine organized the world's first Repair Cafe in the lobby of a movie theatre. "Sustainability discussions are often about ideals, about what could be," Martine said. "This is very hands on, very concrete. It's about doing something together, in the here and now.

Repair Cafes attract people who are not at the center of attention in everyday society, but here they become heroes."

The Netherlands was the perfect place for this idea to take hold. In a small country, long focused on beating back the sea and reclaiming the land, the deeply rooted historical mindset is very much about how to live within limits. Yet make no mistake, prosperity has allowed for plenty of consumer buying by the broad middle class. As Martine says, the Netherlands is no less a throwaway culture than the United States.

The idea caught on almost immediately. The media loved it. Within a year, each of Holland's thirteen provinces had started one or more Repair Cafes. The Dutch Ministry of the Environment decided to fund the creation of a Repair Café Foundation. From there the concept jumped borders and cultures quickly.

The idea is eminently replicable. The first Repair Cafe in the United States popped up in October 2012 in Palo Alto, California (in Silicon Valley — surprise!). In rapid succession, Pittsfield, Massachusetts, and Pasadena, California, followed. Our Repair Cafe in New Paltz, New York, was close behind, the fourth to open within six months. In each of those towns, someone had read that interview with Martine Postma the previous May, reporting on what was then a strictly European phenomenon: "An Effort to Bury a Throwaway Culture One Repair at a Time."

As of this writing, there are more than 150 Repair Cafes in the United States. The largest concentration is in the Northeast, with fifty or so in eastern New York and northern New Jersey and another fifty in Massachusetts and the other New England states. The upper Midwest and the West Coast are the next most "repairing" regions. Sprinkled around the country, you will find regular events in Colorado, Ohio, and the D.C. and Philly areas, plus outposts in Fairbanks, Alaska; Honolulu, Hawaii; Lincoln, Nebraska; Ellensburg, Washington; Moscow, Idaho; Houston, Texas; the Research Triangle of North Carolina; and St. Petersburg, Florida — with wide open spaces in between.

In one relatively small region — the Hudson Valley, Catskills, and Capital District of New York State — we saw more than 120 events in

2019, in forty communities in twelve counties. These events involved the time of more than six hundred volunteers who brought everything from advanced electronics skills to the wherewithal to make a mean cup of tea. The very social "cafe" side of each event thrives on home-baked treats, fruit, coffee, and tea.

This book will explore the reasons for all this growth, the extraordinary appeal of the idea, and why we believe it can — and should — be replicated in some way everywhere.

repair
is/can

mend a broken heart. responsible. give
an object more character and spunk. make
it better than before. give it a second
chance. prolong and save an object's life.
make you self-sufficient. a cool challenge.
promote longevity. be a hobby. problem
solving. the future. cost effective. bring
people together. turn trash into treasure.
teach you something new. meditative. sexy.
tell stories. sustainable. resourceful.
rewarding. create resilient community. save
you money. connect you to people. inspire
your creativity.

repair   Be part of the   Find us on 🅾 🅵
matters   repair community.   repairmatters.ca

One of us, John, worked for many years in communications, as a writer-producer and executive producer of television programming for public broadcasting and cable networks. Always on the lookout for creative ways to build community, he recognized an overlap in the skill sets needed to produce television shows and to organize a repair initiative: both involve bringing together a group of people with diverse skills and backgrounds to work on a common vision. When he moved to the Hudson Valley, asking people for their ideas about starting a Repair Cafe became a kind of "passport" to his new community and a way of sharing interests with people he might otherwise never have met. He describes his role as that of coordinator, communicator, and cheerleader for Repair Cafes in the Hudson Valley, Catskills, and Capital District of New York State, as well as for the repair movement globally. An amateur woodworker since he was a kid, John brings his tools to as many Repair Cafes as he can.

Coauthor Elizabeth is a U.S. Air Force "brat" (her dad served thirty years' active duty) who has lived in at least eight states and two foreign countries. Her mother's mantra, "There's no such thing as a stranger, just friends whose names you don't yet know," led to careers in marketing communications, special events, and the hospitality industry; she wrote several books about entertaining with tea, "the social lubricant." Shortly after she moved to the Hudson Valley, Elizabeth visited a Repair Cafe held in a nearby town. Impressed by the fix-it skills and warm welcome that volunteers extended to all the strangers who walked through the door, clutching wobbly chairs, wonky lamps, and torn clothes, she determined to start the first Repair Cafe in her county. Four years on, she and her team of dedicated volunteers continue to host friends, neighbors, and strangers, offering all a steaming cuppa while they wait to get their beloved but broken items fixed.

John invited Elizabeth to join him as coauthor of this book after reading a year's worth of the follow-up reports she wrote to her volunteers after every Warwick Repair Cafe. The pictures she painted in words captured the spirit and essence of community repair with insight and personality, telling the stories of the people who brought things, and the people who fixed them. John knew that is exactly what this book would need.

A Fixed Thing Is a Beautiful Thing

[
I've got a shrieking blender here! Can you fix it?
— Email from a concerned citizen
]

Ever heard of a Magic Quartz Cooker? They made them in the sixties. Ellen James remembers her mother using one to broil fish year-round on the back porch, "to keep that fishy smell out of the house, don't you know." Ellen brought her broken cooker to the Repair Cafe, our volunteers put their heads together (many repairs are collaborative), and Ellen left impressed and happy. "Swell crowd," she wrote in our comments book.

What else gets fixed at a Repair Cafe? Lamps are item number one in the USA (in Europe, it's coffee makers). Then a lot of vacuum cleaners, CD and DVD players, countertop appliances, pants and skirts, necklaces, picture frames, and wobbly chairs. Beyond that, anything under the sun, really. Elisa and Ray brought their classic-but-not-working electronic "Simon" game (madly popular in the 1980s) so that their teenage daughter Bella, who also came, would be able to play it (and okay, so that Elisa could show off her skills). Kimiko Link's daughter brought her baby doll with a smushed face, and Felicia Casey at our Dolls & Stuffed Animals worktable made her feel better. Meanwhile, high school kids reconfigured laptops, tablets, and smartphones. The joke among our volunteers is, I wonder what's going to walk in the door today?

The "core" repair categories are mechanical, electrical, electronic and digital, clothing and textiles, jewelry, things made of wood, bicycles, and blade sharpening. Gas engines are the one category that most Repair Cafes eschew, for the simple reason that they're dirty and noisy.

Fixing is not an all-or-nothing endeavor. We like to say that there are three possible outcomes for the item you bring. "Repaired" means

the problem was figured out and fixed, and you may have participated in the repair. At the other end of the spectrum is the "Beyond Repair" outcome, where the item isn't fixable for any of a number of reasons. The pronouncement "Tried, Dead, and Done" frees you to recycle or responsibly dispose of a useless thing, with the satisfaction that you followed its useful life to its end. Or you may carry it over to the Kids Take It Apart Table, our popular "learning lab," where it will end its life in pieces. Finally, there's the third, in-between possibility, "Half Repaired" — which is also valuable. Your item wasn't fixed, but your coach identified the issue and suggested possible solutions and a next step. If a replacement part is needed, you might order it from the local hardware store and bring it along to the next Repair Cafe. Or you may now know enough to fix it yourself. The common denominator in all three scenarios is this: you learned something about the way things work. You may have even gained a new appreciation for the stuff in your life.

Who Does the Fixing?

I feel like we were all part of something important. We'll definitely be doing this again!

— Repair Cafe volunteer

We call them "repair coaches." These are guys and gals with significant skills who volunteer their time for three or four hours one Saturday every other month, or every third month. Some run professional repair businesses, and this offers them a way to be out in the community so that people know who they are and what they have to offer. Some are retired, with a lifetime of experience and knowledge. Others are simply passionate about one thing or another: the "lost art" of darning or the intricacies of a pendulum clock. Within each community there are people who bring other skills or passions: metal welding, digital photo restoration, plant care, chair massage, editorial "wordsmithing." Call them "fix-perts" if you like; many repair coaches are people with skills that have been lost to modern convenience, retained from an era when more people worked with their hands. Other skill sets, of course, are wholly of the twenty-first century, such as anything having to do with the latest iPhone or Android release or gaming device. There is a common narrative among repair coaches: when they were kids, they liked to take stuff apart. When they couldn't put it back together, their curiosity was sparked. They were on their way.

Make no mistake: this is often a sophisticated level of repair; it's typical to find current or retired engineers in the mix. Technical skills are necessary. But interpersonal skills are even more important. The connections that people make as they attempt to repair things (and mostly succeed) is not beside the point — it *is* the point. "I find that people are receptive to learning how to make some of the repairs themselves," one of our repair coaches observes. "If I can enable someone to figure out how to do something on their own, I have helped build their confidence and perhaps taught them a few things. People often think they 'can't do anything' and are pleasantly surprised when they realize that a simple repair can be easily done with a little tutoring. It's a win-win for both of us." Early on we received great encouragement and good advice from Peter Mui, the MIT grad who started the network of Fixit Clinics across the United States. He said, "Keep your volunteers happy. Their skills are your linchpin. Good pizza will be a key factor in your success."

We can't guarantee that the item you bring will get fixed. All we can guarantee is that you'll have an interesting time. And so the table is set: You have something broken that you'd like to keep. Repair coaches have the savvy to help you. The level of gratification is high on both sides of the table. Pull up a chair and see what happens.

The Signal We Send

By the time I walked out of there, I thought: This is the way the world should work.
— Manna Jo Greene, Ulster County legislator

The Repair Café International Foundation likes to collect data. We all do. Towns want to know what the measurable impact of all of this activity is. How many? How much? So here are some numbers. A typical Repair Cafe in the United States attracts about fifty people in the space of four hours, many of whom bring two items. Our repair success rate averages anywhere from 70 to 85 percent. In 2019, the Repair Café Foundation collected records for more than 24,000 repair events worldwide, which resulted in an estimated 432,000 repaired products being saved from the "waste mountain" and which, according to the calculation method used by a British researcher, prevented 22.8 million pounds of CO_2 from reaching the atmosphere. (An average person in the Western world causes CO_2 emissions of about 22,000 pounds per year.)

Repair Cafes are good at extending the useful life of everyday items. But as impressive as the growth of repair initiatives has been internationally, no number of laptops and lamps diverted from the waste stream will ever make a difference at the scale needed to transform the global economy or draw down the carbon in our oceans and atmosphere. If that is not the goal, what is?

In conversations with Martine, we've talked a lot about the impact of Repair Cafes, and we believe the data don't capture the movement's true significance. That significance is the *signal* the events generate (to use Martine's appropriate metaphor), the signal received by people who walk into a Repair Cafe for the first time in their town. That signal says, *We are better off when we see our own community in the midst of cooperation, creativity, and downright decency, in a place where goals are achieved and positive outcomes are realized.*

"The value of the Repair Cafe," says William McDonough, an architect and coauthor of the influential book *Cradle to Cradle*, "is that people are going back into a relationship with the material things around them." Evelien H. Tonkens, a sociology professor at the University of Amsterdam, agrees. "It's very much a sign of the times," says Dr. Tonkens, who notes that the Repair Cafe's "anticonsumerist, antimarket, do-it-ourselves ethos" reflects a more general trend to improve the world through grassroots social activism.

And here we can underscore one more attribute about community repair projects: they do not self-select for any political point of view. Everyone has broken stuff, and this speaks to egalitarianism. Sitting down with a neighbor to troubleshoot what's wrong with your stuff helps bridge the partisan divide — or any other divide — that may separate you in another setting.

Repair culture is a tail wagging the dog. It is an active, participatory volunteer gig that animates the larger imperative of sustainability and community.

"LET US RAISE A STANDARD TO WHICH THE WISE AND HONEST CAN REPAIR."

George Washington is said to have spoken these words during the Constitutional Convention at Philadelphia in 1787. Handed down to us as useful guidance, Washington's words are now printed inside every U.S. passport. The word *repair* here means "take refuge" or "find security in." The word *standard* can refer either to a principle or to a military flag — and General George Washington may have meant to invoke both meanings. Which is fine: we repairers do raise a flag to the virtues of wisdom and honesty.

This quote has become our motto, referring to the standard of wisdom and honesty that we see people experience at a Repair Cafe. *Wisdom* is knowledge gained from experience. *Honesty* speaks to the nature of our relationships, to treating each other with respect, as we would wish to be treated. Honesty is the authenticity people experience, the signal they receive, when they walk into a Repair Cafe and "see their own community in the midst of cooperation, creativity, and downright decency." It bridges ideological and political divides. It is essentially patriotic. In a period of divisiveness, we can all look to George Washington for courage, wisdom, and inspiration. And let us not forget that Washington helped lead a revolution of ideas and ideals that changed the world.

Where This Book Will Take Us

Imagine a world worth fighting for, a way forward. It's important to imagine that we can repair. Ideate a world where repair has happened, and work toward that.
— Anna Rose Keefe, conservation assistant,
RISD Museum of Art

This is the first book to attempt to pull together the thousand threads of a rapidly growing movement that is remarkably intergenerational, pervasive, and culturally vibrant. And yet it must be said that we are attempting to capture lightning in a bottle. The repair movement encompasses a fast-moving global community, sharing news and ideas constantly on social media platforms. Repair is in the zeitgeist.

We see the repair movement as both an innovation and a reemergence. To make that case, we will explore the historical and social context of repair. We'll delve into the rich layers of meaning embodied in the ethos of repair and draw lessons about balancing our human economy with "ecological economics." Many of the women and men who do these repairs have thought deeply about why they do it and why it matters, and we will share the eminently practical lessons they've learned. The act of mending also profoundly mirrors the brokenness and healing we experience in human relationships and connects with our sense of individual and social well-being. Some of this wisdom is philosophical and theological, expressed variously through the concepts of *tikkun olam*, Hebrew for "repair of the world," the Zen aesthetic of *wabi-sabi*, the monastic practice of radical hospitality, or the Indigenous worldview known as "re-weaving the basket of life." The wisdom of repair is creative, commonsensical, and — in a throwaway world — radical.

There is nothing proprietary about the idea of people getting together to fix stuff. Peter Mui opened his first Fixit Clinic in Berkeley, California, in 2009, and Vincent Lai held his first Fixers Collective in Brooklyn, New York, in 2010. Since then, community repair initiatives have propagated like some fantastic garden: Repair Labs and Hubs, Fix-It Fridays, Make Do & Mend-It Circles, Restart Parties, Tool Libraries, Men's Sheds and Fix It Sisters Sheds, Tinkerages, Remakeries, and at least one Dare to Repair Cafe. Upcycling, freecycling, and the Maker movement proliferate in all their funky, creative glory. In Berkeley, the Culture of Repair Project defines its mission as "working across sectors to restore repair as a basic social value." In the suburbs, you hear the rallying cry "Bring back shop class and home economics!" There is a strong affinity between Repair Cafes and the Right to Repair movement, which challenges unfair and deceptive company policies that make it difficult, expensive, or impossible for you to repair the things you own. Right to repair initiatives combine social justice, environmental, and DIY activism in the political arena.

Repair is educational by definition, requiring observation, deductive reasoning, knowledge of scientific principles or craft techniques, and creative problem solving. Repair coaches are pretty curious by nature, and most see every item that gets to their worktable as an opportunity to learn something new (although I'll allow that the ump-teenth lamp may be an exception). Still, we find there is a bit of the teacher in most of our volunteers, and the opportunity to mentor would-be repair coaches, including special needs learners, is a strong attribute of repair culture.

The contributions that Repair Cafes and other repair and reuse events make in their communities are all acts of caring, both on the in-dividual level and on the global level as the impacts of climate change become more and more evident. Volunteerism is all around us, but what Repair Cafes offer volunteers can be more meaningful and, judg-ing from the comments we receive, more fun than most. Habitat for Humanity ReStores are natural partners, as many donations need to be "readied" (repaired) for resale. In the private sector, there are sto-ries to tell about how and why some companies, Patagonia and Eileen Fisher among them, have integrated repair and reuse into their corpo-rate culture. We know that this kind of eco-tribalism can create con-sumer bonds and loyalty, and time will tell whether these campaigns are truly a long-term commitment to sustainability.

The Repair Cafe concept has translated well. There are now more than two thousand Repair Cafes in thirty-three countries, with 330 of those starting up in 2019 alone. From their experiences (many post on Instagram), we can see differences in the way societies view volunteerism or embrace the idea of repairing and reusing personal property. *Reparemos* ("we repair") is established in La Paz, Santiago, and Unete, Mexico; and in Temuco, Chile: "Together we repair it. Not always successfully, but free and with love." In India, repair is inexpensive and available in every marketplace, but repair advocate Purna Sarkar in Bengaluru sees their activities as a way to help bridge caste, creed, and religious differences. The Gaia Foundation in London has provocatively redesigned the mantra widely known as the "three Rs" — Reduce, Reuse, Recycle — and expanded it to include seven Rs (see next page). The fixers in Wembley, Australia, say it is eight. Whatever the number, recycling is always the last, the furthest downstream. In the twenty-first century, the pressure is on to rethink business as usual. As social historian Susan Strasser states in her book *Waste and Want*, "Economic development has created persistent assaults on the global ecosystem from air and water pollution and global warming, as well as from solid waste. These problems are urgent, and the solution will not come from going backward in time."

In titling this book *Repair Revolution*, we mean to indicate a change in mindset and a return to social values that is anything but sudden. This revolution has deep cultural and historical roots and has been building for at least ten years. It also requires resolution — the personal decision to improve a situation, inseparable from ethics. "Ours is not the task of fixing the entire world all at once, but of stretching out to mend the part of the world that is within our reach," writes Clarissa Pinkola Estés, author of *Women Who Run with the Wolves*. The repair revolution draws the largest circle possible, to welcome everyone.

The goal of this book is to inspire and encourage people everywhere to start a Repair Cafe — or something like it — in their community. We'll zero in on what's involved and provide a road map for starting your own. At the same time, we know that not everyone wants to take on the task of organizing, and so we encourage you to get involved in any way you'd like, starting, of course, by bringing something that's broken or needs mending. You might think, "Oh, what a nice idea, fixing things for your neighbors." But it's much more than a nice idea, and until you go to a community repair event and feel the generosity, creativity, and sense of purpose in the room, you won't really know what this is. A rewarding experience awaits.

Try a little experiment. Tell someone about the idea of a "community meeting place to bring a beloved but broken item to be repaired, for free." Slow down a little when you say the words "beloved but broken." See how they register with the listener. We think you'll like the response.

The Community Repair Experience

Thanks for all you do for our planet.... Will the zipper lady
be there Saturday?

— Email from a frequent Repair Cafe guest

It's a repair day across the USA. In Palo Alto, California, Peter Skinner,
a Silicon Valley entrepreneur and environmentalist who founded the
first U.S. Repair Cafe in 2012, is helping Repair Cafe volunteers set up
at the Museum of American Heritage. The museum, housed in a home
built in 1907, features an eclectic collection of electrical and mechanical devices and inventions dating from the 1750s through the 1950s. Set
in a residential neighborhood, the building is too small to accommodate the thirty-plus volunteers and approximately one hundred people
who will come seeking repairs, so Skinner and others are erecting tents
on the lawn to shelter the check-in team and the coaches who will work
on bikes and lawn mowers. Another team, including mechanical engineering and product design students from nearby Stanford University,

is setting up shop in the building behind the historic house. These "apprentice fixers" run power cords to the workbenches, each furnished with a vise and tools, where the students will soon be seated next to an experienced fixpert. A half hour before opening, Skinner gathers everyone for an orientation meeting and thanks volunteers and sponsors for their contribution — "a stitch in the fabric of community."

On any second Saturday of any month in Ellensburg, Washington, a small group of five or six friends dedicated to conservation, community, and sustainability — gathered by Repair Cafe organizer Don Shriner, a steam engineer by trade — meet at a restaurant for breakfast at eight AM. Some have taken the day off from work; others have traveled close to a hundred miles to attend. They may not have seen each other for several weeks, but the familiarity with which they greet each other shows their common purpose. Today they are going to help the community and the planet, and they'll help each other become better people by helping others. After breakfast, they drive to the Independent Order of Odd Fellows Cemetery, where a 1,600-square-foot shop stands central amid backhoes, tractors, and mowers. Inside the shop, headstones waiting for names to be added and some already prepared and awaiting placement stand next to tools of the trade laid out on work benches. Shelves lined with welding gear, lubricants, air compressors, and other equipment reveal the face of the many projects that are undertaken there. Ellensburg, Washington, is home to one of North America's oldest rodeos, and so they call their events the Rodeo City Repair Cafe, and the I.O.O.F. Cemetery shop is command central.

On Cape Cod, in Massachusetts, a Fixit Clinic sponsored by the Wellfleet Recycling Committee and Boomerang Bags (whose members stitch donated textiles into sustainable shopping bags to be given away for free) is held in the Wellfleet Public Library's meeting room. Built in the 1930s, the former factory (making curtains, then candles) became a library in 1972. Library Outreach Coordinator Gabrielle Griffis, who is responsible for the setup of the clinic's physical space, creates flyers and other forms of publicity a month in advance of the events. Jed Foley of the Wellfleet Recycling Committee is responsible for recruiting volunteer Fixit coaches. A week before the clinic, coaches meet to discuss their goals, their skills, and the tools that they'll bring to help people fix their things at the library. Griffis, who is also the clinic's official greeter and traffic flow manager, says, "Keeping items out of the landfill is one of the clinic's major goals, but it's not guaranteed — whereas learning is!"

In Bolton, Massachusetts, organizer Ray Pfau, who learned about the Repair Cafe concept from his wife, Catherine, greets Repair Cafe volunteers as they set up in the Florence Sawyer School cafeteria. Unlike the cafe's previous location, the school doesn't charge a custodial fee. Plus, there's space in the large, well-lit room for at least twenty-five volunteers, one hundred fifty people seeking repairs, eight to ten rectangular tables on rollers, and a couple of round tables in the middle where people can sit, snack, and chat. Ray, a former schoolteacher, software engineer, and self-described "general fixer," is kept busy making sure that things are running smoothly, so he doesn't have time to fix things at his own cafe, the second one in Massachusetts. But he enjoys the opportunity to sharpen knives and other implements when he visits one of the other thirty-three Repair Cafes, Fixit Clinics, and other repair events in his state, many of which he helped get started.

Ray's grandson, seventeen-year-old Tyler Bernotas, is the founder and organizer of the Repair Cafe in Phoenixville, Pennsylvania, thirty miles northwest of Philadelphia. When the original location, a makerspace, was no longer available, Bernotas moved his event to the town's Technical College High School, which has ample parking, a helpful staff, and space to spread out as they grow. Currently, the Repair Cafe uses the school's cafeteria, a forty-five by twenty-five-foot room designed to serve sixty students. People seeking repairs sit comfortably at tables, waiting their turn to work with the coaches, or they wander the room, watching the progress of other repairs. The team will attempt to fix almost anything but specializes in bikes, textiles, electronics, lamps, small appliances, and knife and bladed tool sharpening.

Don Fick, who runs his own media company, is the organizer of Repair Cafe NC in North Carolina's Research Triangle. Workshops are held in the Scrap Exchange, an anchor to Durham's emerging creative reuse arts district. Founded in 1991, the Scrap Exchange was established to divert excess materials from business and residential sources. It's a twenty-thousand-square-foot mash-up of thrift store, craft supply, and art gallery, where visitors might find bolts of fabric, lab equipment, electrical switches, and vintage home furnishings. Repair workshops are held in its Design Center, equipped with worktables and sewing machines. The space can accommodate up to twelve active repair projects at one time. With easy access to the materials available for sale, repair coaches and guests frequently source repair parts from the many items in the store. It is common to see scrap metal, wire, and other materials finding new purpose as drawer supports, lamp cords, and other creative reuses.

Repair Cafe NC events are also held in the Cary Senior Center. With just thirty minutes of setup, repair coaches transform an open multipurpose ballroom into a Santa's Workshop of repair. Several eight-foot-long banquet tables, each with one or two coaches, are arranged in a horseshoe pattern, with four to six chairs at each. The Senior Center offers excellent accessibility for guests of all ages. For guests with bulky items, two or three volunteers from Cary's Teen Council are on hand to assist, and they often become involved in repair themselves. With high school college-track curriculums leaving little or no time for industrial arts education, Repair Cafe offers these teens a chance to see the practical benefit and to experience the satisfaction of repair.

> "We celebrate the cafe for its contribution to repair the 'beloved, but broken' items and to create a community crossroads, showing us all that fixing can be fun!"
> — Michael J. Newhard, Mayor, Village of Warwick

In advance of Warwick's Repair Cafe, home to Orange County, New York's first Repair Cafe, the questions have been arriving for days via phone, email, and text: "Can you fix my backpack's busted zipper?" "Can someone sew legs back on a stuffed unicorn?" "Can you sharpen a machete?" We always answer, "We won't know 'til we see it, but if you can carry it in, our team will give it their best shot."

The Repair Cafe doesn't officially start until Saturday morning at ten o'clock, but by quarter after nine, people are already streaming into the parking lot of the Senior Center behind the Town Hall. Just like at a yard sale, there are always "early birds." A man holding a clumsily folded, orange-and-white-striped, long-sleeved shirt says he'd taken it to a dry cleaner earlier that morning to have the worn collar turned, but the young woman behind the counter said, "We don't do that." The man next in line had suggested, "Take it to the Repair Cafe," and here he is. An elderly couple sits, side by side, on the bench outside the building's double doors. She cups a white cardboard box in her hands. He, holding a broken blender, asks, "Who's in charge? Do we need to sign in?"

We thank the visitors for coming and tell them, "We'll be happy to help just as soon as we're set up. Give us about twenty minutes." The volunteer coaches, who live in nine different towns, arrive and begin to unload the tools of their trades — sewing machines, thread, bobbins, fabric scraps, whetstones and oil, boxes stuffed with extension cords, power strips, lamp sockets, wire, nails, screws, assorted glues and clamps, a bike stand. They call out their hellos, hold the doors for each other, ask about families, vacations. But the question on everyone's mind is "What do you think they'll bring in today?" Then, one by one, they move their cars and trucks as far away from the Senior Center's entrance doors as possible to make it easier for the visitors to unload their things.

A couple of volunteers walk to the highway turnoff, just beyond the Town Complex's parking lot entrance, where they plant the plastic yard signs sporting the Hudson Valley Repair Cafe logo, one facing in each direction. Other volunteers post signs inside the Senior Center to indicate various repair stations — "Small Electrics," "Digital Devices and Electronics," "Knife and Tool Sharpening," "Jewelry," "Things Made of Wood," "Textiles and Soft Toys," "Bikes," and so on, as well as funny and inspirational quotes, like "Worry never fixes anything" and "I couldn't repair your brakes, so I made your horn louder." Repair seekers and volunteers often use their cell phones to photograph their favorite signs.

The sewing team members — Liz Bonita, Joan Bono, Mary Bono, Raheli Harper, Regina Shaw, Deanne Singer, and Lenny Valentino —

arrange their tables, supplies stashed underneath, parallel to the electrical outlets spaced along the outside wall. The snack table needs outlets too, for the coffee maker and tea kettle. The jewelry repair coaches — Barb Barron, Cathé Linton, and Suzanne O'Brien — like the natural light in the corner by the piano.

The small electrics team — Larry Bastanza, FixIt Bob Berkowitz, Tom Bonita, Jerry Fischetti (who volunteered for our very first Repair Cafe on his eighty-eighth birthday), Ken Garrison, Frank O'Brien, Jim Pfitzner, and Ken Winterling — sets up across the room from the seamstresses, where they have access to bright orange extension cords and another bank of outlets to plug in their gear. The Kids Take It Apart Table is positioned next to them, opposite the welcome/check-in table, which is stacked with house rules and job ticket forms, baskets of pens, and the donation jar. Fixes are free, but there are expenses — insurance, printing of flyers and signs, repair supplies, snacks for all, and pizza for the volunteers' lunch.

The digital devices team, headed by Rob Shaw, also needs multiple outlets, so the team sets up along the same wall as small electrics. Roger Bergman and Rich White arrange the bike repair station at the back of the room and unfold the metal bike workstand. Fred Rossi, the first of the knife/tool sharpening team to arrive, arranges the sharpening tables in the middle of the room, behind Edwin Winstanley's wooden things and miscellaneous repairs table. All the volunteers, and sometimes several of the early birds seeking repairs, help arrange lines of chairs in front of each set of tables for the visitors.

A member of Sustainable Warwick, our sponsor, might arrive with a collection of small items, brand new or in good repair, and so we set up a give-away table next to the table stocked with DIY and how-to-repair books and magazines. Charles Hemstreet, who manages the Warwick Ecumenical Food Pantry, a community outreach ministry of the Warwick United Methodist Church, stops by to drop off two large rubber tubs, which will be used to collect the anticipated donations of canned and boxed food.

We can smell the coffee now, so it's time to usher our visitors to the welcome/check-in table. Cheryl Karlin, who can knit and explain the house rules at the same time, hands each person a job ticket and asks them to complete the "What's Wrong with It?" section, then sign the liability waiver that states, "If you offer items for repair, you do so at your own risk. Organizers, sponsors, and repair persons are not liable for any physical damage or loss resulting from work performed at the RC. Persons making repairs offer no guarantees and are not liable if objects that are repaired in the RC turn out to not work properly at home."

Visitors are sometimes surprised to learn that Repair Cafes don't offer a drop-off service. We expect people seeking repairs to remain with their items while our volunteers work to fix them. Larry James, a Repair Cafe co-organizer and coach in Lincoln, Nebraska, says that the visitor can help by keeping track of screws or providing an extra pair of hands to hold things steady. There's a dual advantage: "Explaining what I'm doing makes things clearer in my mind, especially when troubleshooting. And if the fix is beyond what we can do, the person will usually be able to understand why."

The welcome/check-in team — which also includes Dee, who volunteers to help multiple organizations; Teresa Gochal, a retired assistant school principal; Nanette Furneau, whose smile is as bright as her eyes; Joan Maxwell, a retired CFO and director of operations; and Lisa Tencza, a school district business office assistant — sets the stage for the whole Repair Cafe experience. They warmly greet visitors and cheerfully explain the process for first-timers. To aid our marketing outreach efforts, they ask visitors how they heard about us and how frequently they've been here, and later, they solicit feedback and ask permission to take photos of happy people holding their freshly fixed items. The team members take turns seating repair seekers in the appropriate fix-it station line to wait their turn (first come, first served), but not before inviting them to visit the snack table. There is fresh fruit and beverages, and thirteen-year-old Ellie, who loves to bake, has just surprised us with a chocolate cake, still warm from the oven, and a bowl of freshly whipped cream to top it off. At another table, a registered dietitian and certified diabetes educator distributes free glucose meters, healthy lifestyle tips, recipes, and truly tasty, healthy apple-walnut snacks.

One of our greeters says hello to Ellie's mom, waiting in the lamps line, and spots the broken blender man's wife perched on a bench behind the Kids Take It Apart Table. The elderly woman is so tiny that her feet don't reach the floor. She looks tired. "Would you like a cup of tea or coffee while you're waiting your turn?" "No, thank you. I don't mind waiting for someone to help me. I had a lot of practice in the hospital." The woman goes on to say that she and her husband were injured in a Thanksgiving Day crash so severe that the rescue team had to use the jaws of life tool to extract him from their car. They were both hospitalized; she has had several surgeries and a long recovery. Asked what she brought to be repaired, the woman lifts a glass and wrought iron sculpture from the white box on the seat beside her. The piece is shaped like a kneeling angel, head bowed over hands folded in prayer. "It's a night light. Her glass skirt lights up. I keep it by my bed to keep me awake long enough to thank God, before I go to sleep, for all the people who have helped me."

"Two Kittens Chewed Wire"

Warwick could open a lamp store with the number of lamps brought to every Repair Cafe. Lamps are the most popular items brought in for repairs throughout the Hudson Valley and in most Repair Cafes in the United States. What's wrong with them? Well, according to today's job tickets, the problems include "flickers," "fixture detached from base," "won't turn on — taken apart years ago," "broken bulb socket," "one side doesn't work," "doesn't work when plugged in," "wobbly base," "two kittens chewed wire," "three-way is a one-way," "heater to lamp conversion," "blown fuse," "loose neck," and "fell apart — put back together wrong?" The woman next in line announces, "See this? This is a dumb lamp! But it sits on my nightstand. I don't want to have to spend eighty dollars on a new one just because I don't know why this one doesn't work." She says that she heard about us from a neighbor who'd had her lamp fixed at the last cafe.

FixIt Bob Berkowitz, a former U.S. Navy Seabee who started a handyman business when he retired from a utility company, helps a nine-year-old girl clutching a lamp that had been given to her by her grandmother. Later he describes what happened next: "I explained to the mother what I did and why, so that she might be able to repair other lamps that have the same symptoms. After a few minutes of diagnosis and a small repair, my young customer was very happy to see the lamp light up and stay lit. I love, love to see children and grownups thrilled that a personal and sentimental item has been repaired and brought back to life."

Ken Winterling, a retired telecommunications engineer, always tries to involve customers in the repair of their devices. Ken shows people how to hold a meter probe on a test point and asks them to read the display. Then he explains how the circuit works, what he's measuring, and the expected reading. When the problem is found, he explains how he located it. After the item is fixed, he has the customers test it again so that they can see for themselves how the meter display looks different on a working device. Winterling got an education one morning when he worked on a table lamp that had belonged to the customer's family for many generations. When he removed the outer cover surrounding the lamp socket, many generations of highly compacted dead bugs tumbled out. And there was something shiny in the powdery pile of bug bits — a single, gold-filigree earring! The lamp owner had no idea who owned the earring. Ken guessed that it had been lost by someone who changed the light bulb long ago.

There are lots of problem clocks in Warwick today. A cuckoo clock is driving its owner cuckoo because it "chimes at 20 minutes to the hour." Another timepiece needs replacement motor-hands installed. The job ticket for another simply states, "It fell." A wooden mantle clock "will not stay running." Ken Garrison, a former high school physics teacher, solves that problem for the owner, who sheepishly admits, "My mechanical error. Wound it in the wrong direction."

The First Step Is Figuring Out What's Wrong

With any repair, the first step is the diagnosis. "Sometimes the challenge is not how to fix an item," says Naomi Aubain at the Repair Cafe in New Paltz, New York, "but in figuring out how to get the owner to tell you exactly what is wrong with it. A common response can be 'It just stopped working!' — usually said with a quizzically innocent look on their face. My first thought is usually 'What did you do to it?' The second is, 'How do I find out?'"

Naomi's favorite example of this phenomenon is the story of the older woman who carried in a chiming pendulum mantle clock that had belonged to her mother. After working well for many years, it had stopped. After examining the clock and fiddling with the key and inner workings, Naomi still couldn't find anything wrong. It was time to play Twenty Questions. But almost immediately, she realized the clock's owner had no idea how it worked. None! Aside from having to wind it each week, not once had she looked inside or examined it in any way. "Okay," thought Naomi, "now I know what to do. It's lesson time." She figured the clock had stopped working because of a sideways motion that interrupted the pendulum's swing. Likely it had been pushed while someone was dusting or rearranging things on the mantle. So her lesson started with the pendulum and how it works. "Who knew you had to be a detective, a psychologist, and a teacher to be a fixer person at the Repair Cafe? It was rewarding to have figured out what was wrong with the clock, even though it was really nothing. Oddly, it was also disappointing to not have actually fixed anything, at least something tangible. I guess I fixed the clock owner's lack of understanding. Hopefully she will remember our little lesson and be able to 'fix' her clock in the future."

Sometimes repairs proceed by trial and error. Charles Goedeke, a retired electrical engineer and organizer of a Repair Cafe in Howard County, Maryland, that travels to different libraries, senior centers, and churches, recalls trying to fix a microwave oven. After commiserating with the other coaches about how hard manufacturers make it to fix such appliances, he asked the customer, "Have you tried bouncing it?" That elicited some quizzical looks, so Charles reached over and bounced it on the counter a couple of times. "A mug of water was produced as a test case. We fired it up, and it worked! As far as I know it's still working."

"Busted Butt" and "Wires Broken"

The small electrics team tackles problems with a can opener, a blender, a label maker, a kelly-green vintage floor fan, a hole punch, a curling iron, a hairdryer ("sparks and smells bad when you turn it on"), a printer, a paper shredder, a weed whacker, three radios — a portable radio ("doesn't work"), a clock radio ("same"), and a third ("tuner string off track") — a Victrola ("buttons pushed"), food processors (both automatic and hand-cranked), a Mr. Coffee machine ("Not hot enough? Coffee too weak"), an adding machine ("When you turn it on it just runs and you can't type in anything"), three vacuum cleaners, a musical jewelry box, an air compressor, a doorbell ("doesn't ring"), a metal horse ("busted butt"), a CD player ("drawer opens and closes by itself"), and a hat ("wires broken"). A woman brings in a rotary dial phone, seeking "advice to make it interactive for 1960s historical society exhibit." Ken Garrison will take it home to fix it for her.

[
"I keep telling people about the amazing amount of cat hair that I've pulled out of vacuums."

— Charles Goedeke
]

Warwick's Repair Cafe, like most, sees vacuum cleaners at every event. "Doesn't work" and "clogged hose" are among the most common complaints. Today, one has a simple diagnosis: "Appears to be working okay — should replace vac bag." Ken Winterling, who volunteers at six different Repair Cafes, tells us about a creative solution to a clogged hose that didn't include an actual repair. An elderly woman brought a vacuum cleaner hose with an attached extension wand to a different Repair Cafe. She blamed her arthritic hands as the reason she couldn't press the release button hard enough to disconnect the wand. Turned out, the latch mechanism was broken, and parts were no longer available because the manufacturer was out of business. So Winterling and Barry Eldridge, who works with Ken at the Repair Cafe in Middletown, New York, put their heads together and discovered that when they turned the nozzle upside down, gravity caused the latch to disengage and the wand could easily be disconnected, even by a senior citizen with arthritic hands. Today, in Warwick, a woman brings in an older model vacuum "'that can go from a wood floor to carpet to tile." The repair coach replaces a missing spring, and as the customer leaves, she waves her job ticket over her head. "Fixed! Thanks! It was going to the curb."

Repairs of electrical appliances and devices are in demand everywhere. "I've been threatening/planning/hoping to go to one of the Hudson Valley Repair Cafes for three years," recalled Robin Romeo. She had been "holding onto broken things with a vague plan and then throwing them out."

Last week my paper shredder refused to shred a twelve-page booklet halfway through the process. I love my paper shredder. It makes junk mail almost as exciting as a check in the mail, so when I saw a Repair Cafe scheduled for the following week (miraculously), I went! Such a lovely community of people — impossible to tell from the look or the vibe, the difference between the owners of broken items and the angels there to fix them. After a brief and comfortable wait, I brought my paper shredder up to the table where the "guy who fixes stuff like that" sat. I handed over my shredder and he looked it up and down, adjusted his glasses, and then — without the slightest hint of irony — said, "You know you can replace these things for around eighty-nine dollars." And then he fixed it! I can't wait to break something again.

Warwick's Repair Cafe team, like others throughout the Hudson Valley, usually sees at least one or two dysfunctional sewing machines. Today, a woman complains that her machine's "bobbin winder won't work." A man brings in a machine with a faulty pressure foot. He's tried, and failed, to fix it for his elderly mother, who relies on it to mend sheets and clothing. Frank O'Brien, a retired telecom operations manager, discovered that it needed only to be oiled. Jackie Carter, who organizes the Repair Cafe at the public library in Moscow, Idaho, says, "I always tell people when they get a sewing machine, 'Get a good used one because the new ones are so lightweight you can throw them across the room' — and that's about what you should do with them."

Rich White, a guy who "can fix whatever anyone who has owned a home for fifty years can do," and Roger Bergman, who owned a bicycle shop for forty-nine years, often team up. "R&R," as we call them, are working on a multicolor, cast iron mechanical bank, circa 1907, that the owner says he gave to his son for Christmas. The action is supposed to involve Teddy Roosevelt pointing his rifle at a black bear cub hiding in a tree trunk, but nothing is happening. After R&R adjust a spring, the president and the bear are again able to play hide and seek. Immediately following that accomplishment, a man arrives with a heavy, metal cheese grater that he says he "bought thirty years ago for one hundred and fifty dollars." Problem? "The suction sucks — need to install new suction cup to secure it to table." Our guys fix that, too. The delighted owner says, "Awesome, perfect!" Roger quips, "Now you can make America grate again!"

WHAT HAPPENS AT REPAIR CAFE DOESN'T STAY AT REPAIR CAFE

Even when Warwick doesn't have a Repair Cafe scheduled, Rich White volunteers, May to September, collecting and refurbishing second-hand bikes to donate to the HRHCare – Alamo Farmworkers Community Center in Goshen, New York, a few miles from Warwick. Mario Fernandez, one of the organization's outreach workers, told Rich that many of the migrant seasonal workers, living on more than fifty farms, depend on donated bikes as their only form of transportation.

Some bikes are donated by friends and neighbors whose children have outgrown them. Others come from the police department's roundup of unclaimed bikes found in parks or along the roads. Driving around town, Rich keeps his eyes peeled for unwanted bikes. Recently, he spotted three bikes at the end of a driveway, parked his car, and knocked on the homeowner's front door to ask permission to take them. A silver one, in such good condition that it needed only to be dusted, estimated value fifteen hundred dollars, came from a woman who volunteers with Rich at another organization, who said that her deceased husband "would be smiling from heaven to know that his bike would go to someone who really needs it." Over the last two years, White has donated thirty-plus refurbished bikes to new owners.

Kid Stuff

[
It is best when we act like we are one family.
— Jay Hart, repair coach, Newburyport, Massachusetts
]

Michele, organizer of the Green Ossining Repair Cafe in Ossining, New York, fondly remembers "hanging out under my family's dining room table as a child, using a screwdriver to loosen and tighten the screws on the chairs, just for the joy of it." Now she finds it fun to work with others to solve problems and create community. "It is amazing to me that in the two years we have been providing these events, we have collectively kept hundreds of items out of the landfill. The feeling of kindness among strangers is a rich community builder. Some people come with loneliness, as well as a need for a new elastic waistband for their pants. They love visiting with the volunteers and sharing stories of their own. People leave feeling that people still do care about each other."

At Repair Cafes, families are always welcome. And families volunteer. In Warwick, Jim Harper, a senior project manager for an engineering website, volunteers with sons Able (eight) and Eli (five) to man the Kids Take It Apart Table — putting things back together not required. "Our boys never complain about going to the RC. Able loves the time he spends at the table," says his mom, Raheli, a volunteer mending and sewing expert. What kinds of things do the kids take apart? Well, today, a woman whose hair dryer can't be fixed is pleased to donate it to what she called the "reuse play station," commenting, "It's better there than in the landfill." And a couple who had things repaired by the small electrics team at the previous cafe stops by just to drop off a cassette recorder, a clock radio, and a camera. Boys and girls wielding tiny screwdrivers dive right in. The mother of a six-year-old boy says that when her son was only four, he took apart the family vacuum cleaner and put it back together all by himself. "We don't have enough stuff for him to work on. He usually can't sit still, but he hasn't moved since he sat down at the kids' table." Pointing to Jim, who is explaining how a glowing miniature light bulb works, she adds, "I think he enjoys it as much as the kids!" At the end of each event, Jim stores everything yet to be taken apart in his basement until the next cafe. Items that have been reduced to bits are dropped off at the Best Buy store or the e-waste recycling center at the County Transfer Station.

Rob Shaw, a systems administrator who works in tech support, brings along his fifteen-year-old daughter, Raven, and his twin, twenty-year-old sons, Nathaniel and Zachary, to learn and help diagnose digital device problems. Today, the team deals with several smartphones, laptops, a tablet that "only charges to 20 percent," and a pair of headphones. They salvage a Macintosh computer ("Disk successfully removed. Hard drive needs replacement"), two DVD players ("Doesn't show video" and "Doesn't play the discs"), and a computer that needs updates. Rob tells the owner of one computer ("just stopped working") that he will "be in touch later with the right part." A computer with a "hidden software" problem is, according to the owner, "made better, anyway." Another customer writes on her job ticket, "Twin boys cleared cell phone storage. Excellent." The family team shows another owner how to delete items to increase his device's speed. Rob's wife, Regina, is an artist and volunteers her sewing skills. "The Repair Cafe is one part of why I moved my family from New Jersey to Warwick. Even if I change one person's outlook on consumerism or turn trash back into treasure, I feel I've made a difference, so I'll keep coming back."

In Newburgh, New York, Damian DePauw, president and CFO of an organization whose mission is to increase civic participation in impoverished communities through volunteering, organizes a Repair Cafe in conjunction with members of the Together We Can Timebank. A dedicated TimeBank member brought in a computer hard drive that had failed many years before. She'd saved the device because it contained photos of her husband, who had passed away five years earlier. Two repair coaches teamed up to get into the hard drive, extract the files, and put them on another drive for her. She teared up as she looked at a few of them and then said that although she had made plans for the rest of the evening, she just wanted to go home to see all the photos of the husband she misses so dearly.

A boy who wanted to fix a part on his game console approached coach Tom Treat at the Repair Cafe in Newburyport, Massachusetts. The boy had already researched what needed to be done, but he didn't have the proper tools to open the console. Tom lent the boy the right-size screwdriver and supported him with a "few well-placed words of encouragement and direction." Then, Tom explained, "he dove in. He wore such a look of empowerment."

Not every kid is comfortable with "hands-on" experiences, but any child can still have a role to play. Colleen M. Johnston, the organizer of the Repair Fair in Milwaukie, Oregon, says, "My youngest son is on the autism spectrum, and he has participated every year as a spectator watching others repair." At the Warwick Repair Cafe, Scott Cheney, a musician who volunteers to fix fretted instruments — guitars, mandolins, ukuleles — has brought along one of his adult guitar students, who is also on the autism spectrum. The duo perform a lively concert for us. At this same event, Scott also appraises an old violin as "useful for a student." A woman waiting to have her knives sharpened overhears and says she knows of a young girl who needs an instrument. She volunteers to deliver the violin to the girl's parents, who are members of her church. The violin's owner is delighted that her deceased grandfather's instrument will bring joy to a new generation.

A Cut Above

> The expectations of life depend upon diligence; the mechanic that would perfect his work must first sharpen his tools.
>
> — Confucius

The blade sharpening station — specializing in non-serrated knives, scissors, and garden tools — is second to lamps in popularity. Today Warwick's team works on a pair of cuticle clippers, a hatchet, a World War II–era machete captured by a U.S. Marine stationed in the Philippines, now used to hack weeds, seven pairs of scissors, a drawer full of assorted kitchen knives, garden shears, grass shears ("screw walks"), a hand pruner, three hedge pruners, lopping shears, and six pairs of other clippers. A tall woman walks in, brandishing a pruning tool at least six feet long. She cackles and says, "I'm the grim reaper! I want to get the saw back on the pole."

Today's sharpening team includes Roger Moss, a beekeeper and bread baker who once operated his own catering business; Fred Rossi, a retired auto parts/machine shop owner and volunteer firefighter; and Brian Fitzsimmons, who runs his own energy-efficient, commercial lighting and controls systems business. One of Fred's visitors is so grateful to have sharp blades again that she tells him, "I was going to go out for dinner, but now that my knives are sharp, I'm going home to cook." Another woman exclaims, "Now all we need is a roast!" Another draws a happy face on her job ticket and scribbles, "Great Advice Too!" A middle-aged man wearing a baseball cap stands in the middle of the room, clutching a three-foot-long pair of freshly sharpened tree loppers to his chest. On his way out, he writes in the guest book: "I love this — everyone here is so warm and friendly. Need to go home and break stuff just so I can come back." A woman tells Brian that he should open a knife-sharpening station at the Sunday farmers' market. "You'd make a lot of money." He smiles and says, "I already have a job. This place is not about money. It's about giving."

Steve Carras, an attorney who loves to cook, divides his time between the sharpening table and working on cracked wooden chairs, gluing the broken hoof on a turquoise blue, Murano-style glass horse, and attaching a wooden birdhouse to a six-foot pole. He volunteers, he says, because "I love to experience the singular joy of repairing and reusing items and demonstrating that anyone — and everyone — can repair or restore everyday household items. I feel it is my duty to work with others toward the goal of greater self-reliance and to fight the onslaught of the 'disposable' goods industry so that future generations don't look back at mine and say, 'Why did you leave us such a mess?'"

Heidi Spinella, a self-employed management consultant, volunteers to repair small items — ceramics, wooden boxes, toys, eyeglasses — at the Newburyport, Massachusetts, Repair Cafe. "My definition of local is planet Earth, so whether I know someone personally or not doesn't matter — we are all related in one way or another. I believe everything has a spirit, and repairing things is a way to pay respect to the invisible source that animates all life."

A woman brought Heidi a set of decorative plates purchased on her Mexican honeymoon thirty years before. They'd hung on her dining room wall, a tribute to love, until her little boy accidentally knocked them down. No one knew how to fix the plates, so they'd been stored in a box for decades. Now, her little boy is a man about to marry, and she wanted to give him the plates as a wedding gift. Heidi and the owner carefully glued all the plates and placed each one in a separate box, surrounded by paper, to keep them vertical until the epoxy set overnight. The woman left beaming.

Edwin Winstanley, a retired clinical chemist who also volunteers for the Catskill Mountain Railroad and the Empire State Railroad Museum, has been presented today with a sneaker ("bottom needs to be glued back on"), a mirror ("one side needs to be glued"), cracked basket handles, an Ethiopian ceramic cook pot with a broken "foot," a piano bench, and several wooden tables. He'll be able to mend them all.

Back during Warwick's very first Repair Cafe, a man with a child's rocker tucked under his arm walked in fifteen minutes before we had to vacate the space for another scheduled event. Told that there wasn't enough time left to repair his rocker, he said, "I only want advice." Edwin examined the rocker's split seat, recommended the appropriate glue, and described how to clamp the seam shut without damaging the wood. "What about the scratches and dents? How do I clean them up?" Edwin, who also volunteers to make repairs at the historical society, winced. "It's up to you, but I wouldn't touch them. You said that the chair belonged to your wife when she was a child? Those scratches are part of its history." The man nodded, and on the way out, dropped twenty dollars in the donation jar. "But we didn't fix it!" said one of the greeters. "That's okay. Now I know what to do."

Many of the people who volunteer for the sewing team, in Warwick and elsewhere, are pros. Deanne Singer, a retired high school teacher, operates a tailoring, alteration, and custom sewing business. Deanne's friend Joan Bono crafts one-of-a-kind teddy bears from discarded fur coats and repairs torn teddy bears, soft toys, and dolls. Mary Bono, no relation to Joan, is an illustrator and graphic designer who sells her vintage button jewelry and tote bags — hand-crocheted with *plarn*, strips cut from used plastic bags — in a local women's craft co-op and her own Etsy site. Katy Banovic once worked for an outdoor gear repair business in Oregon. Now she has her own business providing sewing repairs on outdoor gear and clothing. At repair events in Newburyport, Massachusetts, she does all the repairs on zippers and heavy materials and specializes in tricky sewing problems.

Sewing teams typically work on clothing. Job tickets from previous events in Warwick record that the sewing team has altered, hemmed, mended, or shortened men's and women's pants and shorts, shirts, blouses, uniforms (one of which "needs snaps"), coats and jackets ("hanging loop torn on one side," "does not zip properly," and "button holes unraveling"), holey mittens, a leather catcher's mitt, two torn bathrobes, and a silk, floral-print Japanese kimono ("sleeves too long. Afraid I'll catch on fire at the stove"). The team has also restored and repaired zippers on clothing, backpacks, picnic and pet carriers, and a carrying case for a floor-standing harp. However, the range of textiles and their problems is much wider: moth-eaten sofa pillows and lounge

chair cushions ("chewed by a dog"), a cervical pillow, a torn bar towel imported from an English pub, curtains, a woven rag rug, and a canvas log carrier. Today they craft a queen-sized blanket from two bunk-sized vintage Army blankets. Liz Bonita, a retired nurse who was recruited by her husband, Tom, a retired court administrator, part of the small electrics team, teaches a customer how to properly thread her own machine. Lenny Valentino, who taught herself to sew, encourages another visitor to sit beside her while she demonstrates how to replace a skirt's elastic waistband.

Joan and Mary restore a "headless" teddy bear and reattach another bear's torn ear, a doll's arms, and two legs ripped from a stuffed toy unicorn with a lilac-colored horn. Then a young couple, the woman wearing a sparkling engagement ring, approaches the sewing tables. She carries a black-and-white cloth dog in her palm and says that the toy's nose was chewed off by her living, breathing dog. Her fiancée explains the toy's significance: his bride-to-be had been born prematurely; her parents had tucked the tiny toy into their daughter's isolette. Clearly, this little toy holds a great deal of love. And it's with love that Mary stitches the torn nose back onto the beloved toy's face.

"More than once a parent has come in, followed by a teary-eyed toddler who's holding a frayed, worn, torn 'lovey,'" says Dära Salk, community outreach director and cofounder of a Repair Cafe held at Chicago's second busiest library. "The look on their faces as the little item is carefully repaired by our 'seamstress' is worth more than any of us can say. These are the reasons we get up and out early on a cold, snowy, or rainy Saturday morning." At the Repair Cafe sewing table, love is the thread that binds us.

Dan Barkevich, a repair coach at the Schenectady and Saratoga, New York, Repair Cafes, is an engineer who manages engineers, and he uses the same management skills as a volunteer because "repairing brings life to lifelessness." At his very first cafe, a woman walked in cradling two dolls that had belonged to her for fifty years. They had fallen to pieces decades ago, but she'd kept them, and then she heard about the Repair Cafe and hoped someone there might be able to help. Although he had no experience with dolls, Dan stared at the pair for a long time. Then, with the assistance of the dolls' owner, he used elastic, wire, and zip ties to reconstruct them. Proud of his accomplishment, Dan held the dolls for a moment, then handed them off to the tearful owner. "I will never forget the look she gave me…as if I had just restored a part of her youth."

CAN THIS BE REPAIRED?

Jonathan Ment, who volunteers his carpentry skills at Repair Cafe events hosted by Transition Catskills, is also good with needle and thread. As a kid, he learned to sew patches on his Cub Scout uniform, and he even crafted a felt pillow with a hand-stitched Curious George monkey face on the front. At a recent Repair Cafe, Ment took a break from fixing things for others to show his vintage pillow to the sewing team. He wanted advice on how to mend the worn fabric and damaged stuffing. "I made this with my grandmother over forty years ago sitting at her kitchen table....I'm not sure what to do with it now — or if it can even be repaired." The seamstress and another volunteer took a hard look at the beloved pillow and decided "it's folk art. Don't fix it. Frame it." So Jonathan will use his carpentry skills to build a suitable frame to "display this connection to my childhood and grandmother and other bits of art and memories."

Fixers of Meaningful Things

Warwick's jewelry repair team includes Cathe' Linton, who for several years had a store on the village's main street, selling her own designs and Native American silver pieces. Now she volunteers to serve her community, to stay in touch, and to meet other "fixers of meaningful things." "Everything that comes in here has had a life," she says. "We are not just fixing items. We are repairing souls." Cathe' is joined by Suzanne O'Brien, who sells her collection of "salvaged and refashioned fancies" on Etsy, and sometimes by multitalented Barb, who says, "Random acts of kindness make me feel good." As a young teen, Barb taught herself how to make vases into lamps and beads into jewelry for her mother's store, and at the Repair Cafe she shifts between lamp, jewelry, ceramics, and wooden repairs, depending upon the size of the repair-seeking crowd. This time, the team works on a watch, several bracelets, including a "14K link" ("broken jump ring," "broken metal butterfly wing," "tangled," and "missing loop"). They shorten necklaces and repair a string of pearls ("clasp opens"), several pairs of earrings ("everything came apart," "backward drops," "back fell off," "broken bead"), two rosaries, a mezuzah scroll case, and a miniature, carved wooden elephant with a tangled chain dragging a log.

Just as Suzanne is packing up, an older woman rushes in, clutching a braided silver chain. She has arrived late because she got lost and has been driving in circles for nearly an hour. Choking back tears, she says that she can't afford to take her chain to a jewelry store to be repaired. Nor can she afford to wait a month for the next cafe. The chain has to be fixed today, now, because it supports an engraved cylinder that contains a loved one's ashes. The woman has worn the chain all day, every day, since her grandson's funeral. While Suzanne works on the damaged chain, the grieving grandmother shares the story behind the young man's untimely and tragic death. After the restored chain with the cylinder is hooked once again around her neck, the woman sighs deeply, wipes her eyes with the back of her hand, hugs Suzanne, and says, "You don't know what you've done today!"

Jewelry items such as these seem to be especially meaningful to visitors at all Repair Cafes. Barbara Lane, who worked as an elementary art teacher for more than thirty years, handles a lot of jewelry repairs at the New Paltz, New York, cafe. "Once, a young woman presented me with a bracelet formed with beads made from dried flowers. She teared up as she explained that the flowers were from her husband's funeral. She was so fearful that it could not be repaired when all it needed was a simple jump ring and new clasp. By the end of the repair, we were both in tears. I still think about her, remembering the gratitude that she expressed as she left our table. It's repairs like this that keep me coming back."

"When I fix something for someone, even just a lamp or wobbly chair, it enhances their life, saves them some money, and makes me feel good. For a few moments, I am the person I want to be. That by itself would keep me coming back. Saving things from the landfill is just a bonus." This is from Larry James, co-organizer of the Repair Cafe in Lincoln, Nebraska.

Back in Warwick, a woman, her husband, and his elderly father arrive twenty minutes before Warwick's cafe is closing, with just enough

time to sharpen their dull kitchen knives. The old gentleman sheds his jacket and scarf, arranges his cane, and seats himself to watch. After Brian, Roger, and Fred have sharpened several knives, by hand, on oiled whetstones, the man slowly stands up, pats down and rummages through all his pockets, and triumphantly hands over a battered pocketknife. When it is returned to him, he is visibly delighted with the newly sharpened blade. Then his family collects their cutlery and returns their job tickets to the check-in table, and the woman deposits ten dollars in the now-empty donation jar.

Cash has been counted, bills paid. Charles, the food pantry manager, has returned to collect the donations given throughout the day by our visitors. Now he is packing up boxes and cans, so Lisa, our treasurer, hands the woman's tip to him. "But he's not the one who sharpened our knives!" the woman protests. After Lisa explains who Charles is, the grateful woman takes out her wallet and hands him another twenty dollars for the food pantry.

At the end of any repair day, some of the volunteers need to scoot, but some like to linger. On a Wednesday evening at the Fixers Collective in Brooklyn, New York, after the last customer has left, Vincent Lai, Emily Forman, Joe Holdner, and David Kline sat around exchanging quips.

Vincent: What are we? I'll tell you. We are an ongoing social experiment in aggressive asset recovery and improvisational fixing.

David: In plain English, we're a bunch of tinkerers who like to work on stuff.

Joe: I'm a serial compulsive repairer.

Emily (in her best confessional voice): I'm also a serial compulsive fixer.

Vincent: I've even been called a Toolbox Detective.

Joe: Have you noticed that when you repair a lamp and the light goes on, the owner lights up also?

Emily: Nine times out of ten, it's something so simple, there's just no reason to throw it out. Well, eight times out of ten.

David: It's important to me personally to feel I'm doing something good for the world.

Joe: You try to get people involved, and if we can show someone how it got done, even better.

Vincent: Well, we're offering the world a highly immersive and interactive skill-share.

Emily: The one we did at the school for dogs was really hard. Woof!

Vincent: At the end of the day, everyone knows — or should know — that the most environmentally responsible item you have is the one you already own.

After Warwick's volunteers have packed up their tools and supplies, taken down the signs, carried out the recyclables, reset the room's tables and chairs the way we found them, and turned off the lights, Nick, a seventh-grader, says that he's "had a great time, learned a lot — can fix my lamp at home." Thirteen-year-old Ethan Bele, who also volunteered to acquire community service hours, says, "It's nice to know that with the news saying so many sad and depressing stories, there's a place where there are people who are willing to help you, no matter who you are, for no other reason than to help you in the best way possible. It gives me hope."

The Road
to Sustainability

> Every decently made object, from a house to a lamp post to
> a bridge, spoon or egg cup, is not just a piece of "stuff," but a
> physical embodiment of human energy, a testimony to the
> magical ability of our species to take raw materials and turn
> them into things of use, value and beauty.
>
> — Kevin McCloud, designer

In southwestern Pennsylvania, an archaeological site called Meadow-croft Rockshelter marks an ancient stopping-off place for Paleo-Indians traveling on foot between the Ohio River Valley and the Allegheny highlands, dating back an astonishing sixteen thousand years. Today the site is quite far from any population center and protected from the elements in such a way that it has preserved the longest continuous record of human activity in North America: campfires, arrowheads, shards of pottery, and tools. Anthropologist Lucy Johnson of Vassar College says that we humans are obligate toolmakers: "We cannot exist without tools and are constantly thinking up new ones. Other animals both make and use tools, but the nature and sophistication of our tools are of an entirely different level."

It seems we are also obligate repairers. There is ample evidence that pottery has been both made and repaired by North American Indigenous peoples dating back several thousand years. Archaeologists have found "drilled holes on each side of a crack that had apparently occurred before the vessel was completely broken and discarded. These holes have been interpreted as patching holes, through which a thong of sinew was attached, allowing the vessel to continue to be used, perhaps for storage of dry materials....From this we might say that Indians have been repairing pots for as long as they have had pots."

As our national story progressed, our tools and the way we made them continued to become more complicated. About a hundred miles to the northeast of Rockshelter, there is a bend in the Allegheny River where the river slows. This was homeland to the Erie and Susquehannock peoples and well known as a good place to ford or land a canoe or raft. In the 1820s, white settlers built a charcoal-fired iron "bloomery" and foundry there — a bloomery being the most basic type of furnace for making iron. Producing a fire hot enough to make iron required large amounts of charcoal, and today you will still come upon the chimney-like remains of charcoal furnaces throughout the region. The ratio of hard wood needed to make charcoal is about three to one, and whole valleys were clear-cut to provide it.

This little piece of northwestern Pennsylvania was also known for its prolific "oil seeps," and in 1859, New England investors hired Edwin Drake, a former train conductor, to drill the nation's first commercial oil well in nearby Titusville. Internal combustion engines were still fifty years away, but this subterranean oil was easily refined into kerosene, which was replacing candles and whale oil for lighting homes (we likely have this to thank for the survival of whales as a species), and the petroleum industry began its exponential growth. With it, economic progress was cast as moral progress. It seemed that the earth was ours for the taking, and over the next 150 years technology advanced in unimaginable ways. Petrochemicals gave us synthetics and plastic, and fuel was cheap and abundant. During the Gilded Age, from the Civil War to America's entry into World War I, fortunes were built on the superabundance of timber, mineral wealth, and grazing land. Railroads closed distances and leveled mountain ranges. It was an age of astonishing economic growth and innovation. In the three decades between 1860 and 1890, some half a million patents were issued for new inventions — more than ten times the number issued in the previous seventy years. Manufacturing at a scale never seen before required workers, and millions of people moved from rural America and Europe to the urban centers of the Northeast and Midwest. Everything grew. But this was a growth that depended entirely on extraction and depletion.

Thrift and the Roots of Sustainability

If growth and extraction triumphed as the dominant strain in American business, there has nonetheless always been an alternative story. In 1733, Ben Franklin published the first edition of *Poor Richard's Almanac*, a homespun compendium of calendars and weather predictions, recipes, and practical advice. Almanacs like these were the most widely read secular books in the colonies, and Franklin continued to publish a new edition every year for the next twenty-five years, providing him with a substantial income. Today, *Poor Richard* is mostly remembered for its aphorisms about industry and frugality: "All things are cheap to the saving, dear to the wasteful," "He that is rich need not live sparingly, and he that can live sparingly need not be rich," and in the 1758 almanac, "A penny saved is a penny got" (contrary to popular belief, Franklin never used the word *earned* in this saying).

Until very recently, repairing rather than replacing was a necessity of life. In *A Museum of Early American Tools* and other books, writer and illustrator Eric Sloane chronicles how in the 1800s and early 1900s things were made by hand — with ingenious tools — and then kept in good repair. Sloane does not trade in nostalgia. "Herein lies one of the strangest of American beliefs," he writes, "for we honestly think the old-timers had more time on their hands than we do now. Nothing of course could be farther from the truth." If you lived far from any general store, or if bartering was your essential currency, then making things last was the rule of life for most people — as it still is in much of the world. Self-reliance was a virtue. In 1841 Ralph Waldo Emerson wrote: "It is easy to see that a greater self-reliance must work a revolution in all the offices and relations of men."

> All repairing *must* be done by hand. We can make every
> detail of a watch or of a gun by machinery, but the machine
> cannot mend it when broken, much less a clock or a pistol!
> — Manual of Mending and Repairing (1896)

In the early twentieth century, American society at all levels was enraptured by the thrift movement, a collection of virtues with both individual and social dimensions. In his book *Thrift, the History of an American Cultural Movement*, journalist Andrew L. Yarrow tells a story that has been largely forgotten but that resonates strongly with cultural movements today. The social currents of the time gave it strength. The Industrial Revolution brought egregious income disparities — and there was an unease in the character of many Americans toward the rapid shift in values from self-reliance to the wage economy. Moral reformers sought to "better" the burgeoning working class in the midst of the Roaring Twenties, which arguably brought the first wave of mass-market consumer culture. Credit unions and savings and loan associations encouraged people to set long-term goals and work steadily to meet them. "There is a close intellectual lineage between the thrift movement's antipathy toward waste, push to conserve and belief in stewardship," writes Yarrow, "and the modern idea of environmental sustainability."

The American Education Association and the American Bankers Association, among others, joined forces to promote the message: succeed and live well by earning, saving, and conserving. The YMCA organized National Thrift Week and planned it to begin every year on the birthday of Ben Franklin — the "patron saint of thrift." Boy Scouts recited a Thrift Creed, "In order that I may become a Better American Citizen," and Boy Scout promise number ten was to "avoid waste in every form." Girl Scouts could earn a Thrift Badge and learned the couplet "A Girl Scout patches and darns the rift, for the Laws of Scouting are founded on thrift."

Forebears

John recalls: *My brother and sister and I inherited thrift values from our Midwestern parents. Our mother grew up in a small Iowa town during the Great Depression, and she too knew the rhyme "Use it up, wear it out, make it do, or do without." In an early memory, our mom is showing us photos of the dresses her mother made for her and our aunt — and a little later, photos of them wearing dresses they'd sewed themselves. The pictures were in black and white, of course, and she delighted in describing the colors of the fabrics as she remembered them — and asking us to imagine the colors too.*

Our dad also grew up in a small town, in Wisconsin, and he attended the university in Madison. This is where the ideas of two giants of the modern environmental movement, John Muir and Aldo Leopold, were shaped. Each in his own time articulated principles of sustainability that are fundamental to the story of how we got here, in this time.

John Muir grew up on a farm in Wisconsin with no formal schooling. Farm work was all consuming two-thirds of the year, but during the winter months he had endless hours to invent and tinker. He was mechanically gifted and designed and built elaborate inventions, from wood mostly. Some displayed a wicked sense of humor, such as an alarm clock that tipped his bed up and slid him onto the floor. In 1861 — the year the Civil War broke out — the state university in Madison accepted Muir on the strength of his inventions. Muir's fantastical eight-foot-tall alarm clock / study desk is still on display in the entryway of the State Historical Society Museum in Madison. Muir left the university after his second year for what he would later call the "University of the Wilderness." But before he started out on the epic walks that would take him to the Sierra Nevada, he worked in factories, repairing and renovating equipment, and found he could also make machines more efficient. From the many books and countless magazine articles he published in his lifetime, perhaps the most-quoted expression of his philosophy of ecology and the wisdom of connections is this: "When we try to pick out anything by itself, we find it hitched to everything else in the Universe."

In the 1920s, Aldo Leopold came to the University of Wisconsin from his early career with the U.S. Forest Service. A boyhood of hunting and fishing had taken him in and out of every type of terrain and habitat. As an adult, he opted for bow hunting, which required patience and an acute awareness of one's surroundings. In time, Leopold put his bow aside for a notebook and applied the same keen attention to a different purpose. He did the field work that led to the establishment of the Gila National Forest in New Mexico as the nation's first Wilderness Area. He believed that direct contact with the natural world is crucial to shaping our willingness to extend our ethics beyond our own self-interest. In the 1930s he and his family started their own ecological restoration experiment along the Wisconsin River, planting thousands of pine trees and restoring the prairie habitat on a worn-out farm. In Madison, he researched and ultimately defined a field that had no name yet: wildlife management. He articulated a deeply personal view of land and wildlife conservation that became widely known as the "land ethic." In *A Sand County Almanac* (1948), Leopold wrote: "All ethics so far evolved rest upon a single premise: that the individual is a member of a community of interdependent parts."

Muir and Leopold were forebears of what we now know as "systems thinking" — Muir through observation and intuition, Leopold through observation and disciplined research. In Leopold's words, they understood "that man-made changes are of a different order than evolutionary changes, and have effects more comprehensive than is intended or foreseen."

Building the Consumer Economy

A quite logical challenge to the long-standing traditions of craftsmanship and quality emerged with the Great Depression. There is an inevitable tension between the cost to manufacture a product that will last a good long time and the need to increase sales. In 1932, a New York City real estate broker named Bernard London was among those who argued that the thrifty mindset of mending and saving had produced a "chokehold" on the economy. He addressed that problem in his pamphlet, "Ending the Depression through Planned Obsolescence."

"People everywhere are today disobeying the law of obsolescence," London observed. "Worn out automobiles, radios, and hundreds of other items which would long ago have been discarded and replaced in more normal times, are being made to last another season or two or three, because the public is afraid or has not the funds to buy now." London believed such practices went against the natural order of things. "Furniture and clothing and other commodities should have a span of life, just as humans have. When used for their allotted time, they should be retired, and replaced by fresh merchandise." Possibly most notable of all is his suggestion that this should be managed by the federal government. "It should be the duty of the State as the regulator of business to see that the system functions smoothly, deciding matters for capital and labor and seeing that everybody is sufficiently employed." As historian Giles Slade writes in *Made to Break*, his study of technology and obsolescence in America, "Though the policy was not implemented at that time, all the elements of what would become known as planned obsolescence or 'death dating' were clearly in place by 1932. All that was needed was for them to come together. When exactly this happened is unclear, but by 1950 this combination had long since taken place."

BRAVE NEW WORLD

In 1932, the same year that Bernard London distributed his pamphlet extolling planned obsolescence, Aldous Huxley published *Brave New World*, his novel depicting a different kind of "civilization." In this scene we have an exchange between the Controller and the Savage:

continued on next page

> "Why is it prohibited?" asked the Savage.
>
> The Controller shrugged his shoulders. "Because it's old; that's the chief reason. We haven't any use for old things here."
>
> "Even when they're beautiful?"
>
> "Particularly when they're beautiful. Beauty's attractive, and we don't want people attracted by old things. We want them to like new ones."

The national emergency of World War II rapidly pivoted and ramped up domestic production to meet the nation's all-consuming war aims. Economists disagree about whether the war ended the Great Depression, but it clearly had the effect of "institutionalizing" frugal living, at least for a time. Scrap collecting and recycling became patriotic overnight. One tank required eighteen tons of metal. The nation's wartime motivations were clear — we were all in this together — and participation was extraordinarily high in towns and cities across the nation. Citizens were encouraged to raise their own vegetables by planting "Victory Gardens," and by 1943, about one-third of all the vegetables produced in the United States came from these modest plots in backyards and vacant lots: "Eat what you can, and can what you can't" was just one popular slogan created by advertising copywriters for the Office of War Information. Educational pamphlets on every imaginable home-husbandry subject — including basic repairs — were written, illustrated, and distributed by the U.S. Department of Agriculture, and it is important to say that these programs continue today through cooperative extension offices in all fifty states. After the war, the behaviors that made the scrap drives indisputable morale boosters were mostly abandoned, even as scrap yards became thriving "fringe" businesses located in the poorest section of any town. By 1951 there were already an estimated twenty-five thousand automobile junkyards dotting the American landscape.

In the postwar period, Bernard London's cherished goal was essentially realized when President Eisenhower's chairman of the Council of Economic Advisors, Raymond Saulnier, stated, "The American economy's ultimate purpose is to produce more consumer goods." In an era of perceived limitless resources, this may have made sense. In our own era, we know that this kind of overconsumption is fundamentally unsustainable.

Homecrafting, DIY, and Access to Tools

The virtues of thrift and home economy have been in keeping with the American character for generations. Our natural can-do impulse is rewarded by the deep satisfactions of individual creativity and curiosity, which in turn give us skills and knowledge that others admire in us. Home sewing and home electronics are two examples with broad cultural sweep. Both exploded in popularity in the twentieth century, enabled by entrepreneurs who thought up ways to give amateurs the tools and instructions they would need to do it themselves.

In 1863, in their home in Sterling, Massachusetts, Ellen Butterick told her husband, Ebenezer, a tailor, how useful it would be if dress patterns could be "graded" — that is, if you could buy them in different sizes. At the time, patterns came in only one size, to be used as a guide, and the home seamstress had to enlarge or reduce it.

By the 1860s, women everywhere were making clothes for their families. The Industrial Revolution, which began with the mass production of textiles, had made cloth affordable, and the first home sewing machine had been introduced by Isaac Singer in the United States in 1851. Ebenezer took his wife's idea seriously, and before long, the Buttericks were producing graded patterns out of their home in more than a dozen sizes for both men's and women's clothing. From this simple idea, the Butterick sewing pattern company began a history of innovations that served the interests of home seamstresses (or *sewists*, to use a newer term). By 1900, the Buttericks were receiving thirty thousand letters a week, which they welcomed because they believed that "listening to the customer was the best way to ensure a successful product." They also started one of the first general interest magazines for women, *The Delineator*, which chronicled the activities and accomplishments of progressive women here and abroad and introduced European designs. Many other pattern publishers entered the market, and while the Depression decreased spending power, home sewing sales increased. When World War II mandated textile rationing, pattern makers redesigned their clothing for a slimmer silhouette, shorter lengths, and patterns with fewer pieces. In the sixties, E. Butterick & Company licensed the Vogue name and introduced patterns for Paris couture designs. By the seventies, sewing and knitting magazines were for sale at every supermarket check-out in the nation.

All the while, men and boys pursued their passion for projects requiring tools and a different type of schematic. In natural progression, *Popular Mechanics* began publishing in 1902, the first Heathkit home electronics kits came out immediately after World War II, and *Popular Electronics* followed in 1954. These resources did more than provide instructions on how to build or fix things. They were adept at generating excitement and fueling the dreams of American boys. The cover of the January 1953 issue of *Popular Mechanics* announced: "Wanted: 50,000 Engineers!"

Frank Szenher, a Repair Cafe volunteer and recently retired IBM engineer, suggests that his own boyhood interest is a good example of what led many boys into careers in engineering. "I've wanted to take things apart for as long as I can remember," he says. "As a kid I started asking for radios as birthday and Christmas presents and checking out books from the library about electronics." Frank used circuit diagrams he found in *Popular Electronics*, *Popular Mechanics*, and the *ARRL Amateur Radio Handbook*. He remembers that his first kit was for a Philmore AM transistor radio — which he still has. "I built several transmitters and receivers 'from scratch,' scavenging the parts from old TVs and radios." This kind of learning is still readily available, he says. Several companies in the United States make kits, online user groups are constantly trading information worldwide, and the maker movement is engaging kids nationwide.

In the midst of all this mainstream marketing of how-to information, an influential counterculture version was introduced. In 1968, a writer named Stewart Brand conceived *The Whole Earth Catalog*. It was a profusely illustrated large-format catalog, with listings, reviews, and mail-order information for more than 2,700 books and products, along with essays that reintroduced values such as "Local Dependency" and "Voluntary Simplicity" to a new generation. It promised to provide "Access to Tools," and its statement of purpose was a manifesto of the times: "We are as gods and might as well get good at it.... A realm of intimate personal power is developing — the power of individuals to conduct their own education, find their own inspiration, shape their own environment, and share the adventure with whoever is interested."

Brand described the function of the catalog as an evaluation and access device, and he specified the criteria for inclusion; an item could be listed in the catalog if it had the following characteristics:

1. Useful as a tool
2. Relevant to independent education
3. High quality or low cost
4. Not already common knowledge
5. Easily available by mail

It would be hard to overstate the impact of this publication on the counterculture of the pre-internet world. Steve Jobs, in his 2005 Stanford University commencement speech, famously proclaimed that "*The Whole Earth Catalog* was one of the bibles of my generation.... It was sort of like Google in paperback form, thirty-five years before Google came along: It was idealistic, and overflowing with neat tools and great notions." What seems remarkable, even now, is that the "cultural fix" or corrective offered in *The Whole Earth Catalog* — that is, reclaiming personal agency — captured the spirit of the times so astutely, and almost surgically addressed the social maladies that Brand diagnosed.

HOW TO KEEP YOUR VOLKSWAGEN ALIVE

In 1973, Andrew Willner's ancient and abused Volkswagen bus was breaking down. It was burning almost as much oil as gasoline, and with very little money, he decided to rebuild the engine himself. He knew something about cars and could do a basic tune-up, but, he admitted, "This would be my biggest, scariest project by far."

Andrew was an avid reader of *The Whole Earth Catalog*, and there he found a book, *How to Keep Your Volkswagen Alive: A Manual of Step-by-Step Procedures for the Compleat Idiot* by John Muir (his real name — he was a distant relative of the famous naturalist). "When the book came in the mail, I began the rebuild," he says. "As promised, the book described step-by-step how to remove the engine and take it apart, even telling you to buy the large wrench needed to remove the nut from the crank shaft at Sears, because they would replace any Craftsman tool that broke, and that I would break that wrench."

Following the book's recommended steps, Andrew put down brown paper on the workbench, and drew a line around each part as he took it out. Then the book instructed him to take the resulting basket of pistons, heads, valves, camshaft, and crank shafts to a machine shop to have them milled to new specs. "The book made it clear that I would be ignored at the machine shop if I did not use the exact words and appropriate dimensions — especially because of the culture clash between my hippyish appearance and the machine shop culture. So, I wrote a script based entirely on Muir's advice, memorized it, walked into the shop, recited exactly what was on the script, and handed over the parts with a small wad of cash. I was told to come back in a week. I must have said the right thing as the shiny new looking parts were waiting for me, and the guy behind the counter only gave a passing look to the hairy guy (me) picking up the parts."

Andrew spent the next week, watched by a largely skeptical group of friends, putting the engine back together with the new parts, only to discover one piece that didn't seem to go anywhere. Going back to the book for advice, he found Muir's assurance that leaving out one or two extra pieces wouldn't do the engine much harm. New plugs and wires, new oil filter, exhaust manifolds, and maybe $100 in cash later, the engine turned over and ran for another 150,000 miles. Andrew concludes, "After that, pretty much everyone I knew started rebuilding Volkswagen engines until my grease stained *Manual for the Compleat Idiot* was reduced to compost."

The Age of the Anthropocene

We have been describing some of the trade-offs between the use of natural resources and conservation of natural resources. Looking at it through another lens, social psychologists try to track how changes in economic well-being and other factors drive changes in our attitudes toward nature, that is, how we make decisions about the resources we use, both personally and institutionally. The American public has generally balanced protection of the environment with the desire for economic growth, perhaps with the beauty of our National Park System prominent in their minds. But in a 2016 Gallup poll, the percentage of Americans who identify as "environmentalists" had dropped to 42 percent from a high of 78 percent in 1991. Now we have entered the Age of the Anthropocene, the geological epoch signifying that human activity has become the dominant driver of change for the Earth's climate and ecosystems. Discarded garbage, plastics, and e-waste have risen to unheard-of heights. "With the possible exception of China in the twenty-first century," writes thrift historian Andrew Yarrow, "no society has embarked on so much consumption so feverishly as the United States in the quarter century after World War II."

A number of critics helped define the era by challenging consumerism and blind faith in progress. Journalist Vance Packard's book *The Waste Makers* (1960) exposed the concept of "planned obsolescence" built into products so that they will wear out quickly, while his *Hidden*

Persuaders (1957) revealed the subliminal techniques used in advertising to make us buy stuff we don't really need. The power of "perceived obsolescence" instilled in consumers "the desire to own something a little newer, a little better, a little sooner than is necessary," as so pithily described by industrial designer Brooks Stevens in 1953. In the fifty years from 1920 and 1970, the volume of waste generated in the United States rose five times faster than the population itself. And practically all of it is thrown "away."

The strands of inquiry that led to the concept of sustainability in the twenty-first century (the word was barely used before 1990) are as much social, political, and economic as they are scientific and environmental. In his 1997 book, *The Politics of the Earth*, social theorist John Dryzek gets to the heart of the matter: sustainability is the subject of a broad debate or "discourse" that is attempting to reconcile the conflict between economic and environmental values. In the sixties and seventies, new insights fueled a string of cautionary books that found wide readership: Rachel Carson's *Silent Spring*, Anne and Paul Ehrlich's *The Population Bomb*, Stewart Udall's *The Quiet Crisis*, Barry Commoner's *The Closing Circle*, Garrett Hardin's *The Tragedy of the Commons*, and E.F. Schumacher's *Small Is Beautiful*. The ideas that these writers — mostly scientists — brought to our national consciousness are still with us today. "In many ways," historian Jeremy Caradonna observes, "the sustainable society envisioned by so many is a modernized revival of past wisdom."

> A society in which consumption has to be artificially stimulated to keep production going is a society founded on trash and waste, and such a society is a house built upon sand.
> — Dorothy L. Sayers in *Creed or Chaos* (1947)

Repairing Our Rivers

America's rivers and inland waterways have historically been treated as sewers: the most convenient way to carry away anything unwanted.

Perhaps no modern story illustrates the epic work of environmental repair better than the fight to restore the health of our rivers.

Nineteen sixty-nine was a landmark year in so many ways, and here is one more. On June 22, the Cuyahoga River in Cleveland, Ohio, caught fire. It was national news. To most people it made no sense: how does a river catch fire? However, as we soon learned, this was not the first time. *National Geographic*'s article about the fiftieth anniversary of the fire quotes Frank Samsel, an eighty-nine-year-old Cleveland native who on the day of the fire was piloting his boat, the *Putzfrau* (German for "cleaning lady"), as usual, sucking up chemicals and scooping up debris. "It smelled like a septic tank," he said. "It literally bubbled and produced methane in July and August. It wasn't bad — it was *terrible*. You can't describe it using printable language." A fireboat extinguished the fire in thirty minutes or so, but the controversy it ignited was historic.

That same summer, iconic singer Pete Seeger and his crew began sailing up and down the Hudson River in a 106-foot sloop named the *Clearwater*. Their purpose was to raise awareness of just how dirty and toxic the river water had become. Seeger's idea was simple, says Betsy Garthwaite, a longtime ship's captain and unofficial *Clearwater* historian: "Build an extraordinary boat and people would come in droves to the banks of the neglected Hudson, then described as an 'open sewer,' where they would see its condition for themselves. The sloop might be just the thing, Seeger figured, to show people that the river was beautiful and worth saving."

The idea that the Hudson River could ever be returned to health seemed far-fetched to nearly everyone. Seeger saw it differently. He had experienced the transformative power of music through the social travails of the previous decades, from McCarthyism to the civil rights movement. It was the infectious Pete who had made "If I Had a Hammer," "We Shall Overcome," and "Turn, Turn, Turn" into the inspiring ballads of the movements for civil rights and social justice. Now, in the summer of 1969, Pete and the Hudson River Sloop Singers had a new batch of songs, including Pete's "My Dirty Stream," which became the *Clearwater*'s theme song:

Sailing down my dirty stream
Still I love it and I'll keep the dream
That someday, though maybe not this year
My Hudson River will once again run clear

The day after the Cuyahoga River fire, Cleveland's mayor, Carl Stokes, held a press conference and requested help from the state government to clean up the river. Stokes was the first African American mayor of a major city, and his response caught the attention of the nation, all the more so because just a few months earlier, in January 1969, an oil rig off the coast of Santa Barbara, California, had released a million gallons of oil into the ocean, creating a thirty-five-mile-long slick. Media coverage showing thousands of dead birds and marine animals galvanized public opinion. The modern environmental movement was being born. The first Earth Day was a year away, and soon after came the landmark passage of the Clean Air Act and the Clean Water Act and the creation of the Environmental Protection Agency, all with strong bipartisan support. These were significant changes in national policy, specifically enacted to repair and restore the environmental damage that had proceeded unabated for generations.

Meanwhile, the *Clearwater* was docking at every river town from New York City to Troy, and the Hudson River Sloop Singers gave a concert at each. Hundreds of concerts — and a number of contentious and lengthy lawsuits — later, and the Hudson River slowly began its return to relative health. Further epic battles would be fought for the health of the Hudson, some led by the Hudson River Fisherman's Association, exemplifying what came to be called "blue-collar environmentalism." The resulting court decisions set important precedents for environmental law and policy for rivers across the United States and for the Great Lakes. Back in 1969, Pete had said, "If towns up and down the river start putting in waterfront parks instead of messes, if people all get involved in the work of cleaning up the river, then we'll have something." He lived to see that transformation. Pete Seeger died in 2014, just six months after the death of his wife, Toshi, who was also instrumental to the work.

Today, about seventy species of fish thrive in the Cuyahoga River, along with recreation and real estate. However, mercury and PCBs are still persistent in the river's sediments, and the same toxicity is still to be found in the Hudson and many other American rivers. The work of repairing our rivers continues.

The first recorded fire on the Cuyahoga River was in 1868. Just thirty-seven years earlier, the French historian Alexis de Tocqueville had visited Cleveland en route to New Orleans, and he described the region's waters as the most pristine he had ever seen. In 1835, de Tocqueville wrote in *Democracy in America*: "The great privilege of the Americans is to be able to have repairable mistakes."

Beyond the Recycling Economy

There is plenty at stake where public policy meets the business of where our garbage goes. Since the 1980s, the recycling industry has largely been an export business focused primarily on four commodities: plastic, glass, paper/cardboard, and electronics, mostly shipped in containers to China and remaining remarkably "out of sight, out of mind." And all the while, our own nation's ability to process recyclables — that is to say, to actually recycle materials in the way the public *thinks* we do — has atrophied. Nearly everyone sees recycling as a "bridge" to a sustainable future. It's easy, it feels good, and the message fits nicely into elementary school classrooms. For more than a generation, recycling has received reinforcement from every sector of society, including manufacturers and advertisers, because it seemingly gives us permission to buy everything we want, guilt-free. In fact, the results of a social marketing study conducted at Boston University in 2015 reinforced that supposition, suggesting that when people have the ready option to recycle, they may feel it's okay to use *more* — and so they do.

In November 2017, the organizers of New York State's annual Reduce-Reuse-Recycle conference invited several repair activists to give a presentation about repair as a new "R" word in the materials management lexicon. The conference title was "Keeping Cool in the Age of Climate Change," and the program description of our presentation read: "Repair Cafes offer a unique opportunity to engage communities in taking action to reduce carbon emissions from solid waste." Co-author John was joined by repair organizers from Schenectady, Syracuse, and Buffalo. What we did not know is that a bombshell was about to hit the materials management world. Keeping cool was going to be a challenge.

The bombshell was China's just-announced decision to stop importing most types of foreign waste and to dramatically tighten its standards for impurities in scrap bales. Five years earlier, China had instituted its "Green Fence" rules; but this new and considerably more stringent import policy was given a much more attention-getting name: "National Sword," and the packed conference session that morning was titled "Preparing for the Coming Storm." As Dan Lilkas-Rain, the session moderator, later recalled, "There was a lot of uncertainty in the room about what the policies would mean. We were getting updated information that morning, and the anxieties people were feeling then have played out in a very intense way."

China's National Sword policy went into effect in January 2018, and it disrupted the global market for recyclables. A year later, Fiona Ma, the treasurer of the state of California, told the *New York Times*, "We are in a crisis moment in the recycling movement right now." The Chinese standard has proven to be impossible for most U.S. facilities to meet in the short term. But Neil Seldman, a founder of the Institute for Local Self-Reliance in Washington, D.C., says bluntly, "I think the Chinese have done us a tremendous favor. It is forcing us to clean up our act. Recycling has been the first thing we do. It should be the last thing we do."

The Hidden Value of "Waste"

The role that all of us, as consumers, might play in this is complicated. Brands push single-use, disposable, convenience packaging on us. There is a lack of communication between package designers and recycling facilities to develop materials compatible with North American recycling infrastructure, and so about one in four items that U.S. residents put in recycling bins are not actually recyclable. The feel-good phenomenon known as "wish cycling" decreases the value of truly recyclable material. Recycling still plays an important role in waste reduction and management solutions, but where is the incentive to take care of the things we own — to clean and maintain them — when the cost of buying something new is so cheap? How do we add additional "R"s to the Reduce-Reuse-Recycle mantra when it's hard enough to manage the first three?

Neil Seldman's argument for local resiliency is that almost everything that enters the so-called waste stream has significant value. When we replace the term *waste management* with *resource recovery*, we are talking about the economic principle of value retention. By recovering as much of our garbage as possible and wasting very little, we are rewarded with a rich source of "raw materials" for reuse and remanufacture — and a valuable source of local capital. To prove his point, Seldman offers this analysis of the economic payoff: It's estimated that if just 2 to 5 percent of the materials headed to the landfill were recovered, reused, repaired, or resold, the combined value could be greater than all of the recycling revenue earned from everything else, at today's market prices. (Combined value includes the avoided costs of what you would have to pay to manage those resources in any other way.) The proverbial alchemy of turning trash into treasure is well within our means.

Seldman has seen the alternative to incinerating our garbage or filling up landfill after landfill. It is called a "resource recovery park," essentially an industrial park for companies engaged in recycling, composting, and manufacturing from recycled materials. Their efficiencies are increased because of their proximity to one another. Only a handful of resource recovery parks exist in the United States. Perhaps the best example is the recycling-based business run by the nonprofit St. Vincent de Paul Society of Lane County, in Eugene, Oregon. The operation realizes a "quadruple bottom line": they responsibly reuse and recycle products, provide quality goods and services to the community, provide jobs and job training, and generate revenue to fund other charitable activities. The facility reclaims, repairs, and prepares for reuse a remarkable range of materials. They repair appliances, recover maximum value from e-waste, and upcycle window glass into architectural accents. What's left gets radically recycled, as in their mattress recycling operation, the largest in North America. They even recycle clean polystyrene foam by compressing a forty-foot shipping container's worth down to the size of a single palette of super dense polystyrene — weighing one ton — which they sell for remanufacture. All of this economic activity stays within the local economy, converting what used to be landfilled (44.1 million pounds in 2018) into a continuous supply of local capital with real value. Other examples of the resource recovery park, or "radical reuse center," are Urban Ore in Berkeley, California, which began as a "scavenger organization" in 1980, and Second Chance in Baltimore, Maryland, whose business model focuses on deconstructing buildings, selling the salvaged materials, and creating "green-collar jobs." You have to ask yourself, why doesn't every city and county in the country launch one of these?

The Netherlands is on a path to do exactly that, starting with the creation of "circular craft centers" in ten towns in 2020. "Almost every municipality has an environmental street [where containers are lined up for disposing of electrical appliances, plastics, wood, foam, garden waste, etc.], a thrift store, and a Repair Cafe," the initiative's website (charmingly translated from the Dutch) points out. "But nowhere are those forces combined. This is unfortunate, because it is precisely because of this that more products could be used for longer. And fewer resources would be lost in error. Circular Craft Centers can be valuable in many ways. Not only because there is a focus on repair, high-quality reuse, recycling, and waste separation. Also because such a center provides new employment and learning workplaces." The expectation is that every region in the Netherlands will have a center within five years.

Time to Rethink

IBM staked out the progressive high ground early in the twentieth century when it branded itself with a single word: *Think*. Now sustainability is being reimagined under the new prescriptive: *Rethink*. In the early twentieth century, the thrift movement's anathema to waste and overconsumption penetrated deeply into the culture because of its broad range of motivations: moral self-improvement and sobriety, responsibility and self-sufficiency, economic stability in a time before Social Security, antipathy toward wastefulness, and even land conservation. It took root also because of the wide reach of the interests and stakeholders promoting it: the White House; virtually all government agencies; the banking and insurance industries; Catholic, Protestant, and Jewish hierarchies; women's organizations, men's service clubs, and youth organizations; and on and on. This book contends that in order to make the profound cultural and economic changes needed to respond effectively to the climate crisis, a new ethos must penetrate at least as deeply as the thrift movement did. One encouraging sign of this is in the work of students on college campuses across the country. The Post Landfill Action Network (PLAN) was started at the University of New Hampshire in 2013 to support student-led zero waste projects. Now PLAN is active at more than eighty colleges and universities in the nation.

In the early twenty-first century, the mandate to "rethink" has emerged with an unprecedented urgency. We are sitting on what has been described as a consumption time bomb. The global middle class is more than doubling, a growth that is driving consumption with what economists call high material intensity, that is, the cumulative impact of the materials and energy required to make something, or do something, from cradle to grave. All of this is happening at the same time that climate change is measurably decreasing the global environment's ability to sustain our most fundamental resources. We believe that the repair ethos — with its wide resonance of meanings and applications, is critical to that rethinking.

The "classical" economic model, variously termed the "linear economy," the "materials economy," the "extractive economy," and the "consumer economy," is predicated on the belief that natural resources are unlimited and that markets can solve all environmental problems. But this model is flawed, and here is one reason why. For the last century, economic activity has been measured as gross domestic product (GDP) — a quantification of the total market value of all the goods and services produced in a country or region. The fundamental error in this evaluation is the fact that GDP balance sheets do not account for *all* the costs of producing goods and services. Missing are so-called external costs: unacknowledged and untaxed costs, the hidden costs of doing business that the free market generally ignores. These significant expenses, effectively subsidized by society at large, include the cost of producing clean, "free" drinking water, the cost of sending toxic waste downstream, and the costs of childhood obesity and diabetes linked to diets of snacks and soda.

What is the *true* cost of the twelve-cup coffee maker you just bought for $14.99? When these external costs are factored in, it far exceeds the $14.99 you paid for it. Someone else is paying. To put this at scale, the Institute of Earth, Ocean, and Atmospheric Sciences at Rutgers University analyzed data for the decade from 2007 to September 2017 and identified the social costs of climate change (including extreme weather and the health impacts of burning fossil fuels) in the United States alone to be at least $240 billion every year. The corrective is not a mystery. More than a hundred years ago, British economists recognized that measuring economic activity without an understanding of negative external costs is an error that needs to be fixed; they were tipped off by the extreme air pollution created from burning coal, known as the London Fog. Since then, many methods have been developed to account for the complex environmental and economic impacts of the goods and services we produce. We just haven't chosen to use them.

Why does this matter so much? Because corporate executives and boards are required by law to maximize shareholder value. As long as they are not required to account for the real long-term costs of their operations, they often have no choice but to make decisions that may be shortsighted. In this we recognize the decisions that have led us to the climate crisis, what biologist Garrett Hardin described as the "tragedy of the commons": when the freedom of all to exploit resources vital to the common good of all leads to destruction for all. When economic activity is truly and accurately measured, CEOs, CFOs, and corporate boards will at last be free to make sustainable, long-term decisions — because it will be in their fiduciary interest and their responsibility to do so. As Paul Polman, the former CEO of Unilever and a highly respected voice for corporate responsibility, states: "We need to decouple growth from environmental impact and move financial markets to the long term. CEOs are basically good people. There are no CEOs who want more unemployment, or more people going to bed hungry, or more air pollution. But then why do we behave so miserably? It's because we spend too much time on dealing with the impacts and not with the underlying causes."

Another driver of this change is us. Businesses respond to market conditions, which include incentives determined by consumers. The choices we make and the products we demand fall solidly within our sphere of influence.

> There is no "away" to throw things to. Not on a spaceship. And that's where we're living.
>
> — Garrett Hardin

Economic Foundations for the Future

One of the most commonly accepted definitions of sustainability comes from the United Nations World Commission on Environment: "meeting the needs of the current generation without compromising the ability of future generations to meet their own needs." In response, a range of new economic models has been presented to us with a variety of names and overlapping attributes: regenerative economy, sharing economy, attention economy, artisanal economy, collaborative economy. Aiding a transition to a post-carbon future is part of the dynamic of each of these, but some are more focused on sustainability than others. Plus, transition by any means is not acceptable. It must also be a "just transition" that addresses the vulnerability of populations whose livelihoods will be disrupted and that strives to provide for the well-being of all. Such a transition has virtually no historical precedent.

The economic model that is gaining the most momentum on the world stage now is the "circular economy," predicated on the idea that sustainable biological ecosystems operate in a circular fashion. Waste produced by one part of the system becomes resources for another. This model allows us to design waste and pollution out of our production processes, keep products in use for as long as possible, and radically reuse materials — even down to the molecular level — to regenerate natural systems. This is the vision of "eco-effectiveness" articulated by architect William McDonough and chemist Michael Braungart in their influential 2012 book *Cradle to Cradle: Remaking the Way We Make Things*. In it, they insisted that we ask the most fundamental — and ethical — question: "What is the entire system — cultural, commercial, ecological — of which this made thing, and way of making things, will be a part?"

From 2012 to 2014, the World Economic Forum, the Ellen MacArthur Foundation, and business consulting firm McKinsey & Company produced three volumes of a report entitled *Towards the Circular Economy*, which identified the opportunities for businesses and industries, addressing in sequence durable goods, "fast-moving" consumer goods, and global supply chains. The 2014 report estimated the economic benefits of building circular supply chains could be more than 1 trillion a year in U.S. dollars for the global economy and 100,000 new jobs by 2025. The foundation's 2019 follow-up report further describes a framework of economic resiliency for businesses able to reduce their dependence on raw materials subject to climate risks by implementing strategies — including designs for repairability — to keep materials in use longer.

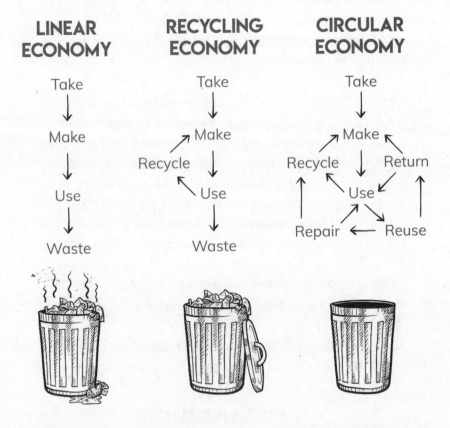

In 2018, the International Resource Panel of the United Nations Environment Program issued a report entitled "Re-defining Value: The Manufacturing Revolution." The report analyzes "re-manufacturing" technologies that reuse, refurbish, and repair the same materials used in the initial manufacture of products, significantly reducing the amount of new material needed: by 80–98 percent for remanufacturing,

82–99 percent for comprehensive refurbishing, *and 94–99 percent for repair.* "Re-thinking how we manufacture industrial products and deal with them at the end of their useful life," the panel claims, "could provide breakthrough environmental, social and economic benefits." A 2019 survey of U.S. business leaders showed a large increase in "circular thinking" — even if what that means is not always well-defined. In the long run, implementation is not something a company can do by itself. Industries will need to work with their supply chain partners, customers, financing partners, and even competitors. How do we imagine this transition might actually happen? The authors of *Towards the Circular Economy* had this to say:

> We do not know how the shift will come about. It would come slowly or in a sudden sweep, as a reaction to external shocks. It may be the outcome of stirring public stimuli or of a killer application, as a silent manufacturing revolution. It could even emerge as grassroots consumer activism, or as voluntary, inclusive industry commitment. History has seen all of these patterns lead to breakthroughs: we do not know which of them will tip consumption into a more regenerative mode. We do expect, however, that the shift will play out between pioneering industry leaders, discriminating, well-informed consumers, and forward-looking public constituencies.

"If it was that easy, it would have been done," says Paul Polman. "It's hard work. The road to change has a lot of skeptics and cynics."

The Trust Factor

John recalls: *When I was a kid, my dad suggested to two of our suburban neighbors that rather than all three families each needing to own a power lawn mower, they should go in together, buy one mower, and share it. This was a pretty radical idea in an era when "lawn pride" said as much about you as the model of the car parked in your driveway. As the principal lawn mower for our family, I don't recall being consulted about this social contract, but I do remember thinking that it made sense, and feeling proud of the role my father played in initiating the neighborly cooperation.*

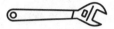

On a rather larger scale, Rachel Botsman, a researcher and lecturer at the London School of Economics, addresses the generational shift toward shared prosperity, in which access is more valued than ownership, and the critical role of trust in that shift. In her 2010 TED Talk, "The Case for Collaborative Consumption," she offered the observation that the typical electric drill is used for only twelve to thirteen minutes per owner in its lifetime. "What you need is the hole, not the drill," she says.

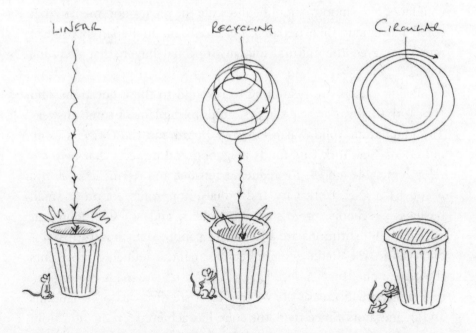

The generation that grew up with peer-to-peer file-sharing is discovering a new belief in the importance of community, such as we see in the growing popularity of Tool Libraries. A society that collaborates through sharing, renting, lending, and bartering things and skills, says Botsman, may well be the defining economic shift of the twenty-first century. Technology has provided us with the means; the key is trust. "Trust between strangers is the social glue, and is the revolutionary component of the share economy," Botsman says.

Trust is also at the heart of the repair ethos, and community repair reinforces the shift toward shared prosperity by emphatically and compellingly creating trust among neighbors who might not otherwise have had the chance to meet.

Rethinking Resource Recovery

"What if all the effort spent on recycling over the last fifty years had been equally distributed over the rest of the R's, including reuse and repair?" asks Joel Newman in his blog for Portland Repair Finder. "What could we do to smooth, simplify, and scale the repair movement? What could movements like Repair Cafe and Right to Repair become if repair achieved the cultural and institutional buy-in that recycling enjoys?"

Policy makers are beginning to respond to these questions, and New York City was among the first cities to implement some answers. The Manhattan Solid Waste Advisory Board and the Citizens Committee for New York City funds neighborhood projects that help develop replicable models for reducing, reusing, and repairing in all five boroughs of New York City. Individuals, nonprofits, for-profit small businesses, schools, professors, researchers, and student groups at educational institutions are all invited to apply. Many observers point out that in the Reduce-Reuse-Recycle mantra, reducing represents the biggest challenge. A decade ago, New York State made it a priority to significantly decrease the volume of waste disposed of at landfills and incinerators. Since then, the state has achieved a reduction from 4.1 pounds per person per day in 2010 to 1.7 pounds projected for 2020 — a difference of more than half. The goal is to reduce that number further, to 0.6 pounds per person per day by 2030. The New York State Department of Environmental Conservation has supported repair as a strategic way to meet those goals, and those of us who signed up for this revolution in sustainability envision several hundred community-run repair initiatives in New York, New Jersey, and Massachusetts within the next five years and many more nationwide, perhaps matching Europe and the UK, where there are more than two thousand repair initiatives. We are setting an example for other states to follow. As they do, the result will be changes in mindset and behavior — and a new kind of materialism. "Repair economies don't regard material things as expendable," writes journalist Katherine Wilson. "They relocate value in the workings, relations and meanings of things."

The Wisdom of Repair

If you do not agree with the phases of the moon, get a ladder and repair it.

— Hausa (Nigerian) proverb

Repare / Repair

Let's begin with the prefix *re-*. It is defined by etymologists as a word-forming element. The *Oxford English Dictionary* takes the position that it is "impossible to attempt a complete record of all the forms resulting from its use; the number of these is practically infinite." The essential meaning of *re-*, from the Old French and Latin, is "back to the original place; again, anew, once more." Its Indo-European derivation is "to turn." And so this spare, two-letter prefix has the power to relate an astonishingly rich constellation of meanings.

Many words have more than one definition, but etymologists claim that *repair* really should be two separate words — *repare* and *repair*.

The fact that we have one word — *repair* — with two meanings is an accident of history.

When we fix or mend a broken or damaged thing, we *repair*, meaning "restore," "rehabilitate," "renovate," "renew," "reinforce," "reconcile," or "redeem." It's the opposite of "wreck," "worsen," or "destroy." The Old French root is *repare*, and it traces back to the Latin "to prepare again," which seems to shuttle back and forth in time ("shall we begin again?"). In its use, *repair* always references and embodies a before and an after. And in common usage, we easily apply this meaning to all kinds of life situations: repairing physical things, repairing a system, repairing relationships, repairing an injustice or inequity, which may include reparations.

But our English word *repair* has a second definition, with an entirely different history. Here the Old French root is *repairer*, with a very specific meaning: it refers to animals that return to their home in a burrow or a den (their *lair*). This word had the misfortune of being similar to *repare* and entering English almost simultaneously.

And so, etymologists say that by rights we really should be using two different words: *repare* to mend and *repair* to return home. "Sorry," says Merriam-Webster, "it's too late to fix this problem." But I delight in the way these two meanings intertwine. It is a deepening. Repair mends and heals, and repair returns us to a place of comfort, nurture, or solace. Repair completes us. Repair calls us home.

> We all have our broken pieces, emotionally, spiritually in this life. Nobody gets away unhurt. We're always trying to find somebody whose broken pieces fit with our broken pieces and something whole emerges.
>
> — Bruce Springsteen

A Connection Has Been Lost

When we started our first Repair Cafes in the Hudson Valley, we figured that most broken items would need replacement parts to get working again. Repairs require parts, right? But as we got into it, a quite different picture emerged. Most machines stop working because a connection has been lost. That connection may be mechanical, electrical, or digital. Two pieces that are supposed to transfer energy and information in a very specific way no longer do. There's a break, a crack, a tear, a short, a fray, a wrinkle, or a stretch. The repair lies in finding and reestablishing that lost connection. In a remarkable number of cases, the "fix" is simply cleaning.

A fix may also have to do with the fit. The term from anatomy is *articulation*, the way bones and ligaments in our bodies are joined to provide structure and strength as well as movement. Within any useful thing, you want the parts to be well articulated: to fit properly so that they interact and adjust as they should. Woodworkers know that joinery is essential to the craft, and the goal is always that joints be snug and solid. If not, chairs will wobble, tables will skew, and drawers won't pull as they were designed to. To make the metaphorical leap, all of these kinds of connection and articulation extend to our social and economic world, and to all of the businesses, institutions, organizations, and activities that give order to our everyday lives.

Quite a few of our repair coaches are engineers, and they will gladly, even gleefully, point you to the second law of thermodynamics: the entropy of any isolated system always increases. A physicist will talk about entropy in terms of energy, a biologist in terms of organization, but in all cases it runs in one direction only: systems run down, things fall into disorder. But these definitions apply to a closed system, and it is the job of the repairer to open up the system, the object in front of them, and put energy into it, to restore order and to "fix it." "My experience of the world is that things left to themselves don't get right," said biologist T. H. Huxley a hundred years ago. Don Grice, whose career was at IBM and who has become deeply invested in the repair ethic, likes to tease: "We really should call these Entropy Reduction Cafes, but I suspect that wouldn't attract too many people."

Broken World Thinking

In his essay "Rethinking Repair," Steven Jackson, a professor of information and science and technology studies at Cornell, introduces a thought experiment he calls "broken world thinking." Which world do we live in? he provocatively asks. "Is it the imaginary nineteenth-century world of progress and advance, novelty and invention, open frontiers and endless development? Or the twenty-first-century world of risk and uncertainty, growth and decay, and fragmentation, dissolution, and breakdown?" Depending on where you choose to look, you will find ample evidence of both, but I think Jackson wants us to consider more than a choice between nostalgia and the real world. This is not simply a glass-half-empty, glass-half-full observation. He is asking us to get real about the world around us.

It is a great irony that here in the twenty-first century more people than ever before are living in prosperity, while at the same time, whole cultures are seeing their homelands becoming uninhabitable, and the extinction of perhaps a million species in the coming decades is underway. These two realities coexist and are relentlessly feeding a positive feedback loop of resource depletion and ecological instability.

Broken world thinking asks two things of us: a clear-eyed acknowledgment that the world we have built has outpaced our ability to maintain it, and a "deep wonder and appreciation of the subtle arts of repair" that are critical to reestablishing and maintaining stability and balance, and essential to "new combinations and new possibilities."

Jackson calls repair a "fulcrum" between these two worlds, arguing that innovation in actual practice is limited unless it is extended, sustained, and completed through repair. By paying attention to both parts of this worldview, we find a mindset that is hopeful and realistic, and that demands productive, even audacious, responses and solutions in every sector of society.

> Repair is a radical act of resistance to the unmaking of our environment and our world.
>
> Repair is a humble act of resistance to the unmaking of our environment and our world.

Both are true.

REPAIR AND RELATIVITY

Repair is an inescapably timely phenomenon, bridging past and future in distinctive and sometimes surprising ways. It accounts for the durability of the old, but also the appearance of the new. It fills in the moments of hope and fear in which bridges from old worlds to new worlds are built, and the continuity of order, value and meaning gets woven, one tenuous thread at a time. And it does all this quietly, humbly, and all the time.

— Steven J. Jackson, *Rethinking Repair*

Always, the family of repair activities shares the aim of maintaining some kind of continuity with the past in the face of breaks or ruptures to that continuity.

— Elizabeth V. Spelman, *Repair:
The Impulse to Restore in a Fragile World*

Time is visible in a person's clothing, and repairing it is essentially about preserving a relationship. Sometimes the garment will have been the property of someone who has died, so repairing it enables the relationship to continue. The act of mending artfully is a form of caring and memorialization.

— Celia Pym, *I Didn't Ever See the Point of Invisible Mending*

Tinkering

You can trace the idea of "tinkering" back hundreds of years. In history and in folklore, to "tink" was to rivet, and a tinker was an itinerant fixer of pots and pans and other mainstays of kitchen and domestic life. Blade sharpening was also a specialty. And so tinkers would present their skills to the women of the house who oversaw such matters. In their best light, tinkers were resourceful and perhaps a good source of local news and gossip as they traveled around. But they lived on the

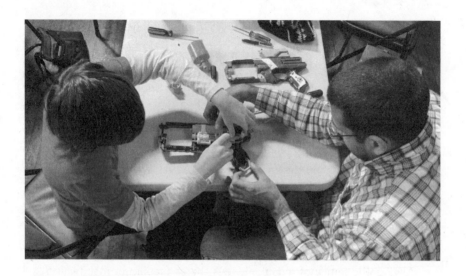

fringes, and folklore is full of stories of tinkers who were not always to be trusted, or who might be tinged with magic. In the mid-twentieth century, *tinker* transformed into *tinkerer*, and the epithet "basement or backyard tinkerer" — the husband usually — called up the dictionary definition of the verb *tinker*: "an attempt to repair or improve…often to no useful effect." The romance was gone.

Fast-forward to this generation — when tinkering occupies an entirely different realm. The "tinkering mindset" embodies a seemingly intuitive understanding of broken world thinking. It has been described as technical work with a cultural attitude. Tinkering has also become a potent form of storytelling, mythmaking, entertainment, and performance. David Malki! (yes, he spells his name with an exclamation point) is a writer and illustrator in Los Angeles who has created a website called Wondermark. There you will find his weekly comic strips and his "nominally essential" and very tongue-in-cheek *Tinkerer's Handbook: The Magazine for People Who Cannot Leave Well Enough Alone*, in which he encourages us to "Take It Apart" and issues his Rallying Cry for a Generation: "Let us meddle." Malki! delights in tinkering's steampunk connotations, and he champions all manner of creativity and repair as a rebellion against idleness and entropy.

In her fascinating 2017 book *Tinkering*, Australian journalist

Katherine Wilson analyzes a culture of individuals with "an impulsive habit of material problem solving." She profiles the kinds of tinkerers you will find in every postindustrial society. Tinkering across the globe reveals the cross-cultural passion for questioning and challenging how we engage with the material world. Many tinkerers think of the mending, adapting, creating, modifying, repurposing, and improvising they do in their homes simply as "unremarkable, ordinary, obvious and common-sense living." Others quite consciously see tinkering as a social movement, "idealized as a radical and transformative act against powerful forces." In her research, Wilson says she came to realize that "this ineffable thing called tinkering had its roots and branches in social justice, civil liberties, digital communities, legal frontiers and urban sustainability." The global tinkering community, just like the global repair and maker communities, is highly social and networked.

The Institute for the Future in Palo Alto, California, has also examined this seemingly archaic practice. Research director David Pescovitz writes: "Despite its fascination with things and bits, tinkering is resolutely human-focused: you don't make things 'better' in some dry technical sense, you make them work better for you. Tinkers modify everything from cars, computers, and cellphones, to virtual worlds and computer code. They are driven by a desire to experiment, to make existing technologies more useful, and to customize them to better suit users' needs." And in Pescovitz's blog, technology forecaster Alex Pang adds: "Tinkering offers a way of engaging with today's needs while also keeping an eye on the future consequences of our choices. The same technological and social trends that have made tinkering appealing seem poised to make it even more pervasive and powerful in the future. Today we tinker with things; tomorrow we will tinker with the world."

Repairing shares all of these attributes, and repairing and tinkering overlap and reinforce each other in all kinds of ways. Do our skilled volunteers at Repair Cafes and Fixit Clinics see themselves as tinkerers? Some clearly do, although we can allow for differences in personality and points of view. The engineers and former engineers among them, used to working in very top-down environments, may not embrace the tinkerer characterization, which tends to be very bottom-up, but none-theless they will share many viewpoints broadly, such as the value of reverse engineering and the "work-around." Repair coaches routinely are faced with the challenge of finding a way to make a fix without the benefit of a new part or the ideal tool — and so they improvise. "It's the ability to look at things maybe two degrees off-center," says repair coach Tom Joscelyn. "Suddenly solutions come." The other side of the coin? Some tinkerers might prefer to work alone, while at repair events, we encourage collaboration. Working-around and working together are strategies that increase our repair success rate.

And what about the kids? Erik Hoover, a professional woodworker and repair coach in the Hudson Valley, says: "My sixteen-year-old son sometimes comes to me and says, 'Hey Dad, you want to tinker?' He brings home old electronics, like gaming consoles, from our Transfer Station — a great resource for tinkerers. As a consumer of sophis-ticated technology, he couldn't believe, for example, how primitive speaker wires are. And it's just great to watch him peel back the lay-ers of the analogue insides of something and figure it out. He's got nerve."

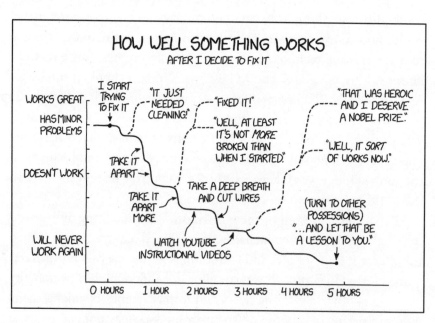

Maintenance

John recalls: *My first real summer job was before college at a small chemical plant in New Jersey. I learned to drive a barrel-lift and I worked on the bottling assembly line when that cranked up, but mostly I got to be the maintenance man's assistant. Everything I can claim to know about electricity and plumbing I learned from Jim that summer. It was an education I have valued ever since. But I also remember in grade school how we all smirked when someone called our school janitor a "maintenance engineer." We knew he swept the floors; I had no appreciation for everything else he did. Until I was the one sweeping the floors at my chemical plant job.*

Throughout history, maintenance and repair have been the most widespread types of technical expertise by far. Most people would be surprised to learn that today worldwide, engineers who are devoted to maintenance outnumber those involved with design or innovation by about three to one. And that does not begin to include the enormous number of independent repairs carried out in the home and in every nook and cranny of our lives. The degree to which we take this for granted is remarkable. We notice maintenance mostly in its absence, of course — when things break. But the role of maintenance has rapidly evolved from a taken-for-granted aspect of our world into a central strategic concern. The power grid in the United States has been called the most sophisticated machine ever invented, and experts agree that it is in critical need of modernization. (The fact that this is actually being accomplished as a condition for integrating wind and solar energy is not acknowledged often enough.) The prospect of system failure or sabotage to the power grid or the internet is something most of us don't want to think about.

Maintenance engineers offer a cost-benefit analysis they call the "iceberg model." At the tip of the iceberg, in plain sight, are all the traditional direct costs of maintenance: labor and materials, contracts, and overheads. Hidden below the surface is 80 percent of the iceberg, the costs that come as a result of reduced asset life, lower-quality performance, higher energy costs, lost production, wasted resources, late deliveries, safety risks, and environmental costs. A full cost-accounting will show that the indirect costs may add up to as much as five times the direct costs. The bottom line is that avoiding or delaying maintenance means a loss of profit and lower sustainability, which is why the phrase "deferred maintenance" means so much to investors.

In the United States, professionals and academics in the field have organized as the Maintainers, and in Europe an annual Festival of Maintenance is "a celebration of those who maintain different parts of our world, and how they do it, recognizing the often hidden work done in repair, custodianship, stewardship, tending and caring for the things that matter." But as recently as 2007, David Edgerton, perhaps our foremost historian of technology, was able to dismiss the efficacy of repair in our economy: "In rich countries, as far as domestic equipment is concerned…repair no longer exists — from electric toasters to fridges, repair is hardly worth carrying out — and not surprisingly the networks of retailer/repairers are long gone. A new toaster retails for less than an hour of repair time."

Edgerton also identifies the result of this in world trade: second-hand goods move from rich countries where they're being thrown "away" because they're no longer working properly or wanted, to poorer countries that have not lost their culture of repair and maintenance. You can bring just about anything to a city market in an emerging economy and get it fixed. Ugo Valauri, a cofounder of Restart — the repair movement in the UK — says, "We've been inspired by different practices elsewhere in the world, where some of us have traveled — Kenya, India, and Cuba — and meeting people who would never think to throw things away. They maintain them and repair them. That is the mindset we want."

It is often the case that items brought to us for repair are not really broken, but simply haven't been cared for in the most common-sense ways. Occasional cleaning (from vacuum cleaners to laptops), descaling (coffee makers), or lubricating (most things with moving parts) is often enough to keep a product functioning for a good long time. It is true that, years ago, "maintenance free" became a selling point, and manufacturers would have you believe their product requires no care. This of course is not entirely true, yet it has enabled a further level of de-skilling. The majority of vacuum cleaners left on curbs likely just need to be unclogged. Marine Postma observes, and we certainly agree, that many people no longer see maintenance as a self-evident task to be taken care of at home, as part of everyday life, which underscores the general lack of repair knowledge in society.

> Stories about making new things are ten a penny. Less common are stories about keeping things as good as new.
> — *The Economist*

As with so many things, surprises can be costly, and there is a critical difference between anticipating events and reacting to events, with the strategic benefit always accruing to those who look ahead. The more complex the system, the greater the risk of the unexpected. Maintenance engineers identify four categories of repair that are concurrent in their industry. *Preventative maintenance* aims to detect and correct latent faults before they become operational faults. *Corrective maintenance* responds to failures. *Adaptive maintenance* is a response to changes in the environment. And the goal of *perfective maintenance* is to eliminate inefficiencies and improve performance, which can elevate maintenance from an operational overhead to a profit contributor. Some maintenance consulting firms expand the list to include, for example, "failure-finding maintenance," which focuses on backup equipment that isn't required to function until something else has failed. An example of this is your home smoke detector, which your fire department reminds you to test every October. Homeowners will benefit from all of these practices too, of course. *AARP* magazine recommends that you set aside 1 percent of your home's value each year for maintenance and repairs.

Wabi-Sabi?

How are we to reconcile the precise demands of maintenance in our modern world with the Japanese aesthetic philosophy of *wabi-sabi*, which finds beauty in imperfection? To repair something is not to make it new again, but to renew its purpose and function. Many of the visitors to our Repair Cafes are already aware of this distinction. When Marie Young brought her lightweight folding shopping cart to our very first Repair Cafe in the Hudson Valley, the hub of one wheel was broken and beyond repair. The fix was to fabricate a replacement hub with a circle of wood. It was imperfect, practical, and beautiful, all at the same time. Marie said, "Looks wonderful to me. I need that darn cart!"

Perhaps without realizing it, Marie had found a homespun way to express the Japanese aesthetic philosophy of *wabi-sabi*, which prizes the beauty of imperfection. "We live in a world of things," architect and scholar Leonard Koren writes. "Discoloration, rust, nicks, dents, peeling and other forms of attrition are a testament to histories of use and misuse. Wabi-sabi is exactly about the delicate balance between the pleasure we get from things and the pleasure we get from freedom from things."

Wabi-sabi is associated with Zen Buddhism, and the language used to talk about it, when it is used at all, is poetic rather than technical. The *wabi-sabi* worldview is a choice: to take pleasure in things that are imperfect, impermanent, and unpretentious. You cannot insist on the beauty of rust or the simplicity of peeling paint. It is voluntary. Things *wabi-sabi* may be unconventional and incomplete, oddly misshapen, or even ugly to some, and this explains the phrase "Beauty can be coaxed out of ugliness." You can make a pretty good party game out of it too: to start, just point to an object and ask, "Wabi-sabi?"

Craeft

In his introduction to *Diary of an Early American Boy, 1805* (the text of which includes the actual verbatim diary of Noah Blake, who lived in a small New England town), historian and illustrator Eric Sloane writes, "The good things of the past were not so often *articles* as the *manner in which people lived* or *the things that people thought.* This, of course, is still true; the fine TV sets and modern kitchen appliances we prize now will be junk within a matter of years; the lasting examples of our time will turn out to be the *ways that we live* or the *things that we think."*

Repair culture asks us to take greater notice of how the things in our lives were made and whose hands they passed through before coming into ours. The historic Locust Lawn House and Farm in Gardiner, New York, regularly holds events they call "The Timeless Art of Repair." Local experts demonstrate "antique skills": pewter ware and metalwork, wood planing and joinery, darning, felting, and other waning arts. Right next to the tinsmith is someone changing the belt on a vacuum cleaner or fixing a coffee maker. It's a juxtaposition that engages people's curiosity and gets them thinking about what is well made and what is not.

In his book *Craeft*, British archaeologist and medieval historian Alexander Langlands explores the deeper meanings of a thousand-year-old English word mostly lost in its original usage: "It should be more than just about making. It is the power, the force, the knowledge and the wisdom behind making — the *craeft* behind it…an extended definition where a sense of 'wisdom' and 'resourcefulness' surpass in importance the notion of 'physical skill.'" Langlands looks at the true trajectory of craft production like so:

Tended landscape → *sustainable production of raw materials* → *intelligently processed* → *beautifully made* → *fit for purpose* → *fondly used* → *ingeniously reused* → *considerately discarded* → *given back to the earth*

This vision is at the heart of the circular or regenerative economy: choosing materials that will last, understanding their properties, and knowing how to care for them. Repairing and reusing the things we own is far more "resource efficient" than recycling. Think about it: when we repair something, everything that was needed to make it is preserved and intact, embodied within it: the energy, the materials, all of the time and talents required to manufacture it. When we recycle, much of that is lost. When we throw something "away" and buy something new, *all* of that is lost.

But the loss may run even deeper. In her book *Lifting Depression*, Kelly Lambert, a behavioral neuroscience researcher, writes, "What I've discovered is that there's a critical link between symptoms of depression and key areas of the brain involved with motivation, pleasure, movement and thought." She calls it an "effort-driven rewards circuit" that is "generated by doing certain types of physical activities, especially ones that involve your hands, which give us an emotional sense of well-being." When our lives are full of "effortless-driven rewards" — a consumer culture that doesn't require much in the way of knowledge or imagination — Lambert believes the conditions for unhappiness may be more prevalent.

Britain's Health Ministry, in response to statistics that revealed the "mass prescribing" of antidepressants for one in six adults, is supporting programs that expand opportunities for people to work with their hands. Men's Sheds is a prime example; it's a movement that started in Australia and has spread throughout the United Kingdom, and is now augmented with Fix It Sisters Sheds. The negative impact of loneliness and isolation on a person's health and well-being is well established, and the informal groups of guys and women who call themselves "shedders" are responding by getting together to tinker, build, repair, share skills, and spend time. This way of addressing twenty-first-century social needs may not entail the traditions and slow mastering of technique that characterize *craeft*, but it nonetheless provides, in Langlands's words, "a hand-eye-head-heart-body coordination that furnishes us with a meaningful understanding of the materiality of our world."

> Forget your perfect offering. There is a crack in everything. That's how the light gets in.
>
> — Leonard Cohen, "Anthem"

Mending Made Visible

Historically, of course, clothing repairs that attracted attention were an embarrassment, a sign of poverty or want. Today, visible mending has emerged as a creative trend that's bridging generations, from experienced seamstresses and fiber artists to kids and punks. Simply stated, visible mending is mending that is meant to be noticed. Seamstresses with their sewing machines at Repair Cafes are always busy, but we find that visible mending engages people in a different way. In her essay "Mendfulness and the Long Journey to Repair," visible mending crafter and author Katrina Rodabaugh adopts the word *mendfulness*. "It simply implies there is an intersection between mending and being mindful. That there is an intention to repair but furthermore to pay attention or to witness, to be thoughtful, and then to attempt to act from this place."

Dawn Elliott, a historian and Repair Cafe hand-sewing expert, counsels simply: "If your desire is a garment that is repairable, go for buttons or snaps. Stay away from zippers. And accept that repairs likely will not be invisible." Dawn can teach you *darning* (anchor yarn in the fabric at the edge of a hole, carry it across the gap and anchor it on the other side, and fill the hole with crisscrossing running stitches) or *felting* (separate, tangle, and relock yarn or wool fibers by stabbing them repeatedly with a felting hook).

Now imagine using those same techniques, but with different fibers of contrasting colors. It is flat-out fun to see the way groups gather around the textile table. Raheli Harper, who shows our visitors these skills at the Repair Cafe in Warwick, New York, takes delight in the freedom of mending that's colorful and clever. "Mending embraces the fact that when we wear clothes on our bodies we are wearing them out. We embrace the whole imperfect story of our lives — we make mistakes, we tear our clothes and/or lives. And yet we also have the tools to heal and recover. For me, mending is a practice to embrace and celebrate our imperfect damaged selves and a road to healing those breaks." Plus, the strong pull of fashion has always included the way we use it to construct our identity, and so mending as a personal statement actually fulfills some of the same symbolic and psychological satisfaction we get when we shop.

You will now find mending circles and workshops in every part of the country, a sign that the appeal of mending in groups of friends around a table has taken hold. Sashiko embroidery, a popular technique for simple and durable patching, uses a universal running stitch

OH DARN IT!

We simply can't let those pesky moths win
LET'S WEAR OUR REPAIRS LIKE MEDALS

Bring your moth-eaten wool garments along and I'll show you how to make a feature of those moth holes. Don't hide them, enhance them with coloured patches & darning. I provide needles, yarns, patches and scissors .... You bring something to mend.   Sally Walton

SUNDAY 8th Oct 10 - 12 noon
£10 each limited to 10 people

BOOK BY EMAIL sallyswalton@icloud.com

Taking place at The Crown.

and thicker thread and is easy to learn. Mending circles nestle very comfortably within Repair Cafes, and we like to introduce hand-sewing DIY workshops with the question: "Your mother (or grandmother) knew. Do you?"

The cross-generational appeal is especially striking. Lisa Z. Morgan, department head for apparel design at the Rhode Island School of Design, says she senses a revolution through the needle and thread. Students she's working with are hyperaware of the wastefulness and toxicity in the fast-fashion industry, and they see it as "fighting talk to be repairing, reworking, remaking and mending." Their passion emerges out of individual commitments that are political, ethical, or personal, and for some students, it is a way of coping with anxieties about the future. Plus they get to hang out and be creative without having to spend money. Lisa even sees it in the punk-skater-tagging subculture as she watches her son and some of his friends stitching the jeans they've torn skateboarding, "like miniature swords they're wielding with thread." Badges of honor. You will find thousands of examples of visible mending on Instagram and Pinterest.

FIX THE WORLD IN COLORS

The concept of repair as a cultural and political expression came from activist artists. In Amsterdam in 2008, the artist collective Platform21 started with the idea that "repair is underestimated as a creative, cultural and economic force." They proceeded to organize exhibitions (which Martine Postma covered as a journalist and was inspired by), outfit a "repair truck" to take to street fairs, and hold a Most Remarkable Repair Contest, with the first prize going to a woman who repaired the plastic bags that got caught in her bicycle tires. That same year in Brooklyn, New York, an interdisciplinary arts venue known as Proteus Gowanus started its Fixers Collective in response to the 2008 recession and to "promote a counter-ethos that values functionality, simplicity, and ingenuity and that respects age, persistence and adequacy."

But a year before either of those projects, Berlin artist Jan Vormann started filling crumbling niches of buildings and streetscapes with Legos of all colors. From the beginning, Jan hoped others would pick up on the idea, and indeed it has become a worldwide participatory phenomenon. "Fix the world in colors," he declares, and on the website he created, dispatchwork.info, you will find an interactive map showing the hundreds of places where Lego repairs have been made, many with pictures and the story of why the spot was chosen. One reads:

> Jan gave me a bag of LEGO, before I travelled to South Kurdistan for the art project 'Space 21.' I promised to find a place for his work. When I visited the Amna Suraka (the red museum), the former prison of Saddam Hussein's intelligence service, where the Kurds were tortured until the liberation in 1991, I felt that this place had a very sad energy that needed Jan's positive and colourful work as a symbol for a brighter future. When you walk through the main entrance of Amna Suraka you find the Dispatchwork at the building in front of you on the upper left side of the facade.

Agency

In social science, *agency* is the ability of individuals to act on their intentions to make something happen. These actions take place within social, economic, and environmental structures that enable or limit our agency, both as individuals and as groups. This is perhaps the most fundamental way of examining the human condition, and repair and reuse are one small way we can be agents of change in our lives. The impulse here is to reclaim something we may feel we've lost. "Control of my world has been taken away from me, and I want it back." Cracked smartphone screens, unresponsive coffee makers, printers that won't print — we'd like to fix them, but when repair is not an option we end up replacing them instead. We feel trapped by planned obsolescence. Repair culture aims to establish the agency of repair and reuse as social norms, as a way of challenging and remaking the ecology of our economy.

In his book *Shop Class as Soulcraft*, Matthew Crawford considers the merits of "individual agency in a shared world." He admires the self-reliance that repair and maintenance offer us, and he wonderfully describes the way we feel when we become competent in our chosen activity, the excitement of seeing the practical results of our efforts. Individual agency, he says, is at the core of being human. But Crawford also cautions against the kind of self-reliance or agency that is self-absorbed. When we get to a place where we feel our judgments are truer and better, it is usually because we have sought the wisdom of others who are more experienced than we are. "For in fact we are basically dependent beings: one upon another in a world that is not of our making."

Here in the Age of the Anthropocene, we are facing the imperative for shared agency on a global scale. In 2017, Paul Hawken edited *Drawdown*, a book with the ambitious goal of providing a blueprint for "drawing down" the carbon in our oceans and atmosphere — that is, reversing global warming in our shared world. Project Drawdown breaks down this huge challenge into one hundred strategies and contends that most of the tools and ideas we need are already in use around the globe. Once a year, Project Drawdown brings together a couple hundred climate educators and activists at Omega Institute in Rhinebeck,

New York. In 2018, Martine Postma was invited to speak about repair as a Drawdown strategy. The organizers titled her presentation "Repair Cafe: Creating Agency through Fixing Stuff and Strengthening Communities" and positioned it in this way: "The full range and beneficial impact of climate solutions have not been explained in a way that bridges the divide between urgency and agency. As a result, the aspirations of people who want to enact meaningful solutions remain largely untapped."

At the conference, Martine built her case for the agency of repair as an experienced journalist does, brick by brick. Repair is not, she conceded, the fastest way to reduce global warming, but it does directly address a modern problem we all recognize: "Things break, and when they do, most people just don't know what to do anymore. They have no repair skills, they have no tools, and no time to focus on the subject. And so, when something breaks, they feel helpless." At the same time, she said, there are people in every community who do know how to make repairs, and who are so fond of tinkering that they are more than happy to help their neighbors and try to fix things together.

Repair Cafes have been Martine's singular contribution, fitting together our individual and social characters like the convex and concave sides of a curve. "Repair Cafe connects people with their common sense and their inner feeling of what's right," she said at the conclusion of her presentation. "When you take the time to make a repair, you realize that it's actually a very normal thing to do. And when you succeed, it makes you feel strong. It empowers you, and when communities are empowered they're capable of achieving more together. That's the kind of mindset we need for a more sustainable future."

Tikkun Olam

Somewhere in the teachings of every wisdom tradition on earth is the admonition to "make whole that which is broken." In Judaism, it is *tikkun olam,* "repair of the world." It is said that in the eyes of God, an object that has been repaired is more holy than one that is new. There is an interpretation in Judaism of the world as we see it and of how it came to be; it is a retelling of the Genesis story by the sixteenth-century mystic

Isaac Luria. In his vision, Luria saw that God filled the entire universe completely and perfectly and that the world could only be created by somehow making a space for life. Luria imagined that God contracted, like a series of containers within containers, and by becoming smaller and smaller, God allowed a new creation to emerge. When the enormous energy and potential of that creation finally exploded outward, sparks of the divine scattered throughout the universe: the universe we see. The teachings that follow from this, in the wisdom tradition of the Kabbalah, tell us that we are to gather the shards and the sparks and bring them back together. This is the meaning of *tikkun olam*. *Olam*, or "world," comes from the same root as *hidden*, and so the repair we are asked to accomplish requires that we see the sacred hidden within the ordinary — the wholeness that exists in all things, everywhere.

This specific idea of "seeing the sacred in the ordinary" was the premise of a television series called *New Morning* that coauthor John produced for six seasons. It was a radically interfaith, intercultural, and intergenerational program that told stories of people from all walks of life, sharing their sense of everyday spirituality: a Boston pie shop owner, a Chicano radio station DJ, an urban ecologist in Atlanta. A regular voice in the programs was Irwin Kula, an eighth-generation rabbi and author of *Yearnings: Embracing the Sacred Messiness of Life*.

"So often in religion we start with a stain or a sin or moral judgment because that's where the brokenness is supposed to be," Irwin says, "instead of recognizing that, no, the normal course of life is that we mess up and things get broken. There's a wisdom in that brokenness, and once we see that, we can actually get to fixing it."

Irwin identifies the two levels of *tikkun olam*. The first is repair of the self, our interior world. When we are disconnected from the center of our own consciousness, we are also disconnected from the divine. The second layer is repair of the external world. It is our responsibility to "manifest and enact" compassion and justice in the world. "We see our separateness from each other as the cause of poverty, injustice, and suffering," Irwin writes. "Broken shards are everywhere waiting for us to retrieve them and to put them back together. But what if, in lamenting the world's brokenness and working toward Oneness, we extinguish those sparks? Suppose in our drive to love the whole we exile the parts? What if the shattering itself is the point?"

This emphasis on the dignity of the pieces and the parts is indeed true wherever repair takes place. Examining the parts is essential to the process. Without them, pieces of the puzzle — important parts of the story — are missing, even if, or especially when, it turns out a piece needs to be replaced. Wholeness isn't uniformity — wholeness is multiplicity. "Repair Cafe makes it okay and laudable and, to use a more religious word, praiseworthy to bring your broken stuff. When you can still dignify the broken, that's when you can actually work on it. Beloved and broken, not broken and broken. To be human together is to fix things together."

In Hebrew, the image of the word for *blessing* is a wellspring, the flow between the human and the divine. "The metaphor is so rich,"

Irwin says. "Through our actions at the repair table, we're opening the flow. We're repairing the circuit, and both sides — the human and the divine — are there already. A place of knowledge and community. *Tikkun olam* Cafes."

BY THE TIME YOU ARE REAL

One afternoon at Repair Cafe, a boy of six or seven years old brought in his stuffed puppy for repair. He told us that he would fall asleep every night by pressing and stroking the ear between his fingers, and the fabric of its ear was now worn with use. Caroline, who specializes in handwork, took good care in mending the toy. When she was done, the boy wrote in our comments book: "They fixed my dog's ear and he feels a lot better and my dog is happy and so am I." This exchange prompted Don Grice (who does digital photo restorations) to recall this excerpt from *The Velveteen Rabbit* by Margery Williams, one of his favorite books:

"Real isn't how you are made," said the Skin Horse. "It's a thing that happens to you. When a child loves you for a long, long time, not just to play with, but REALLY loves you, then you become Real."

"Does it hurt?" asked the Rabbit.

"Sometimes," said the Skin Horse, for he was always truthful. "When you are Real you don't mind being hurt."

"Does it happen all at once, like being wound up," he asked, "or bit by bit?"

"It doesn't happen all at once," said the Skin Horse. "You become. It takes a long time. That's why it doesn't happen often to people who break easily, or have sharp edges, or who have to be carefully kept. Generally, by the time you are Real, most of your hair has been loved off, and your eyes drop out and you get loose in the joints and very shabby. But these things don't matter at all, because once you are Real you can't be ugly, except to people who don't understand."

The Right to Repair

The cover is cracked. It is time to rip it off, look directly at the inner workings, and begin to fix things for ourselves.
— Matthew B. Crawford, *Shop Class as Soulcraft*

In 2009, Matthew Crawford's book *Shop Class as Soulcraft* crept onto the bestseller list and into the public imagination. Crawford is a motorcycle mechanic and repair shop owner in Richmond, Virginia, who unexpectedly enough also holds a doctorate in political philosophy. He evoked the worldview of another book that urged readers to play closer attention to what is valuable in their lives, Robert Pirsig's *Zen and the Art of Motorcycle Maintenance*, published thirty-five years earlier. Crawford's stated approach was "an inquiry into the value of work." His book's aim was to examine "the experience of making things and fixing things…and to consider what is at stake when such experiences recede from our common life."

By the time Crawford's book appeared, an online open-source

repair manual known as iFixit had already been out in the world for several years, spurring computer technicians and tinkerers to keep pace with the relentless stream of digital products entering the marketplace. Kyle Wiens and Luke Soules were still students at California Polytechnic State University in 2003, when they founded iFixit to be the tip of the spear challenging the tech industry from the user's side. Kyle had begun compiling a collection of pithy statements like "Repair is war on entropy," "If you can't fix it, you don't own it," and "We have the right to devices that can be opened." Together, these axioms revealed a developing philosophy but fell short of making a larger, coherent statement.

Then Kyle came across the "repair manifesto" created in 2009 by Platform21, the design collective based in Amsterdam that had also inspired Martine Postma. Some of the statements in the manifesto read more like stage directions for performance art than a political agenda: "Repair survives fashion." "This isn't about money, it's about a mentality." "You can repair anything, even a plastic bag."

But Kyle recognized an affinity and sketched out the first version of iFixit's own Repair Manifesto, articulating the repair ethos in a way that was exciting and clearly attuned to tech culture. A logo of a raised fist clutching a wrench suggested the kind of anarchism celebrated in Edward Abbey's novel *The Monkey Wrench Gang*, which opens with an epigraph by Walt Whitman: "Resist much. Obey little." The IFixit Repair Manifesto was both a call to action and a declaration of independence for the burgeoning repair movement: *We hold these truths to be self-evident...*

The Repair Manifesto went viral almost immediately, encouraged by iFixit's open-source philosophy. Kyle's purpose was to build community around a powerful set of ideas, and the collection of truisms gathered under the "wrench held high" banner stuck. "Before we came along and started doing this, there was not interest in repair as a holistic umbrella that applies to everything," Kyle told us. "That's what's radical about what we're doing, what Repair Cafe is doing, and everybody else. We are identifying and seeing acts of repair as fundamentally the same across all disciplines." Kyle's Repair Manifesto has now been translated into twenty languages, and you will see iFixit's poster shared and displayed in work spaces and classrooms all around the world.

REPAIR MANIFESTO

WE HOLD THESE TRUTHS TO BE SELF-EVIDENT

IF YOU CAN'T FIX IT, YOU DON'T OWN IT.

REPAIR IS BETTER THAN RECYCLING

Making our things last longer is both more efficient and more cost-effective than mining them for raw materials.

REPAIR SAVES YOU MONEY

Fixing things is often free, and usually cheaper than replacing them. Doing the repair yourself saves you money.

REPAIR TEACHES ENGINEERING

The best way to find out how something works is to take it apart.

REPAIR SAVES THE PLANET

Earth has limited resources. Eventually we will run out. The best way to be efficient is to reuse what we already have.

REPAIR CONNECTS PEOPLE AND THINGS | **REPAIR IS WAR ON ENTROPY** | **REPAIR IS SUSTAINABLE**

WE HAVE THE RIGHT:

TO DEVICES THAT CAN BE OPENED | TO CHOOSE OUR OWN REPAIR TECHNICIAN | TO NON-PROPRIETARY FASTENERS

TO REPAIR DOCUMENTATION FOR **EVERYTHING**

TO REMOVE 'DO NOT REMOVE' STICKERS

TO REPLACE **ANY & ALL** CONSUMABLES OURSELVES | TO TROUBLESHOOTING INSTRUCTIONS & FLOWCHARTS

TO REPAIR THINGS IN THE PRIVACY OF OUR OWN HOMES | TO ERROR CODES & WIRING DIAGRAMS | TO AVAILABLE, REASONABLY-PRICED SERVICE PARTS

BECAUSE REPAIR IS INDEPENDENCE SAVES MONEY & RESOURCES | REQUIRES CREATIVITY | MAKES CONSUMERS INTO CONTRIBUTORS | INSPIRES PRIDE IN OWNERSHIP

Repair as a Political Act

"Tossing things out instead of fixing them has far-reaching consequences — for consumers, for the economy, and for the environment," writes repair activist Gay Gordon-Byrne in the essay entitled "Why We Must Fight for the Right to Repair Our Electronics," which she co-authored with Kyle Wiens. "Indeed, a future in which nothing ever gets repaired isn't bright for anyone except the people trying to sell you new products. And many of us are not prepared to accept that future without a fight." As a Repair Cafe volunteer in England put it, "When fixing items is actively discouraged by manufacturers, repair becomes a political act."

The ideas expressed by Gay and Kyle represent the guiding philosophy behind the growing Right to Repair movement, an initiative that has been spreading for several years in North America and Europe. The basic legal principle is this: if you own it, you have the right to repair it. We might take this right for granted until we discover that many products are designed so they cannot be repaired by you or me or any repair shop not licensed by the manufacturer, if at all. Many corporations want to capture additional profits when you bring the broken item to them for repair, or when you have no choice but to buy a new one.

Many of our repair coaches, for example, are familiar with "the printer conversation." Here's how it goes: When someone lugs in a broken printer, often purchased not so long ago, they are often disappointed by our relatively low success rate in getting it to work again. The ready explanation for this problem is, to many, a revelation: Printers are made as cheaply as possible and may even be sold below cost. This is okay with the company behind the brand because the real profit lies in selling you the ink, "the most expensive liquid in the world." Marketers call this the "razor and blades model." As a result, poorly made and quickly discarded printers are the bane of Repair Cafes — and landfills — everywhere.

To further complicate matters, an astonishing array of products now contain embedded software, which manufacturers protect from consumers as intellectual property, making troubleshooting and repair nearly impossible. The first challenge to this emerging state of affairs came in the early 2000s, when carmakers were refusing to sell computer diagnostics to independent auto repair shops. After a decade of effort, an association of independent auto care companies, led by Aaron Lowe, convinced the Massachusetts legislature to challenge that position. In 2012, Massachusetts passed the Motor Vehicle Owners' Right to Repair Act, requiring carmakers to give independents access to the same diagnostic tools they provide to their franchised dealers. In 2014, to avoid a series of protracted legal battles over the issue nationally, the automotive industry capitulated. The president of the Association of Global Automakers admitted that "a patchwork of 50 differing state bills, each with its own interpretations and compliance parameters, doesn't make sense." The Massachusetts law became the national standard. This was a significant win for the nascent Right to Repair movement and for consumers. Turns out, Right to Repair legislation is very popular with voters; the ballot referendum that preceded the Massachusetts law passed with 86 percent of the vote.

In December 2016, at the request of Congress, the U.S. Copyright Office weighed in. After a year-long study, it issued a report concluding that "the spread of copyrighted software...embedded in everyday products...raises particular concerns about consumers' right to make legitimate use of those works." The Copyright Office also cited the use of "complex and opaque language to frustrate reasonable user expectations" and found these concerns "particularly acute with respect to products that have not required software in the past." Moreover, the study argued that federal copyright law couldn't be used as an excuse to prevent consumers from making their own repairs.

Framed this way, the legal right to repair can be seen as a consumer protection issue, and it is specifically allowed by U.S. copyright law. The problem arises when manufacturers try to circumvent the rules. As an article in *Consumer Reports* put it, "Can a company that sold you something use its patent on that product to control how you choose to use it *after* you buy it?"

Some companies are employing tactics that effectively prevent or seriously limit consumer options. Digital locks and restrictive end user agreements are among the practices that benefit only the manufacturer. An editorial in the *New York Times* in April 2019 stated the situation plainly. "The growing complexity of electronic devices means that people need help from manufacturers. And companies have taken advantage of that shift in power."

You see this type of deceptive practice reflected in all kinds of David and Goliath stories. And indeed, consumers are fighting back. Farmers are "hacking" their tractors to make the sort of repair that John Deere prohibits in its "end user agreement." Ryan Finlay, who has worked with appliances for years, wrote his analysis of the "made to break" points in home appliances (refrigerators, dishwashers, washing machines, and dryers), titled "They Used to Last 50 Years." He's cofounded a company to build the market for quality used appliances. Austin McConnell, a YouTube blogger in Springfield, Missouri, made a video called "Ink Cartridges Are a Scam," based on his experience as an over-the-phone technical support person and supported by additional research. The video has been viewed more than five million times. His message: "It's high time we did something about this. Join me in starting the revolution." And Jessa Jones has done just that. She's become a heroine of the repair movement by starting a company called iPad Rehab — a mail-in business that gained a national reputation as the "go-to" place for motherboard repair. Her goal was to teach these repair skills to other stay-at-home moms, give them a place to practice, and instill them with confidence. "The stay-at-home-mom community is huge and full of talent," Jessa says. "If Apple doesn't want to repair, fine. But we do."

HIERARCHY OF REMEDIES

When a product stops working as intended, the owner has a variety of options. In Europe they call this a "hierarchy of remedies," which might look something like this:

What Consumers Can Do

- Check the obvious: Try a different outlet, wiggle the cord, clean it.
- Consult the user's guide. (Some products, for example, have a reset button, separate from the on/off switch.)
- Act on the product warranty, if it is in force. (Right to Repair advocates counsel: politely decline extended warranties.)
- Open it up: Do you see something that doesn't look right? A clog, a leak, a broken part? See appendix 1 for recommended online sources for DIY repair advice.
- Bring the product to a community repair event, or take it to an independent repair person in your town.
- Return it to where you bought it and, depending on store policy, exchange it.
- Ship it to a factory-authorized repair service.
- Buy a new one.

What Manufacturers Can Do

- Ensure that the owner's manual is available and posted online.
- Make any diagnostic software available to consumers.
- Make replacement parts available to consumers.
- Make any necessary specialized tools ("funny screwdrivers") available to consumers.

Everyone agrees that companies should be able to reasonably charge for these things, but information and access are essential to an open marketplace for repairs. What is not acceptable is for companies to seek to create a monopoly on repair by keeping information about the product and its components behind the shield of "proprietary" property.

The Battle Lines

What has emerged around the repair movement is a power struggle between the technology companies — the global economy's largest corporations — and consumers fighting for the right to an open market for repair. Kyle Wiens says, "As the industry gets bigger, there's more and more money in the internet of things, which means there is more money to prevent these kinds of [consumer protection] laws." Tech companies, by one estimate, are outspending other interests in their lobbying efforts by a margin of nearly 30 to 1.

But consumer advocates have been active for many years. Gay Gordon-Byrne began her career buying, selling, and leasing large enterprise computers. She started a company that compiled a database of computer failures based on repair records. Her clients were the companies that did the repairs. In 2010, when Oracle bought Sun Microsystems and said, "We're no longer interested in facilitating repairs," her customers lost 30 percent of their business overnight. She said, "This is wrong" and volunteered with a trade association committee that, three years later, started the Digital Right to Repair Coalition, with Gay as its executive director. The coalition's goal is to represent the interests of everyone involved in the repair and reuse of technology, from DIY hobbyists to independent repair technicians.

Another repair warrior is Nathan Proctor, a policy director with the U.S. Public Interest Research Group who describes himself as a "career public interest campaigner." He explained his advocacy this way: "We saw Right to Repair as a strategic place in which people are actually having a conversation about taking back control of the stuff in their lives. People are reinvesting in local skills and local businesses and local resilience, pushing back against the consolidation of Main Street and asking what it means to live within our ecological boundaries. Repair invites that conversation in a lot of different places."

The remedy, all agree, will be not through the courts but with legislation. The persuasive logic of Right to Repair laws for all types of consumer products is now working its way through twenty-five state houses: Minnesota, Michigan, New Hampshire, Massachusetts, New York, and

California among them. Support
among lawmakers has been remarkably bipartisan. The resistance has
mostly played out behind closed
doors, with tech industry lobbyists.
Repair Cafes and Fixit Clinics are
significant grassroots allies in fur-
thering the Right to Repair lobbying
effort. When state representatives
hear from a community repair volunteer, they are getting the perspective
of an expert, who often gives them
their first real understanding of how
the repair economy is working in
their district and how many lives it

touches. At a press conference in May 2018, Joe Morelle, the majority
leader of the New York State Assembly at the time (he is now a con-
gressman), responded to a reporter: "The big question is why it hasn't
happened already. And don't get me wrong, we have some big opponents
in certain areas. They visit us quite frequently on it. But this is the time
to do it because we need to save ownership rights in New York State and
protect our environment."

Somewhat surprisingly, many of the legislative proposals receiving
special attention are in response to the experiences of farmers. Elizabeth Warren, a senator from Massachusetts and an architect of the
federal Consumer Financial Protection Bureau, has advocated for a
national Right to Repair law to ensure farmers' right to repair their
own equipment. When she proposed the legislation in March 2019, she
put it in the context of leveling the playing field for consumers and
corporations. "A company puts out sophisticated equipment and then
says if it breaks…you don't get to repair it at home. You don't get to
take it to a shop in town where there are three competing places. Both
of those keep costs down for small farms. Instead, you've got to take
it back to the one company that sold it to you, and they can charge

whatever they want to charge. Because as long as the thing is broken you can't get any use out of it."

A follow-up survey of more than one thousand registered voters conducted by the research group Data for Progress in May 2019 asked the following question: Would you support or oppose a policy allowing farmers to repair equipment they own, rather than to have an authorized agent make repairs for them? More than 70 percent of respondents, including Republicans, Democrats, and independents, supported such legislation.

The media also took notice. The *New York Times* editorial board opined, "Mrs. Warren has the right idea, but she did not go far enough. The owners of consumer electronic products deserve the same protection as farmers," and concluded, "An open marketplace for repairs benefits consumers, independent retailers and the environment. Modern devices are increasingly complicated; that concept is not." Other newspapers around the country agreed. The *Pittsburgh Post-Gazette* stated that "right-to-repair policy is a smart plan that would have a tangible impact on millions of Americans."

Nix the Fix?

In July 2019 the Federal Trade Commission hosted "Nixing the Fix: A Workshop on Repair Restrictions," a public symposium in Washington, D.C., to look at how the advancing technology of consumer products was affecting adherence to federal statutes. The statutes discussed included the Magnuson-Moss Warranty Act of 1975, which was enacted to prevent manufacturers from using disclaimers on warranties in an unfair or misleading manner. In her introduction to the workshop, Commissioner Christine Wilson began by asking who in the room had watched the late 1980s TV show *MacGyver*. Delighted at the number of hands that went up, Christine said that MacGyver's practical application of scientific knowledge and inventive use of common items had always inspired her. "But," she said, "in today's connected world even MacGyver may have had a bit more difficulty getting out of sticky situations. I'm not sure he could fix a smashed smartphone with gum

and a paperclip." She then noted how complicated repair questions have become, and that the purpose of the workshop was to assess the dynamics of the repair market in light of the bedrock principle of the Federal Trade Commission: robust competition provides the greatest benefits for the consumer.

In advance of the workshop, FTC staff had issued ten "questions for inquiry," seeking to discover (1) the prevalence of certain types of repair restrictions, (2) whether consumers understand the existence and the effects of repair restrictions, (3) the effect of repair restrictions on the repair market in the United States, and (4) the impact that manufacturers' repair restrictions have on small and local businesses. The workshop drew participants from a wide range of fields, who shared their perspectives with the commission and the public. Among them:

- The CEO of a Minnesota company that resells large digital devices. When a manufacturer refuses to provide aftermarket support, she pointed out, the sale dies, the customer is angry, and the equipment goes to the landfill.

- A Vermont independent repair shop owner, seven years out of college, whose business is increasingly stymied by devices that are "completely sealed, batteries glued in." At stake, she said, is a whole sector of small business. Her biggest concern: "What will technology cost in ten years, and who will be left behind?"

- A federal safety and risk management expert who believes we are in a "fourth industrial age, the exponential age," in which "dumb metal boxes" are long gone and we are "balancing cost, complexity, sustainability, and life-cycle management." The question is: "Who should repair what, and when?" His answer: "It depends."

- An automotive manufacturer's association rep who helped craft the 2012 Massachusetts Memorandum of Understanding between carmakers and the trade groups representing independent auto repair shops. He said, "Dealer-only repairs? We've rejected this argument as a society."

- A rep from the Association of Home Appliance Manufacturers, who raised safety issues related to DIY repair, cautioned that insurance rates might rise, and reminded everyone that Right to Repair laws have yet to be adopted in a single state. She was chastened, however, by a state senator from Vermont, who cited research indicating that appliances that used to last thirty years now last an average of thirteen, and who noted that legislation is being drafted carefully in order to withstand anticipated legal challenges.

- A Republican state senator from Minnesota who was the lead sponsor of Right to Repair legislation in his state, who affirmed, "Consumers are demanding this, and I say to the corporate interests here in the room: 'No' is not going to work. There will be legislation in my state, with or without you."

> Every day in the United States, more than 416,000 smartphones are disposed of.
> — Environmental Protection Agency

THE LONELY MAYTAG REPAIRMAN

In 1967, the Maytag Corporation of Newton, Iowa, introduced a character in its television commercials that has become a cherished part of Americana. "Ol' Lonely" was played memorably by actor Jesse White as a good-hearted Maytag repairman who simply didn't have much work to do — all because of the remarkable quality of the machines he was trained to service. The first black-and-white, thirty-second ad, titled "Drill Instructor," is an acknowledged advertising classic. Here we see Ol' Lonely address his new Maytag recruits in a tough voice. "I'm gonna give it to you straight," he says — although you can tell right away that he's really a softie. Pointing to the "rugged motor" and "almost indestructible pump" inside a Maytag washing machine, he tells his repair recruits that in fact they'll spend most of their time waiting for a service call that

continued on next page

never comes. That's when he picks up a small toolbox: the Maytag survival kit, filled with playing cards, crossword puzzles, and beadwork to fill their lonely hours. When actor Gordon Jump took over the role in 1987, Maytag's sales pitch still centered on dependability, promising that the consumer washers and dryers were "built to last longer and need fewer repairs." In an era of stiff competition, Maytag rose to number three among appliance manufacturers. Then, in 2006, the Whirlpool Corporation bought both Maytag and KitchenAid. Maytag commercials changed, and so did the product. In 2007, Whirlpool held a nationwide search for an actor to play its new repairman, seeking a "more relevant look and contemporary feel" for the character. By 2014, the repairman was handsome, wore tailored blues, and through animation-assisted actions, performed the same tasks as the machine he represented, with the emphasis now focused squarely on efficiency and convenience.

The nostalgia we may feel now for Ol' Lonely is not for a simpler time but for appliances that once had a life expectancy of longer than the six, eight, or perhaps ten years estimated for many of today's washing machines, clothes dryers, dishwashers, and refrigerators, which often need a repairman within the first two or three years.

I Fix, You Fix, We Fix

Peter Mui of Fixit Clinics and Kyle Wiens of iFixit, both based in California, have partnered to strategize ways to pressure for this kind of fundamental change. Their emphasis is less on community repair and more on ways to significantly increase the number of people with the knowledge required to make repairs. "How do you change the material economy of the world?" Kyle asks. "How do we get everyone thinking about this in a serious way?" Peter answers:

Once people start repairing, they start asking questions like "What went wrong?," "Can it be fixed?," and "How might it have been designed differently to avoid breaking in the first place?" That last question is where we're ultimately going with Fixit Clinic: to encourage products designed with maintenance, serviceability, and repairability in mind. As consumers, we're going to have to start demanding those things; at Fixit Clinic we trust that improvements in product quality and durability will come through a broader understanding and dialogue around how things are made now.

Any plan to build a vibrant repair economy will require product access and information. In 2003, iFixit set out to build the community of fixers by enlisting them to the cause. First, iFixit issued a call to action to product users and tech geeks everywhere: to do a "teardown," that is, to get inside any product, take it apart step-by-step, and document in words and pictures how they did it. "Our goal," Kyle says, "is to hijack the new product release cycle and get people thinking about product longevity from day one."

New product releases are like catnip to tech hotshots around the world, and they compete for bragging rights to be the first to get inside every significant new product and report on what they find. It's the kind of fervor that has accompanied the automotive industry for generations, but these are digital rights activists fixed on blowing the whistle on designs that shut out users and make tech less repairable. The iFixit team has deep experience, and when they announce their newest teardown on Twitter, along with their repairability score, it is definitive.

From the start, Kyle's call to action was basically "Teach others." Find a problem, figure out how to fix it, and write a repair guide to explain it. The self-described goal was to create a "free guide to fixing everything, written by everyone." The results fall anywhere between a heavily illustrated blog post and a technical manual, and iFixit Repair Guides are now arguably the most reliable single source of product-specific repair information. The world of YouTube how-to videos has exploded also, and all these various online sites have created a global repair community and an invaluable resource for community repairers.

The scale of these resources is impressive. On iFixit.com you can search more than fifty-nine thousand Repair Guides, covering more than twenty-one thousand devices (within any device there are multiple repairs that might be needed), and hundreds of brands in every digital and electronic product category, including a growing number of appliances, car and truck models, and, more recently, an apparel category from zipper jackets to eyeglasses. iFixit.com will also sell you parts and tools, including those "funny screwdrivers" and a very useful tool called a "spudger" that is used for separating pressure-fit plastic components without damaging them.

Because the guides are the result of bona fide reverse engineering and the instructions are produced by iFixit and not the manufacturer, iFixit hasn't accessed or published proprietary information. All of the guides are made available under the open source Creative Commons license, and the site is wiki-based to allow crowdsourced content editing. As a creator or user of the guides, you can share, copy, and redistribute the material in any medium or format, and you can adapt it — remix, transform, or build on it, and form collaborative teams. iFixit's Tech Writing Project has been adopted by more than eighty schools and colleges. "Getting students to think about the longevity of products is a sea change," says Marty Rippens, who's running the program. The site also highlights professionals who can do the job for you; iFixit champions the act of repair as a job creator.

All of this sharing of repair know-how represents a full-on challenge to the hegemony of the technology companies. The point is to fill what Kyle calls "the ecosystem hole" that the companies have dug by manufacturing millions of devices without any end-of-life maintenance and disposal strategy. "I think of ourselves as an operating system to the repair world," he says, "providing information, knowledge, and tools to help make it possible for you to go out and do the repairs. But we're not the ones turning the screwdriver. You are."

You will find a user's guide to navigating the world of online repair resources in appendix 1.

Building a Repair Economy

Repair and maintenance will make its way back into the fabric of everyday life only when professional repair is reestablished as a viable and attractive career path. Reclaiming repair as a profession is critical to establishing a repair economy. An important advantage is that repair is predominantly local — recalling one of Neil Seldman's axioms for resource management: localize the industry; nothing should travel far.

The proliferation of main street computer and digital device repair businesses and the appearance of smartphone repair kiosks in every mall in the nation have been steadily growing this segment of the market. Apple's initiative with Best Buy to provide the kind of repair you could previously find only at the few-and-far-between Apple Stores, Motorola's partnering with iFixit to provide repair kits for its phones, and HP's posting step-by-step repair videos to its YouTube channel are all significant moves to scale at the corporate level. The emphasis on electronic products is justified — the electronics industry is in a hot competition with the garment industry to be the fastest growing waste stream. But the real potential for an economic shot in the arm lies in developing a thriving repair sector that offers a much broader menu of repairs.

In Portland, Oregon, an organization called Portland Repair Finder is providing a central resource that links people to repairs. Its mission might be a model for every city and county: "Dedicated to helping more people fix more things. We make tools, knowledge, and resources easier to find, and help tell the stories behind repair work." The Portland Repair Finder locator map shows the wide range of repair businesses and nonprofits in their orbit.

In New York City, Sandra Goldmark and a group of backstage theatre artisans founded Fixup in 2013 to help rebuild the repair economy. How exactly? By creating pop-up repair shops that provide work for professionals of all stripes. By creating an apprenticeship program. By holding workshops to build excitement around repair. Fixup repairs are not free but they are reasonable — their website has their pricing. In 2018 they expanded to develop "Good Stuff" — a retail experience that combines repair, reuse, and smart, sustainable design all in one space. "This is the future of stuff!" they proudly proclaim. If repair is to be a first option in the "hierarchy of remedies," then this is the kind of collaborative repair culture communities need.

The Open Repair Alliance

The open-source repair culture represented by iFixit and others is a growing global phenomenon. In 2017, the environmental ministers of the member states of the European Union approved a set of recommendations, called the Ecodesign Directive, to increase the "resource efficiency" of mainstream appliances: lighting, televisions, washing machines, dishwashers, and refrigerators. The document begins with the observation that 80 percent of the environmental impacts made by

products are determined at the design stage. "Europe's 'take-make-use-throw' economy is costing consumers money and depleting the world of finite resources. Better product policy can help Europe transition towards a circular economy, where waste is prevented and products are designed to be reused or recycled."

Repair culture is in the thick of this push. In 2018, five organizations joined together to form the international Open Repair Alliance, challenging the common definition of *prosperity* as purely economic. Their members include the Repair Café International Foundation, based in Amsterdam; iFixit and Fixit Clinics in the United States; the Germany-based Anstiftung Foundation, which coordinates a network of seven hundred Repair Cafes and brings a strong focus on repair in education; and Restart, based in London and active throughout the UK and Europe (its motto is "Don't despair, just repair").

In late 2018, the European Commission considerably weakened the proposals of the Ecodesign Directive, and critics easily demonstrated that the revisions mirrored the language and interests of industry. In response, Restart, Repair Cafe, and iFixit activists drafted the Manchester Declaration. "We are part of a growing movement pushing for our Right to Repair worldwide," the document asserted, "alongside independent repair businesses and citizens frustrated with the early obsolescence of most of today's products."

In October 2019, a substantial and somewhat surprising breakthrough was achieved that seemed to respond to those demands directly. The European Commission approved new rules for appliance manufacturers that were, as the BBC reported, "prompted by complaints from consumers across Europe and North America infuriated by machines that break down when they are just out of warranty." New standards will take effect in 2021 requiring appliance makers to extend the life expectancy of lighting fixtures, washing machines, dishwashers, and refrigerators, and to provide spare parts for up to ten years. One important aspect of the legislation falls short, however: companies can limit consumers' access to parts and remove consumer-repaired products from warranty. Stephane Arditi of the European Environment Bureau told the BBC: "When repair activities stay in the hands of a few firms, we're missing an opportunity to make it more affordable and readily available. Small independent repairers can make a great contribution to the economy and our society. We need to help them do their job."

Individual European countries are adopting other kinds of repair-friendly policy initiatives too. These include Sweden's tax breaks on repairs, to nudge consumers to take a second look before throwing things away, and France's proposed product sticker requirement, which, in addition to energy use, would provide both the estimated life expectancy of appliances and electronics and a one-to-ten rating for repairability. The direction this is heading is to make planned obsolescence flat-out illegal, but the hope is that the market itself will provide that incentive.

A key strategy in lobbying for these kinds of policies is collecting information that sustainability organizations can use to pressure manufacturers to develop better designed, more resource-efficient products. To this end, the Repair Café Foundation created a first-of-its-kind platform called RepairMonitor. Restart in the UK has developed their Fixometer. The Open Repair Alliance is establishing an "open standard" to make it easy to collect and share data on electronics repair among many different groups. By collectively analyzing this information, the alliance will be able to extract insights to strengthen the push for repair.

Is this broadening coalition merely another social movement that will come and go in the long arc of history? Governments are responding slowly to the profound changes reported by climate scientists around the world. We don't know how the dynamics of extreme weather events, for example, will force entrenched industries to transition to a postcarbon economy, but we are seeing rapidly growing political pressure for climate action from the younger generations. Those who identify with the repair movement see the repair mindset, the right to repair, and all that they imply for consumer and cultural behaviors as vital to the transition. Isn't this the nondystopian future we all hope for, in which civilization has learned from its mistakes?

Whether your motivation is to take control of your stuff, satisfy your curiosity, show off what you know, find something to do with your hands, find something to do for your neighbors, stick it to the big corporations, push back against obscene consumerism and waste, or draw down the carbon in our atmosphere and oceans — your town can have a community repair project too.

Repairing in Place

Reform, correct, repair, cure, heal, doctor, fix, patch, recondition, renovate, revamp, and rebuild. Oh, I could write a novel on each of these words and its necessary place at the intersection of art, fashion, and ecology. Let alone its place in our kitchens. In our gardens. In our art studios. In our communities and legislation and infrastructure.

— Katrina Rodabaugh,
Mendfulness and the Long Journey to Repair

Home as the Center of Repair

Repairs are born of necessity and oftentimes must be made anywhere: in towns seeking strategies for revival and transition, in libraries reclaiming their place in the town center, in social innovations such as Tool Libraries and TimeBanks, in classrooms and in museums, at a nearly lost burial ground, and on a historic sailing ship. But perhaps the place to begin is closer at hand. As Elizabeth Spelman writes in *Repair: The Impulse to Restore in a Fragile World*, the truest center of repair has always been in our own homes, a "veritable repair shop" for our bodies and spirits, responding to the "steady flow of crises arising from the vulnerability of the human heart and from the fragility of the web of human relationships": skinned knees, broken toys, mended seams, busted windows, stuff that stops working, and never-ending housework. And too often, as we know, the home is also the backdrop for domestic violence.

Modern living has been steadily "de-skilling" us for decades. We demand convenience, and we all need more time. (You've probably seen the clever meme: "What I really need is another day between Saturday and Sunday.") But that is changing. Millennials are now driving the demand for re-skilling, seeking opportunities to regain the knowledge that might have skipped a generation. Add to that the fact that in the United States today, single female homeowners outnumber single male homeowners two to one, and breadwinning mothers are increasingly the norm in U.S. homes. The number of how-to resources for female homeowners has grown exponentially. See Jane Drill, the DIY home improvement channel on YouTube, is a good example of what's available — for women and for men — today.

A homeowner's work is never done. Let's leave it at that, and go outside, into the commons.

Positive Proximity

In 1994, Dar Williams was a talented young singer-songwriter touring the country with her guitar and an extraordinary collection of songs. Her first full-length album, *The Honesty Room*, was just out, and she was playing the coffeehouse circuit that had been established in the sixties, had languished from the mid-seventies to the mid-eighties, and by the mid-nineties was seeing a comeback. Hers was a high order of song craft, and before long Joan Baez, among others, would be recording her songs.

That circuit took Dar to just about every state in the lower forty-eight. She visited quite a few college towns, but mostly postindustrial cities that had lost their core industry and major employers a decade or two earlier and were struggling to find a way back to some measure of prosperity, and perhaps relevancy, in the twenty-first century. Dar was in each town only a day or two, and what she found were audiences tenaciously holding on to their optimism. "The towns were empty," she told us. "The malls, the big boxes, and the exodus of factories had happened all at once, and the public square was overgrown. Nobody knew which way was up."

Dar's experiences inspired the images in her song "Bought and Sold," a portrait of what's been called "the malling of America," leaving empty storefronts on Main Street.

> Well we're heading for a past that you can leave and not defend
> Where the downtowns hold the sadness of "You can't go back again"
> It's there you'll find the rust and debtors
> Motel signs with missing letters
> Cause there's a monster on the outskirts
> Says it knows what your town needs
> Then it eats it up like nothing and it won't spit out the seeds

Dar started taking notes, and when she returned to those towns a year later, she found herself becoming more and more interested in how change happens. Soon she had evolved into a student of social dynamics. "I got to see what works, and that helped to keep me inspired," she explained. She recalled a dinner in Charlottesville, Virginia, with friends, one of whom, Hal Movius, writes books about conflict resolution. During dinner Hal asked a question: "What do you think determines the relationships we'll have in our towns?"

Dar said, "Values." No.

"Politics?" No again.

"Hobbies?" Wrong.

Then Hal said, "Proximity. That's all."

In time, Dar began to think that visiting this collection of towns repeatedly had given her a unique opportunity to write about the social dynamic she came to think of as "positive proximity." She describes this dynamic in her book *What I Found in a Thousand Towns*. In towns that are thriving, Dar found an essential ingredient, an extension of the "proximity principle" recognized in social psychology and described by her friend Hal: individuals are more likely to form interpersonal relations with people who are close by. It's an idea so intuitive it hardly needs stating, except that…everyone is so busy, and in our wired world, real connections are not to be taken for granted.

Dar didn't set out to write a handbook — she's a storyteller, after all — but her book is full of instructive and insightful case studies, captured in her subtitle: *A Traveling Musician's Guide to Rebuilding America's Communities, One Coffee Shop, Dog Run, and Open-Mike Night at a Time*. She structured the book into three sections: "Place," "Identity Building," and "Translation." "Placemaking" has become a familiar idea in town planning; it's the creation of public spaces where strangers can become acquaintances, discover common interests, and have conversations that may lead to collaborative ideas. "Identity building" is about the way bridges get built from one part of the community to another — between business owners who are parents and want to see more activities for their kids; pastors, rabbis, and imams who recognize their common ground; town officeholders who aren't in it for themselves; artists and entrepreneurs. One well-known challenge is bridging the divide between longtime residents and newcomers.

Dar's third ingredient for positive proximity is "translation," the way we announce ourselves to the world and all the ways the world can find us. Dar focuses on two kinds of translation that are as old as civilization: partnership building and the role of "conscious bridgers," people who take pleasure in connecting people. Where once we saw a town of strangers, now we see a town where almost everybody knows *somebody who can*. "This is social capital, and when it starts to build, it keeps building — and keeps *variegating*," Dar explained, using a word that nicely combines economy with ecology. No one is saying that restoring community and repairing generation-old divides is easy; and job losses, social isolation, and the opioid epidemic, among other problems, have devastated whole communities. The challenges are huge, and towns need powerful strategies. Dar captures a fine distinction when she writes, "Some people even go from saying 'I live here' to 'I'm from here.'"

There is a Repair Cafe at the library in the town next to Dar's home in Cold Spring, New York, one at her local farmers' market, and another one ten miles up the Hudson River in the community room of a low-income apartment building. Dar continued:

Let's look at what Repair Cafe is doing. It's creating a lot of face-to-face conversations. It models a citizen who has a sense of sharing and good will, which gives people a sense that where they live is populated by friendly, accommodating people, not judgmental, exclusive people. Those things add up to a sense of social trust.

Another cool thing about Repair Cafe is that it's not saccharine and it's not condescending. It's not exactly "charitable" in the way we usually think. It gets people engaged with mechanics and side-by-side good gritty stuff. The opposite of division is not unity, it's collaboration. That's what I see at Repair Cafes.

Dar quotes her friend Beth Macy, who has written extensively about the decline of small towns in her books *Factory Man* and *Dopesick*: "Communities thrive when there is a diverse range of equal voices." The truism of "When you've got your health, you've got just about everything" has its parallel for cities and towns: when you have affordable housing that is a walkable or bus-able distance to healthy food, you've got just about everything.

These are the things that build civic self-esteem, the "beating heart" that's able to stand up to "the monster on the outskirts [that] says it knows what your town needs." "You don't have to do any of this," Dar says. "It's just that when you do these things, you will have so much more than you do already."

Transition Towns

In 2005, Rob Hopkins was back home in England from extended travels in Asia, and he was teaching the principles of permaculture: ways to design beneficial relationships by emulating natural systems. The question that consumed him was, How can communities become stronger in a future that is far less dependent on fossil fuels? Years earlier, on a trip to the Hunza Valley in northern Pakistan, he'd found a social and economic fabric that was not dependent on trucking things in from the outside world. Hopkins described his reaction: "In this remote valley I felt a yearning for something I couldn't quite put my finger on but which I now see as being resilience: a culture based on its ability to function indefinitely and to live within its limits, and able to thrive for having done so." But he also observed that sacks of nitrogen fertilizer and cement were already appearing, along with refined sugar products and drinks.

Hopkins and his students in England began working on a road map to help communities revitalize their local food systems, strengthen their local economy, and create a just transition to a postcarbon future. Since 2005, the Transition Town movement has grown internationally, with more than twelve hundred initiatives in fifty countries — towns where people come together to initiate positive social change. There's an emphasis on practical projects; you want people to see what you do and be inspired by it. You want to give people different ways to get involved. You're looking for the intersection where community needs meet the skills and passions the group has to offer.

Transition Towns have embraced the fundamental attributes of the repair movement. Sharing skills is at the core of their resilience, and sharing skills, of course, is fundamental to the repair movement. When the first Transition Town–sponsored Repair Cafe in the nation launched in Pasadena, California, in 2013, partnering with the Arroyo S.E.C.O. Network of Time Banks in Los Angeles, they learned that clothing repairs were both the most needed and the most offered skill. "The following month we held our first Repair Cafe with seven sewing machines running for three hours!" says Transition Pasadena's Therese Brummel. "It was a huge success. The following month we decided to focus on electronic appliances. Again, a huge success. Forty-five events later, we offer just about anything you can think of."

And so Repair Cafes are thriving alongside "blitz gardens" (planted by a small army of volunteers in a single weekend, "occupying" every part of town), re-skilling workshops, healthy food networks, and the other strategies included in the 2019 book *10 Stories of Transition in the U.S.: Inspiring Examples of Community Resilience Building*. Not surprisingly, the second chapter in the book is titled "The Spread of Repair Cafes."

Twenty-First-Century Libraries

For generations, libraries have been an essential part of democracy in America. In 1790, Ben Franklin facilitated the first public library when he donated his books to the Massachusetts town that named itself after him, and the residents voted to make those books freely available, establishing the institutional paradigm for the sharing economy. In his book *Palaces for the People*, sociologist Eric Klinenberg delivers an inspiring account of the vital role libraries play in providing "social infrastructure" — informal places that enable mutual support; that allow people to become acquainted, to check in on each other, and to take the pulse of the neighborhood. A place, for example, that gives children the chance to fall in love with reading. "Social infrastructure influences seemingly mundane but actually consequential patterns," Klinenberg writes. "It affects everyone." It also requires attention and investment, and just like hard infrastructure, social infrastructure must be maintained. When it is not, we see the domino effects of weakening social bonds.

Librarians have emerged as champions of community repair. It offers them the kind of programming they especially value: hands-on learning that is intergenerational and that brings new faces into the library. The idea of starting a Repair Cafe at the Mamakating Library in New York's Catskills region was an outcome of a series of discussions initiated by the Sullivan County Human Rights Commission in the spring of 2016. They called it "Dialogue2Change," and the purpose was to inspire outside-the-box solutions to poverty in the area. Someone had heard about "these free Repair Cafes," and Library Director Peggy Johansen was intrigued. She visited the closest one, which happened to be at another library twenty-five miles away in Gardiner. "It was just perfect for what we were trying to do," she says. Their first Repair Cafe, with the support of the local Lions Club and the Lady Lions, got started that summer.

"I'm not sure we're reaching enough people yet to address people's needs across the socioeconomic spectrum of the whole area," Peggy says, "but we'll keep doing it. We're all subject to the bombardment of commercials that want to sell you something that is new, new, new. In this county we have dollar stores sprouting like weeds. The mindset to think, 'I have something worthy of repair,' doesn't come easily."

Libraries have always been our "community crossroads." You will find quiet at a library, of course, but you will also find countless invitations to learn with others and from others. Ironically, the limitless and mostly free information available online has led some to believe that libraries are less relevant, less deserving of public funding. Branch libraries, in particular, have suffered in recent years. But it is precisely in an era when we are wedded to our handheld devices that we need what libraries give our neighborhoods. Was there an era when libraries became static and lost their knack for bringing people through their doors? Perhaps, but if so, that time is long gone. Libraries are back — and if you have spent two minutes looking at the programs being offered day in and day out by your local librarians, you know that they deserve your support.

On the West Side of Chicago, at the Austin Branch Public Library, Ray Kinsey hosts summertime Repair Cafes as part of his teen program. "This is the first Repair Cafe, of more than a thousand worldwide, to locate in a predominantly Black community," he told the *Austin Weekly News*. Ray says that growing up he was lucky enough to be able to tag along with older guys who could fix things. It was a bonding experience. Now, he's giving kids the chance to learn from the older volunteers at their neighborhood library and earn community service credits for school. "You can develop a skill and patience instead of just following society's tendency of instant gratification," Ray says. "You can fix something instead of throwing it away to a landfill." Ray is also a recording artist and rapper, with four albums to his credit, and he excels at offering the kids opportunities to tell their stories. "Empathy in our profession is just as important as the information. When young black boys walk in, it helps them to see a young black male librarian who raps. Libraries can help you be you in your highest form."

Today, librarians everywhere are reinventing their spaces and their services to be "twenty-first-century libraries," with an emphasis on learning experiences. They have become "libraries of things." Your library is likely lending out one or more of these items: free family passes to your region's zoo and museums, ukuleles, fishing rods, croquet sets, microscopes, mobile Wi-Fi hot spots, American Girl dolls, and sewing machines. And that's a starter list. What's more, Rebekkah Smith Aldrich, a founding member of the American Library Association Sustainability Roundtable, wants libraries to also be sustainability leaders in their communities. "In library-speak, we catalog items and you can check them out. But what if you could catalog people and expertise? So that if you want to know about beekeeping or furniture refinishing, you can do a search, find a book or a DVD, but also find a neighbor who's willing to talk to you." She says Repair Cafes and Fixit Clinics are manifesting exactly that idea in a growing number of libraries by connecting people with knowledge through other people. "I'm so excited when I see another library anywhere in the country hosting a repair program. It's happening, and it's empowering people to really own the world around them."

Tool Libraries

The twenty-first century has brought on an expansion of the sharing economy, which is not only a cultural change shaped by context but also a generational change, from Millennials to Gen Z, born between the 1980s and 2010. A common value is that experience matters more than ownership, and this idea is contributing to consumer and lifestyle choices that are critical to growing the circular economy. But it was way before Gen Z, forty years ago, that a social innovation emerged that has been reinforcing the repair movement ever since: Tool Libraries.

A Tool Library is exactly what it sounds like: a place to "check out" tools — from ladders and expensive power tools to the basic staples of carpentry, painting, and gardening — just as you would check out books. You access the things you need when you need them — especially those that would be expensive to buy — without cluttering up your home. Unlike tool rental businesses, most Tool Libraries are nonprofit membership organizations (typical annual dues run about fifty dollars a year), and along with the tools, they offer expert advice, workshops, programs for kids, and occasionally parties with live bands. In short, a vibe.

In early 2018, Tessa Vierk, who has a background in culinary arts, decided that Chicago needed a Tool Library. She started by researching existing "tool institutions" for best practices and inspiration. Both Tessa and her cofounder, Jim Benton, are in their thirties and are Midwest natives who moved away for a few years and then came back. They feel fiercely rooted. Their language is threaded with intention:

Tessa: I want to create a space for self-directed learning, self-sufficiency, and resource equity.
Jim: All people should have access to the things they need to thrive.

We wanted to know why their generation has embraced Tool Libraries. "People are looking for ways to ask critical questions about how they're living their lives," says Tessa. "They're thinking about their waste, and existing structures don't offer a lot of solutions to that. People in our generation are more familiar with the idea of group ownership, and they don't feel they need to have something all to themselves." It's also simply practical. There's no room in an apartment for tools. Her friends in the city don't have houses with garages, and "space is money."

THE "GREAT TOOL LIBRARY SHOUT-OUT"

On the Chicago Tool Library's Instagram page on five consecutive days, Tessa Vierk profiled the Tool Libraries upon whose shoulders they hoped to sit. Here's how the feed reads:

Day 1: The Tool Library
in Downstate Bloomington, Illinois

West Bloomington Revitalization Project
Tool Library

Our first Tool Library friends! Check out just 3 of their awesome initiatives among many: When you volunteer to fix bikes, you earn a bike of your own! College students build benches for bus stops! Their "Veggie Oasis" provides free healthy food!

Day 2: "BPL DIY," the Tool Lending Library at the Berkeley Public Library in California

One of the granddaddy tool institutions, with a tool inventory we dream about — helping people get their hands on tools since 1979. And it's a real public library! You can check out a tool just as easily as a DVD of *Ace Ventura: Pet Detective*. Win!

Day 3: Denver Tool Library

Model missionaries for the tool library gospel because, dang, do they make it look fun! We aren't totally convinced that anybody can beat their silly vibes, but we'd really love to be wrong. We are inspired by the welcoming, playful space you've created — a true community gathering place.

Day 4: HNL Tool Library in Honolulu

Inspired and impressed by their commitment to the tool library as a vehicle for environmental activism and as a stronghold for circular economies. They are great about educating the public about how sharing tools redirects waste and prevents needless consumerism.

Day 5: Baltimore's Station North Tool Library

Like us, they set out to explore and experience as many tool libraries as possible before deciding on a system best for Baltimore. Unlike us, they did this on a motorcycle trip across the country. We aspire to be that swashbuckling. We are also starry-eyed over their inclusion of textile arts in their tool library. They have a loom, knitting classes and natural dye classes!

Coauthor John visited the Chicago Tool Library in July 2019, a month before they opened their doors, and helped Tessa and Jim build shelves. The Tool Library is located in a renovated industrial building that's home to a variety of creators and fabricators, lending instant community and neighborly support. Their ground floor space has high ceilings, cement floors, and perhaps best of all, a loading dock. The kick-off party, with tacos, Lagunitas, and music, was the week before Labor Day. By then, Tessa and Jim had attracted a core of volunteer tool geeks, run a crowdfunding campaign to add to their start-up nut, and received donations of more than three hundred tools of all types.

All of this was communicated by Tessa in more than a hundred Instagram posts that set a creative and engaging tone. "The amazing thing about Chicago is that there's a huge artist and fabricator population of a younger generation. I'm confident we'll grow a network of experts for all the trades and crafts that we can draw on."

Tessa and Jim want their policies to be welcoming to families with young kids. They consciously designed their logo without tool imagery, so no one would think of this as a you-better-know-what-you're-doing-when-you-come-in-here kind of place. They want it to be an "Oh, you have a question? Come on in!" kind of place, like a public library. In fact, their dream is to be acquired by the Chicago Public Library. "Chicago is very segregated racially and socioeconomically by neighborhood. We want to make this replicable because we want other neighborhoods in Chicago to have one too," Tessa says. "Every tool library is a product of the community it calls home."

Repair in the Classroom

A middle school science teacher I know delights in telling this story about the mechanical advantage of using simple tools: She presented her eighth-grade class with a wooden board with a nail partially driven into it. She then held up a carpenter's hammer and asked for a volunteer to remove the nail. Hilarity ensued as the student tried to use the "claw" part of the hammer to "unscrew" the nail. The class coached him on how to remove the nail by using the hammer claw as it was intended, as a lever. Similarly, a surprising number of kids have never actually seen a hammer or a screwdriver in use. And so we arrive at a key observation: many young people simply don't realize that things can be repaired. What they know of the world is that when something breaks, you throw it away and get a new one. Practically speaking, a shift toward sustainability and the circular economy requires an increase in "repair literacy" — people's basic ability to maintain the things they own. This awareness may build over time, but as a report by the Repair Café Foundation concludes, "the real change will come when the learning of repair skills gets a place in education again."

In the last few years there has been an outcry in some quarters about the fact that shop class and home economics have all but disappeared from our public high schools. The feeling is that perhaps we've lost something of value. It was in 1908 that Ellen H. Richards founded the American Home Economics Association, culturally right in step with the thrift movement. The association reached its peak of influence during the 1950s, with the expectation that women would learn to be housewives and homemakers. In the 1990s, "home ec" became known as "FCS" (family and consumer sciences), and classes teaching "Life Skills" continued to reflect the times.

The concept of sustainability was introduced to these courses in the early 2000s, but in the decade that followed there was a drop of nearly 40 percent in the number of students taking FCS classes. This decrease came with the advent of the Common Core curriculum in public education, when programs that weren't amenable to test scores — especially those that required a budget for materials — were being reevaluated. High school–level short courses that introduce life skills that children are not learning at home (sometimes called "adulting classes") are popular in many parts of the country. Topics include cooking and textiles, healthy living, family life, personal money management, and "anything else that touches the home and heart." But these programs often lose out to computer literacy and STEM classes in the competition for funding.

The story of shop class is different. Beginning in the 1980s, there was a steady decline in high school–level "trade-related" classes due to state funding cuts and the push for more students to enter degree programs. But the picture that Matthew Crawford presented in his 2009 book *Shop Class as Soulcraft*, of a public education system providing few opportunities for hands-on learning, has fortunately evolved significantly. There has been a nationwide expansion of vocational high schools and tech schools, offering a wide range of career pathway programs — jobs that pay well and that we all depend on. Training for the renewable energy sector — building wind and solar systems — is also driving these programs. Still, we can acknowledge that when high school students separate into different tracks, they lose the opportunity to learn basic skills along with the classmates they've grown up with, as well as the healthy male mentorship that shop class teachers traditionally provided.

In the Netherlands, a curriculum called "Repair in the Classroom" has been developed, with corporate support, for three age levels between six and twelve years old. It is available to anyone in multiple languages through the Repair Café Foundation. The plan provides two prep lessons to be taught by the teacher, after which a "practical" lesson brings repair coaches from the community into the classroom to work with the kids on broken things they've brought from home. Volunteer repair coaches are asked to guide the troubleshooting process and encourage curiosity. Imagine kids you know responding to these class discussion questions:

- What happens at home if something breaks?
- Do your parents sometimes repair things?
- If you throw away broken objects, what happens to these things? Where do they go?
- Where do new things come from?
- What is necessary to make all these things?

- Do you think it's possible for everyone in the whole world to have as many things as you do?

In the United States, public schools can't often accommodate repair as a classroom activity, but in independent schools, where teachers have the time and latitude to incorporate innovative programs, it is embraced. At the Waldorf School of Saratoga Springs, New York, Michael Whitney is the practical arts teacher. He's been a carpenter, designer, and artist all his adult life. "I fix things for people so they will tell a story about how somebody fixed it," he says with a smile. A couple of years ago, he decided to offer "Tinker Week with Mr. Whitney," a class for his eighth-, ninth-, and tenth-grade students. It was five days of fixing things from the school classrooms and community, to save money for the school and to prove to his kids that you don't always have to "just buy a new one."

Mr. Whitney's idea caught on. "After we presented the hundred or so items the students fixed that week, the twelfth graders, who were not part of this opportunity, came to me and asked if they could do it too. A few minutes later, the idea of 'the Fix-it Club' was born." The club meets after school on Fridays to fix broken items like wooden trains from the kindergarten classrooms and broken seatbacks from the campus lecture hall. Now the club is ongoing and has an eager student following. "I could talk for hours about the fun we've had in Fix-it Club."

Jump to the Culture of Repair Project in Berkeley, California, which collaborates with the Transition Berkeley Repair Café and the Fixit Clinic at the Berkeley Public Library and was instrumental in helping both programs get started. Vita Wells, who founded the Culture of Repair, is from south Texas, "hailing from a long line of fixers and doers." The fact that she holds degrees from both Yale Divinity School and the Yale School of Management will give you an idea of the depth she aspires to: ethics and social structures that will be subversive enough to compete with consumer culture, and seductive enough to revive the fixer and doer mentality she grew up with. Culture of Repair is "working to transform our culture into one that more readily repairs than it purchases," she writes. "A culture that repairs because that's just what you do." Wells is working toward a repair sensibility that is deeply embedded, as cultural values always are.

In 2018, Culture of Repair began collaborating with Agency by Design in Oakland, which has a well-established maker-centered professional development program for teachers with Maker Ed, an organization supporting maker-centered learning across the country. They've developed "hands-on learning routines" that focus on three core "maker capacities": the ability to look closely, explore complexity, and find opportunity. For example, in 2019, Shraddha Soparawala, a math teacher, created a class called "The Art of Repair" at a charter school in the Fruitvale neighborhood of Oakland. The student population reflects the demographics of the community: 10 percent are in special education, 70 percent are multilingual learners, and 92 percent receive free and reduced lunch. The kids watched YouTube videos of different kinds of repairs, and Shraddha devised repair projects for them to try. "It is very easy for them to get discouraged and want to move on to a different project," she says. "I want to gear their experiences so that they are getting more 'at bats.' This will build their expertise and their confidence as repairers. In my view, 'failing forward' is a critical component of developing a repair mindset."

These are classroom experiences that excite Vita. "This is just the beginning," she says. "I'm confident that the combination of the momentum behind Maker education, combined with the imperative and urgent momentum behind addressing environmental issues, will draw repair into mainstream education relatively quickly."

HOUSTON, WE'VE HAD A PROBLEM

If there is one story about repair that captures the imagination of middle schoolers, it is the story of how the *Apollo 13* spacecraft was fixed 248,655 miles from home. In April 1970, as the spacecraft's command module neared the moon, an oxygen tank exploded, and mission commander Jim Lovell calmly radioed back home: "Houston, we've had a problem." He and fellow astronauts Fred Haise and Jack Swigert were in immediate peril. There was a critical loss of oxygen and electrical power. The decision was made to leave the command module and move into the lunar module as a "lifeboat." But that craft was designed for only two people.

Maintaining the balance in the "atmosphere" inside a spacecraft is a major design consideration, and the filter that absorbs CO_2 is a critical part of that design. The three *Apollo 13* astronauts, now crowded inside the lunar module, absolutely needed the additional air filters from the command module. But the filters were not interchangeable; the command module filters were rectangular, while the lunar module filters were circular. With very low power, in a very cold cabin, with oxygen falling and CO_2 rising, the astronauts worked with engineers on the ground on the fix: a makeshift adapter fashioned from plastic packaging, an air hose from a spare spacesuit, a tube sock, and yes, you guessed it, duct tape. The repair was actually much more complicated than it sounds, and it worked. For the rest of the seventy-two-hour return flight, all systems held steady, barely. For a long stretch the entire spacecraft was running on about the same amount of electricity as it takes to run a toaster. *Apollo 13* did not reach the moon, but the legacy of the flight is told and retold as NASA's "successful failure."

This prompts the not-so-trivial question: Why are the jokes about duct tape being able to temporarily fix almost anything…actually true? The secret of duct tape lies in its versatility and tensile strength. Sandwiched between the poly coating and the adhesive layer is a strong layer of cotton mesh, which reinforces the tape in the same way rebar reinforces concrete. Yet because the threads are uniformly horizontal and vertical, duct tape can be easily torn by hand — no tools needed. Duct tape was standard equipment on Apollo space missions beginning with *Apollo 11*, and it would be called on again for a critical fix to the Lunar Rover on *Apollo 17*.

Repair in the Museum

When *Repair and Design Futures* opened in the fall of 2018 at the RISD Museum (part of the Rhode Island School of Design), its purpose was announced as you entered: "This exhibition investigates mending as material intervention, metaphor, and call to action." The curator, Kate Irvin, says the idea for the exhibition began to take shape when she noticed that students who visited the museum with their classes were most interested in items you might find at the bottom of the collection drawers in most other museums — the neglected, messily mended, or even sweat-stained items. One student told her why: "It allows me in." Kate intuitively understood their impulse to seek out well-worn, mended, and sometimes humble items. "That's where the excitement is bubbling up. The 'back' is what they want to see. It's where you might find a clue to the mysterious history of a piece." Kate sums it up simply: "They recognize a good story."

At about the same time, Brian Goldberg, who teaches in the RISD Department of Architecture, was becoming interested in how repairs are carried out in everyday life. He was bothered by the way the discipline of architecture tends to repress, or at least downplay, the work of cleaning, maintaining, and repairing. In architecture, Goldberg says, a "build it and move on" mindset often predominates. He and Kate began to consider what an exhibition about repair could encompass.

Kate had recently acquired an example of traditional Japanese *boro* textiles (*boro* translates to "tatters" — and boro garments are made from various saved pieces of fabric patched together). Kate says, "I was seeing the design world paying a lot of attention to these mended, broken, and loved garments with deep, deep narratives, and I wanted to understand this fascination. What is this moment?"

Brian continues: "And I thought to myself, this is remarkable. Kate's actually invested in and highlighting all the conditions that I think of curators as working to repress and hide — the signs of wear and use and mending and affection. The experiences and marks of time."

Anna Rose Keefe is a twenty-something conservation assistant for the museum. She saw that the exhibition would present a very different kind of interaction with the past. "As conservators we are encouraged to train the visitor's eye away from the damaged place." Anna Rose is very aware of that delicate balance — the tension between the goal of making sure something is around for the next century and "meeting the object where it is." It is heavily context dependent.

One piece in the exhibition is a hunter's tunic from Mali. The exhibition catalog tells us it was made by Fode Keita, an important hunter and historian/storyteller. "Every time he wore this," explains Anna Rose, "he believed it made him stronger, because of the supernatural energy of the hunt. It is dyed with a bark used for medicinal purposes." Keita repaired the tunic himself with materials at hand — including pink plastic to patch a hole. Typically, art conservators would have worked to adhere the pieces to make them stable. But, says Kate, "in this we see the accumulated power in the rawness of the patches, and it's not our job to interfere with that."

Lisa Z. Morgan, who teaches apparel design, takes us to see a pair of stockings included in the exhibition: calf-length cotton knit stockings owned by Ann Katherine Kittredge Taylor, a Victorian woman, wife, and mother born in 1834. Lisa speculates that they appear to have been a treasured pair — perhaps Kate's only pair of like stockings — because of the repairs we see: repeated darning at the toes, with whole patches added on the heels, made over a period of years. "For me," says Lisa, "what is really beautiful is envisioning it on her legs, because from ankle up it's going to look quite immaculate, but then, in taking off the shoe or boot, you're aware of how much work she's having to do to keep up appearances, of what's hidden. What we reveal on the surfaces of ourselves, what we present, can be very different from the upset or the discourse and discomfort we might be having to navigate every day."

Brian looks down at his own well-worn boots. They are not yet part of the museum's collection, he jokes, although he has promised them as a gift. Brian's boots are both practical and biographical. As soon as he grew big enough, his father handed down a pair of his own shoes, along with instruction for their regular cleaning and polishing, plus one oddity: his father believed that shoes should be worn only every other day in the belief that they need a day to dry out. As an adult,

Brian has continued his father's habit. He owns two identical pairs of boots, which he alternates and wears nearly everywhere. "I long ago lost track of how many times they've been resoled. In use and wear they have recorded and marked time, situations otherwise unnoted and forgotten. Maintaining their utility and purpose has become a covenant." Brian sees in the work of maintenance and care a respect for what the object has supported or made possible, and he's also aware of "the energy embedded in its form," from the cow to the cobbler to the store, "the entire system of production, distribution, and consumption that allowed me to exchange paper money for a pair of boots."

> The future of museums is inside our own homes.
> — Nobel prize–winning novelist Orhan Pamuk

Kate walks us across the gallery, showing us three framed scenes made from scraps of cloth in bright reds, yellows, greens, blues, and browns. These are *arpilleras* — appliqué-style pictures made by Chilean women during the 1970s and 1980s, the era of General Augusto Pinochet's brutal military dictatorship. The pictures are full of people, and at first look they are not so different from the folk art tourists brought home from Chile before Pinochet. "But look closer," says Kate, "All three *arpilleras* document protests by women who carry posters with the faces of missing husbands, fathers, sons, and brothers. They are raising banners of opposition at a prison, at a closed factory, at a TV station taken over by the government." Kate explains that the authorities paid no attention to this folk art made by poor women and had no clue that each *arpillera* was a subversive statement or that the pieces were being secreted out of Chile and brought to activist meetings and fundraisers around the world. "That is their beauty and power, and the reason they are here," says Kate. "This is social repair. This shows the power of the stitch."

Meanwhile, the Long Island Children's Museum in Garden City, New York, features an award-winning hands-on exhibit called "Broken? Fix It!" which invites children and adults to "get inside the repair process." One item in the exhibit is a plastic dinosaur accompanied by a sign that reads: "Plastic toys often break. Glue can bond pieces back together, but adding a dowel makes for a stronger fix. A pencil makes a good dowel."

A boy learning about repair culture through a repaired plastic dinosaur at the Long Island Children's Museum.

A Hard-Working Boat

The *Clearwater* is a 106-foot-long, bluff-bowed, shallow-draft, gaff-rigged, single-masted Hudson River sloop. The keel was laid in South Bristol, Maine, in October 1968, and the *Clearwater* was launched in May 1969. It was Pete Seeger's singular vision to build a historic-looking boat so that people could experience the Hudson River, learn about it, and care about it. He'd first seen the sloops in a book published in 1908. This type of sloop evolved from an original Dutch design, specifically for navigation on the Hudson River. Alexander Hamilton wrote the first of his *Federalist Papers* while taking passage on one. None had survived the advent of steamboats and railroads for moving cargo and passengers on the river between New York City and Troy, and the *Clearwater* was the first Hudson River sloop to be built in more than a hundred years.

After not quite seven summers of "sailing in the industrial sewer" the river had become, the *Clearwater* needed its first major restoration. From that point on, the sloop's captain and crew put into place continuous and rigorous preventative maintenance measures. In 2004, the *Clearwater* was added to the National Register of Historic Places for its role in "articulating, publicizing and defining the American environmental movement." Two years later, the foredeck and the rigging were replaced. All of this work was led by Jim Kricker, master shipwright. "A boat like the *Clearwater*, it's a hard-working boat. You just have to anticipate at some point, or at several points, much more than routine maintenance during the course of its life. You're going to have to do major rebuilds on it."

Starting in 2009, three entire winters were devoted to reconstructing the hull and replacing all the wood below the waterline at the sloop's home port in Kingston, New York. The work was beautifully documented in the film *Restoring the Clearwater*, where you hear from the crew and the craftspeople doing the work — some experienced, some apprenticing.

At what point do we recognize that all of this repairing, restoring, and maintaining rises to another level? At what point is it *sustaining*? Pete Seeger's *Clearwater* has long since become a symbol of something much bigger than a sailing ship. "The nucleus is the boat," says longtime *Clearwater* member and ship's captain Steve Schwartz. "My God, the thing is so beautiful, so lovely, that people will do extraordinary things to be connected to it and keep it going." Over the last fifty years, by virtue of the nonprofit organization Hudson River Sloop Clearwater, thousands of people from all over the world have come to see her, to sail on her, to learn about the river from her, to crew on her, and even to learn from Jim Kricker how to rebuild her. "I have seen many people who started on the crew just as volunteers, who have come up and who I now consider to be master craftsmen, able to carry on the tradition to build and rebuild. Having artifacts and objects in museums is great, but unless you can preserve the skills that went into making those, you're missing half the picture." All of these activities are sustaining a way of life: the life of the river and the river towns, and by extension, the life of our world. On the day in 2004 that *Clearwater* was named to the National Register of Historic Places, Pete Seeger, then eighty-five years old, told a reporter something important about the legacy of a wooden boat that has been sailing for thirty-five years. He may have helped plant the seed to build the boat, Pete said, but "you should consider that the essential art of civilization is maintenance."

Sacred Space

The city of Kingston, in Ulster County, New York, is one hundred miles north of New York City and sixty miles south of Albany, where the Catskill Mountains meet the Hudson River. It was burned by the British in 1777 and was the first capital of New York State. By 1790, there were about thirty thousand people living in Ulster County. Ten percent were enslaved Africans.

Several currents are now affecting life in this city. After three decades of economic stasis following the closing of IBM's Kingston campus, people are moving up from New York City, along with developers, and gentrification is underway. Rapid changes in this small city have prompted a discussion about affordable housing and creative forms of collective land ownership. In 2018 the Kingston City Land Bank was established to maintain a range of affordability in the city's housing stock and to guide the development of neighborhoods. It is in the process of converting thirty-seven properties to affordable housing, with more to come. A tenant's union has organized, city and county policies are in place to protect the rights of immigrants, and there are questions about who will actually benefit from a multimillion-dollar "uptown" development.

In the midst of these changes, a small private property was in pre-fore-closure proceedings in a neighborhood near the oldest part of the city: an uncared-for stucco house on Pine Street with a nondescript backyard, 70 by 225 feet. Few knew that starting in 1750 or so, this plot without grave markers or tombstones had served as a burial ground for enslaved and freed Blacks. Church burials had been denied to enslaved people in New York since 1697, and instead, "common ground" sites like this one were designated for their use. By the late 1800s, the burial ground on Pine Street was forgotten, the house was built, and there was even a plan to pave the yard for parking. Then in 1990, Ed Ford, the city's historian, noticed some script on an 1870 map, designating the site as a "coloured burial ground." Archaeological analysis confirmed it, but the property remained in private hands for nearly thirty years. In 2019 the property was listed at auction, sparking a community-wide effort to reclaim it. Through the efforts of many, including Harambee (a new community organization whose name means "all pull together" in Swahili) and preservation nonprofit Scenic Hudson, the Pine Street African Burial Ground was finally purchased and protected by the Kingston Land Trust. A paid educational program enabled city youth, ages fourteen to eighteen, to learn about and then teach the community about their local history and culture, and to help establish the burial ground as an interpretive site.

The Pine Street land protection effort has been held up by many as a tangible act of repair at the heart of the community's aspirations for restorative justice. In her book *Repair: Redeeming the Promise of Abolition*, legal scholar Katherine Franke makes the case for community land trusts as a way to bring "substantial reinvestment in communities that have essentially been abandoned by modern society," and as one model for reparations. Micah Blumenthal, a community activist involved with all of these efforts, agrees.

> Right over there on Pine Street is proof of the people who worked this land, who were forced to work this land — an honest recognition of our history and a way to repair the holes in our collective memory, just as we would for any form of sickness. Can we recognize the history of harm, especially when it's gone unacknowledged and unrepaired and is still causing harm? We love to talk about freedom as a nation, but freedom and responsibility are intertwined. Maybe we have the responsibility to recognize that harm was done and to say, "What am I going to do about it?"

Micah reflects, "What we move toward is a more even distribution of not only wealth but, more importantly, power. That's the world I want to see, the world I want to live in."

Repairing Is Caring

In taking up repair...we prompt a conversation and inquiry into the ethics and practice of care — of things, but also of each other, our environment and our communities.
— Brian Goldberg, Rhode Island School of Design

Let's take simple hospitality as our starting point. As Repair Cafe hosts, we gladly welcome our invited guests. A Repair Cafe extends two invitations. The first is, "Let's see about repairing that thing you've brought there." And the second, "In the meantime, would you like a cup of coffee or tea?" Important things happen over a warm beverage — and at a repair worktable. Barbara Lane, who does jewelry repairs, puts it this way: "*No* job is insignificant. People bring in some weird things to be repaired, and it is not up to us to judge what is worthy or not worthy to be 'fixed.' I surmise that many people use the Repair Cafe as a means to get out of their house and have some interaction with other human beings — humans who will listen to them, laugh a little, and maybe even cry with them."

Martine Postma decided to use the word *café* because she wanted to be sure people understand that they are coming into an informal and convivial social space. As much as we focus on repair, the "cafe side" is essential to our purpose. The attention we pay to community repair as a social gathering is not beside the point — it *is* the point. In the UK, the Restart project calls their events *parties* "because they have a fun, ad-hoc spirit where all are welcome to meet, mingle, and share in the fun of repair."

Long before she'd ever heard of a Repair Cafe, much less started one, coauthor Elizabeth Knight was the tea sommelier for the St. Regis Hotel (the original Saint Regis was the patron saint of hospitality and social workers) on New York's Fifth Avenue. Prior to that, she'd written books about tea — the plant, the drink, the meal, the experience. She lived for a time in London, the home of the afternoon tea ceremony, and witnessed tea grown, blended, processed, and packaged in countries around the world. She learned that in China, tea is so essential to daily life that even during the Communist Revolution, when true tea was scarce, people served each other cups of hot water to keep their social connections alive. There, it's still considered bad form to pour your own tea; it means that no one cares about you. The same holds true in London, where she often saw one man, of a group of businessmen seated around a table, ask, "Shall I be Mum?" before pouring the steaming-hot "social-lubricant" into everyone's cup. In Japan, the daughter of a tea master who had studied the way of tea for fifty years told Elizabeth that the point of the ritual is to focus attention on the fleeting moment. In the words of the sixteenth-century tea master Sen-Rikyū: "This occasion and this meeting may come only once in a lifetime; therefore it should be highly valued." The sentiment of this may seem overstated for someone who has brought their blender to be repaired, but in our experience, it fits well the experience of the people who bring a profoundly beloved item for our attention — and there are many.

Radical Hospitality

Then there is the practice known as radical hospitality, which asks much more. The idea comes down to us from the *Rule of Saint Benedict*, a set of fifth-century monastic precepts written by Benedict of Nursia for the monks living under Benedictine rule. Christine Valters Paintner, a prolific writer on spirituality and creativity, says, "Benedict's Rule is a foundational expression of the principle of hospitality at work: Instead of being able to say that God appears only in what is familiar, only in the people who make me feel comfortable and safe and look like me, hospitality calls on us to extend ourselves, to risk."

Since 2013, the Repair Cafe in New Paltz, New York, has been hosted by the United Methodist Church, and every Sunday morning, Pastor Jennifer Berry invites the congregation to Communion with these words:

> Every color of the earth, every corner of the globe, old or young, you are welcome. Able to come on your own two feet, needing the help of canes, crutches, or prosthetics or the strong arm of a neighbor, or needing the elements brought to you, are welcome. Whatever your sexual orientation, however you are dressed, you are welcome. If you feel you are worthy, you are welcome. If you feel you are unworthy, Christ Jesus welcomes you to his table.

This is a beautiful expression of "radical hospitality." And although we are likely to think that something radical is "extreme," the word's true first meaning is "from the root." So, rather than thinking of radical hospitality as something out of the norm, we can consider it a fundamental practice, "arising from the source." Jeanette Nakada, baker, seamstress, and founder of the Repair Cafe in Lincoln, Nebraska, says, "We intentionally located in the oldest part of the city, a high-density area with a vibrant, eclectic population that includes many renters as well as immigrants, refugees, and neighbors with lower incomes. Inviting others to bring things to us means we won't be strangers very long. We know a good number of those former strangers will visit us again and will become familiar faces."

We only have what we give.
— Chilean novelist Isabel Allende

Self-Sufficiency Is Self-Evident

In the Forrestal Heights public housing complex in the City of Beacon, New York, the U.S. Department of Housing and Urban Development funds a program called "Resident Opportunity and Self-Sufficiency." As part of this program, a Repair Cafe is set up in the Community Room from time to time, and neighbors from the nearly 250 apartments can bring things to be repaired. When people don't have extra money to buy and replace things, a free service like this is cost-effective. It's also a welcome reason to get out of their apartments and be sociable with their neighbors — a mix of seniors, families, and a few singles. The "hurdle of pride" may make some hesitate to bring something broken, but Noah Hargett, the program coordinator, mostly discounts that. He wants people coming in from everywhere in the city. "It breathes in more life, brings in new stories. People get to see who we are and what we're doing here, instead of just driving by."

"This is the thing," says Kingston resident Teryl Mickens. "When we care to repair items, we are caring for our children, your children and all of our grandchildren. Clothing, electronics, jewelry — whatever you bring. Folks, especially those who are poor, are conditioned to throwing away the old and broken, and buying the new and shiny. I've learned a lot by seeing people repair, repurpose, and reconsider their own paid-for possessions." Jordan Scruggs, a Methodist deacon active in a program called Kingston Midtown Rising, says self-sufficiency is a self-evident community goal. "This is more than just an opportunity to fix broken things. It's also an opportunity to fix broken systems and relationships. The Repair Cafe is organized around the ethos of skill sharing. That's a mutually beneficial and empowering thing. It creates opportunities to nurture neighborly networks. It calls on the invaluable wealth of community knowledge and know-how."

> Her gratitude was enormous. It's like a contact high. You feed off of that. It feels like a blessing. Those are the small important things in life I think you can easily miss, and at the Repair Cafe it's just one after another like that.
> — Patty, sewing volunteer at Repair PDX, Portland, Oregon

ELECTRICIAN'S DAUGHTER

Jo Schilling's dad was an independent electrical contractor and a fifty-year member of the International Brotherhood of Electrical Workers Local 494 in Milwaukee. "Ever since I was a little girl," she says, "I loved my dad's workshop." He showed her how to use tools properly, starting with a coping saw. "Electrical wire was the thread and fabric of my life!"

Her whole family made things. They grew and preserved food, repaired and reconstructed things. "I learned at a young age how to create and make things out of the materials that were close at hand." When Jo was fifteen, her dad gave her a shoemaker's treadle sewing machine because she wanted to work with leather and make purses and moccasins and belts. When she was thirty, he gave her a heavy-duty vise for her basement workbench. "He was so happy," she says. "He just felt I needed that to keep the house going. He was right. I've used it a lot." Jo has always been the one to take care of her house.

Along the way, she met a songwriter who was so impressed with her skills that he wrote a song about her, in the voice of Jo's daughter Natalie.

My Mom's an electrician's daughter
I'm so glad my grandpa taught her
How to use the tools he bought her
Anything that gives us trouble
Mom can fix it on the double

Jo's dad loved to ask questions of complete strangers. So does she. Her dad had an endless curiosity about what makes things tick. So does she. "One of the key things I do when something needs repair," says Jo, "is to think, okay, this was working before. What has changed, and why? I work backwards from there to figure it out." Just like her dad.

continued on next page

Mama grab the wrench
Mama grab the screwdriver
Fix the thing herself
Or if she don't know how to
She'll call someone else
Mama's never too proud to

And when Jo does have a repairman in, she's right there, learning everything she can. "My dad always told me that a hardware store contains a wealth of knowledge. When he passed, I knew that taking a project to the guys at my hardware store would mean I've got someone else to figure it out with."

"Giving me these skills was his way of sharing his love with me. He taught me what he knew. And even now, when I'm trying to fix something, I try to channel him and think: How would Dad approach this repair?"

Mom's an electrician's daughter
Box of tools my grandpa bought her
Sitting on a bench in the basement
Filled with magic and amazement!

Bicycle Samaritans

Two categories weigh in heavily on the "make-a-difference" repair scale: bicycles and digital devices. Bicycles are a vital means of transportation for many people in U.S. cities and even more so around the world. When Dave Panico, an electrical engineer, was shown "a huge jumbled pile of bikes" that had been donated to the soon-to-be-opened Habitat for Humanity ReStore in Kingston, New York, he thought, "I can't stand to see them sent to a landfill. I believe we are stewards of the earth and the environment." Combined with Habitat's mission to give folks a "hand up," repairing the bikes seemed to Dave like a perfect way to help people and the environment. It didn't hurt that he's an avid cyclist. He assembled a small team of like-minded folks to meet on Wednesday nights and start working through them. Four years later, they've restored more than three hundred bikes.

There are bicycle repair "samaritans" like these all over the world.

"The first year we did this, all the bikes got stolen from an un-locked building," recalls Bill Shader. "And I mean *all* the bikes we'd spent the last several months fixing up." That was in Pittsburgh in the early 2000s. The city had put out the call for used bicycles in any condition, and Bill says in those days about half the bikes that came in were better sold for scrap. Over time, things improved. The group of cycling enthusiasts who volunteered to do the work got better at it, bicycle shops started donating parts, and a foundation with programs overseas got involved.

The used bicycle economy is more layered than you might think. Bill helps break it down for us. The players are metal scavengers, bi-cycle shop owners, police and public works departments, recreation programs, social services nonprofits, the overseas market — and guys like him. Let's look at the source first: the scavengers. There are people everywhere who drive the county roads looking for scrap metal to sell. Older bikes made from steel typically weigh twenty to thirty pounds. A kids' mountain bike bought at a department store might weigh thirty-five pounds. The metal scavengers Bill knows will apply their best judgment, and if they think a bike is too good to scrap, they'll drop it off in his driveway. The police get involved by picking up the skeletons of derelict bikes, often left padlocked to a fence somewhere. Bill's township holds an annual cleanup day, when generations of bicycles get fished out of basements and garages, the kids who once rode them having grown up and moved away. Many bicycle store owners recognize their role as well and are an invaluable source of parts. The local weekly or *Penny-Saver* will carry occasional reminders for donations, and Bill says he still gets calls from people who saw a feature article titled "Pedal Power" that ran in their monthly lifestyle magazine six years ago.

Wherever they come from, the bikes get collected in a workspace. In Bill's township, fifteen miles south of Pittsburgh, the space is a garage bay at the Department of Public Works. Then the triage happens. "Pump-ups" need the least work; clean them and they're ready to go. Bikes that have been sitting out in the weather may be fine mechanically but need new cables and lube. It's rare to have to replace chains or spokes. A real time-consuming job is getting the rust off the rims. "When you get a bike that's just too much work," Bill says, "it becomes parts. Do you have any idea how many sizes of seat posts there are?"

The "pipeline," as Bill calls it (his career was in construction management), leads to the distributors, those who get the bikes to their future home. The main distinction there is whether bikes are given free to children's homes and social services clients, or resold to provide a revenue stream for a nonprofit. Bill is willing to split his inventory between the two. A foundation called Brother to Brother ships all over the world, to places where a bicycle makes the difference between a recipient's ability to get to a job four miles away or a job that's triple that distance. Or a bike that will increase the number of homes a healthcare worker can reach in a day. The demand is always greater than what Bill and other bicycle samaritans like him can possibly supply.

There is a big buildup to the holiday season at the end of the year. "By then, I've had my fill," Bill says. "But then you get a bike that mechanically is ready to go but is a bit rusty. You look at it and you think, 'If a kid got this on Christmas, is he going to be happy?' So you spend the extra time. It's obviously a used bike, but it's a good-looking used bike. I've done what I can, then I'm happy."

REPAIR CAFE GLASGOW'S "PRAMAGEDDON"

Scotland's Repair Cafe Glasgow launched Pram Project in 2019 to help parents and children in need of vital transport. They put out a call for donations of prams (better known in the United States as baby strollers) and were inundated with requests for drop-offs and pickups. They posted this on their Instagram in August 2019: *"Pramageddon* has truly been upon us over the last two weeks." Since then they have been fine-tuning their process of collecting, receiving, cleaning, and repairing the prams and then getting them out to families who need them.

One sure source of prams has been the large St. Enoch Centre shopping mall in Glasgow, where unwanted prams are simply left abandoned. The prams are steam-cleaned, repaired to ensure they are safe, and then given to families. What started as a collection drive to meet an immediate need has grown into a long-term project with many partners. One partner is Refuweegee, a radical hospitality initiative started by a group of Glaswegians in 2015 to provide community-made "welcome packs" to "forcibly displaced people arriving in Glasgow." As often as needed, they include a pram with the welcome pack.

"We know that it can make people's lives a hell of a lot easier," says Lauren Crilly, Repair Cafe Glasgow's communications officer, "and we hope we will be able to provide families across Glasgow with as many pre-loved prams as possible."

Repair Cafe Glasgow's founder Jon Dawes (left) and Anne Ledgerwood of St. Enoch Centre with two unwanted prams recovered by Pram Project and ready to be steam-cleaned.

Inclusive Repair

Repairing brings people together who otherwise might never find themselves in the same room. Time and time again, it provides opportunities for enhancing individual and collective well-being. But a subtle and interesting new dynamic has emerged. With growing frequency, people with autism have been participating in community repair events. What is attracting them?

Frank Szenher, a retired IBM engineer, started bringing a couple of high school kids to our Repair Cafes, where they quickly became regulars. "Through a youth mentoring program, I've been working with kids on the autism spectrum. Andrew is a computer whiz and is now attending community college. Michael was in a school-to-work program called Youth Soft Skills Empowerment. I volunteered to tutor him in electronics twice a week for his senior year. And then I was his job coach during his trial employment as a repair technician at a record store. Now he's repairing vintage audio equipment full time. Amazing how the demand for that has returned!"

General statements about people with autism may often give you the wrong idea, simply because of the wide range of variability among autistics and other neurodivergents (NDs) — a broader term describing people with neurological characteristics outside the norm. Even the experience of one person can change, depending on the activity, the environment, and their recent experiences.

A person with autism may show up to a repair event for the same reason as anyone else: something has stopped working. But for her or him this may be much more than an inconvenience; it can be a big deal. Suddenly having to learn to use a new device is discomfiting. Discovering that there is a place where you might get your familiar device working again is not trivial. It is consequential in ways others may not grasp.

Panda Méry is active with Restart in England. As an ND, he's been able to communicate his own experiences and help others understand the strategies autistics may employ in their day-to-day lives. In blog posts and podcasts, he relates why repair activities and, more specifically, community repair events are so well suited to NDs. Why have they been seeking out repair events, and what is their experience of repairing?

First, Panda explains, there is an attraction to technical things. Problem solving and close observation are enjoyable for many autistics, especially when you're using your hands and tools. These activities invite intense focus, particularly in the diagnostic stage. In a sense, Panda says, you welcome the object into your social sphere, and a kind of conversation ensues. How is the device reacting, and how can you test it, question it, probe for answers? Of course, the person who brought the item is also there — a complete stranger, exactly the kind of social situation that is often challenging for NDs. And this is where Panda observes a therapeutic accommodation: "As soon as I have something in my hands, I am more comfortable talking to people." Small talk can emerge easily from that unselfconscious "flow state" — and small talk is good social connectivity.

A completed repair is a shared joy and a meaningful experience (you helped the device live longer!) And when something isn't repairable, it might be a "small tragedy," but it also more likely adds to your storehouse of patience. Panda points out two other dynamics that organizers should be aware of when working with ND repair coaches. NDs tend not to be collaborative repairers. Once they have "entered the fix," they won't be noticing what's happening at other tables and will be unlikely to invite another coach in on their "conversation" with the item. They may also be more persistent than other coaches in their quest to make a repair, which means they'll need more time and will likely see fewer items. They'll also likely be happier if there is no line at their table, and people aren't hovering.

Repairing also offers the opportunity to design specific events for people with specific goals and needs, including NDs. An organization in Florida has developed a first-of-its-kind repair program for adults with autism.

Earth to Autism

When Leanne Scalli was in fourth grade, she wanted to be an environmental scientist. She grew up to earn her doctorate in social science instead, and she now works with adults with autism in St. Petersburg, Florida. When she had the opportunity to start her own program,

images of the Earth kept coming to her. "I've always been really passionate about taking care of the planet, and I thought, what if we put
those two things together? Put autism to work on environmental issues." In 2017, Earth to Autism, or E2A, formed as a nonprofit.

Their first Repair Cafe was an experiment. People with autism
don't typically experience the world as a communal place, and there
are precious few opportunities for them to work together. A Repair
Cafe would be asking them to look around the room and recognize
that they had all come for a common purpose. Their interest in repair
and affinity for gadgets is not in question. "Electronics, video games,
and bicycles too, are all fascinating to a lot of people with autism," says
Leanne. "But what's so great about Repair Cafe for E2A is the social
component." It is a misconception that adults with autism don't want
to socialize, and communicating with someone about the item they've
brought to be fixed is a unique opportunity for reciprocal conversation.

Eighty-five percent of adults with autism in the United States
are unemployed. The mission of Earth to Autism is to teach pre-
employment skills for green industry careers. Leanne has seen the demand for digital repair growing, and she hopes demand will grow for
other kinds of repairs too. Earth to Autism started its "Ambassador
in Training" program in 2019 to teach a range of repair skills. Each
trainee, or ambassador, has a mentor, and experts from the greater
Tampa area volunteer to work with them. There is now an E2A Repair
Cafe every month; here their training gets put to immediate use, and
they are the experts. Technical skills combine with the soft skills of self-
awareness. Arianna Reybitz helped coordinate the first Repair Cafes,
and she credits Leanne with helping her gain the confidence she
needed to be hired as biology lab instructor at St. Petersburg College.
She continues working with E2A, and she and her mom repair jewelry at the Repair Cafes. "It's cool now that they are happening every
month. More people can get their things fixed, get to meet each other.
We'll be noticed a lot more, and get more people to join our group."

All told, a community repair experience can offer multiple gains to
people with autism. You are out of your house, interacting with others
and making friends. You are focusing your intelligence in ways that are

satisfying to you and appreciated by others. And if the event has been organized to meet your needs reasonably well, you may want to come back. The repair movement globally is working to make its events as inclusive as possible to everyone.

Too Good to Toss

Many projects inhabit the same social ecosystem as community repair but do not involve any actual repair of things. Rather, their purpose is to repair the social fabric through acts of caring and sharing or to provide counterweights to waste. Most are straightforward in concept and highly replicable. Towns all across the land have some version of a spring cleanup week, when the Department of Public Works will haul away just about anything residents put out on the curb. But before that can happen, people come from as far away as they wish and roam the streets at night in their pickups on a grand scavenger hunt, sorting through the curbside piles for the usable and the fixable. It's an unofficial but tolerated way to keep a significant volume of stuff out of the landfill, and everyone wins.

Now imagine a highly organized, community-spirited variation that provides a public space to collect and share unwanted goods with those who could use them. In the light of day! The town of Warwick, New York, holds one such event every spring. It's held in a park on the closest weekend to Earth Day and prior to their annual bulk trash pickup. They call it "Too Good to Toss," and to pull it off, all they need is a few good organizers, the full cooperation of the town and village, and about a hundred volunteers who fit the job description: positive, welcoming, respectful, flexible, helpful. Acceptable items for donation must be clean and in full working order, with all the parts. Unacceptable items include auto parts, TVs, computers, grills, large appliances, and other items deemed unacceptable by the Department of Public Works. Saturday is drop-off day, Sunday is come-take-it-away-for-free day, and hundreds of people come. The Salvation Army, Big Brothers Big Sisters of America, the Humane Society, and local charities take things too. The number of donations and shoppers has increased every year, and still, when it's all over, less than one-half of one dumpster of unwanted stuff is left over. Anything recyclable is pulled out of that before the remainder is hauled away, and one community's waste is reduced from a mountain to a molehill.

Swap/Meet

Clothing swaps have become a vibrant part of the sharing economy in Portland, Oregon. One version, organized by Swap Positive, is called "free fashion & frugal fun." Their rules read, in part: "You agree that you *will not sell anything* that you received at any Free Swap. Re-sellers, hoarders, and factious people will be asked to leave. People who come to free swaps have found that as they have given freely of what they no longer need, they have received freely cool new stuff! Plus, remainders are donated to organizations that will give them away for free, so everyone is a philanthropist!"

Sarah Guldenbrein has swapped clothes at the Portland free swap and is also a sewing volunteer at Repair PDX — the Repair Cafe in Portland. As a graduate student in sociology, she wrote her master's thesis about both experiences, seeking insight into how these social innovations give people an alternative to the negative effects of "fast fashion." She interviewed participants at a number of events and found that their reasons for coming were, of course, varied: to save money, for the opportunity to connect with like-minded people, for the "pleasure of refreshing their wardrobe," and so on. Participants included "hard-core" middle-aged shoppers and also younger people with limited resources who are looking for a "slow fashion" alternative. Sarah found that to some extent, their personal motivations also aligned with the larger goals of degrowth ("reducing the ecological impact of the global economy to a sustainable level") and decommodification ("a shift away from production and profits and towards well-being and care"). And while she observed that the participants in the clothing swaps were predominantly white, college-educated, and young, she concluded that "in a social climate where many feel paralyzed by the magnitude of change that is required, degrowth offers a glimmer of optimism, and the promise of actionable change."

Brands Taking Stands

Repair and repairability have caught the attention of many companies pledged to the "triple bottom line" of people, planet, and profits, as well as the 250,000 or so business members of the American Sustainable Business Council. Philip Kotler and Christian Sarkar made a case for "brand activism" in the *Marketing Journal*, noting that "Millennials have high expectations for brands....Many would like brands to show concern not just for profits but for the communities they serve, and the world we live in." And in a Q&A published in the *Wall Street Journal Online*, Paul Alexander, chief marketing officer of Eastern Bank, said, "Brand purpose of this nature is a marathon, not a sprint. Tying it to outcomes takes time, and everybody wants case studies showing positive results. The proof will come when those who step out on this plank thrive. That's what's going to convince hearts and minds. Let's put it this way: I'm cautiously pessimistic. I'm hopeful more brands will consider it, but I'm cognizant of the real world."

It is common knowledge that the fossil fuel industry, for one, has been engaged in brand activism for many years, successfully fomenting doubt about climate science, exactly as Big Tobacco did for smoking. And the hegemony of Big Tech in electronics and appliances has a corollary in the phenomenon of "perceived obsolescence" in the garment industry. In her book *True Wealth*, Juliet Schor addresses the psychology underlying fast-fashion marketing, which she says "fosters an unhealthy dissatisfaction with what one has and anxiety about falling behind." Mending and visible mending are creative and outspoken responses to textile waste and toxicity, but as designer and scientist Mark Liu writes, "the scale of fast fashion is so massive it can easily eclipse other sustainability initiatives." Here the question becomes, How will the fashion industry ever care enough about the citizen consumers of the world to "slow down" and work to repair itself?

"We're trying to take responsibility. We need to move from a use-and-discard economy to a reuse economy," says Eileen Fisher, who founded her company in 1984 with $350 in start-up money and created her now iconic "breezy and unbothered" brand with pieces made from organic fibers. The irony is that over time, Fisher faced up to the fact that *organic* is not synonymous with *sustainable*. It takes 713 gallons of water to make one cotton shirt, organic or no. So the company created its "Renew" brand, made from clothing bought back from its customers. This is not a small-scale effort. In May 2018, the company reclaimed its millionth garment, and it continues to collect as many as three thousand garments each week. More significantly, the company is now focused on the process of remanufacturing: creating new raw material by dismantling and machine-felting garments at its "Tiny Factory" in Irvington, New York.

H&M Group (Hennes & Mauritz) is the Swedish multinational clothing-retail company that largely created the fast-fashion business model. In 2016, it announced a recycling initiative that was a carbon copy of Eileen Fisher's, but when challenged over the results, H&M admitted that less than 1 percent of its clothing included recycled fibers. Mind you, H&M's annual revenue is more than twenty-five billion dollars, while Eileen Fisher's is on the order of three hundred million dollars. But here is the interesting development: local media reports that reps from H&M have been spending time at Eileen Fisher's remanufacturing factory. "We realized that we need to share what we know," Fisher says. "We need to teach other people, because we're like a drop in the bucket. We're one mid-sized company, and that's great, but unless the rest of the industry follows then we're not going to solve the problem." The industry is responding. At the October 2019 Textile Exchange Sustainability Conference in Vancouver, British Columbia, H&M Group and IKEA, the other Swedish retail giant, announced a collaboration on a large-scale study to review chemical content in postconsumer textile recycling, with the "ambition to become 100% circular and renewable."

In 2015, the Patagonia clothing company launched its "Worn Wear" project. The project's "mobile repair wagons" visit towns and college campuses across the United States and Europe — driven by peripatetic "sewists" who will mend one clothing item of any kind per visitor. At a stop at Bard College in Annandale-on-Hudson, New York, designer and product developer Denise Neil told us how many innovations in clothing manufacture actually move through the industry: it is at the factory level. "We work with different factories, and they may recommend our ideas about how to make things more sustainably to other companies, such as better ways to reinforce seams or to reduce production scrap with smarter pattern design. Likewise, they make recommendations to us all the time. It's a give and take of sharing best practices." The difference is whether those practices are about making things more cheaply, as has been the norm, or about making things that last. The very next day, Denise would be visiting Eileen Fisher's remanufacturing factory to exchange ideas for making things that last. "We're always wanting to learn," she says.

Rose Marcario, CEO of Patagonia, has been quoted widely, saying,

"Why is repair such a radical act? Fixing something we might otherwise throw away is almost inconceivable to many in the heyday of fast fashion and rapidly advancing technology, but the impact is enormous. As individual consumers, the single best thing we can do for the planet is to keep our stuff in use longer."

And the single best way to keep stuff in use longer is to give people a practical alternative to throwing it away. The solution is obvious: start a community repair project in *your* town. In the next chapter, we provide you with the conceptual and practical tools to do just that.

How Do I Get One of These in My Town?

It makes you feel good to get your own things repaired rather than buying something new.

— Repair Cafe customer

I f you've ever had an item fixed at a community repair event, experienced the joy of having a broken but beloved item restored to use, or read or heard about the repair revolution in the media, you might be tempted to ask, "How do I get one of these in my town?"

The answer is right in front of you, close to where you live. First-time visitors often tell the event organizer, "This is *so* great!" "*So* cool!" "*So* fun!" Then they ask, "Could you bring your team and do this in my town?" The answer is, "Glad you like it! And sorry, but no." Because one size doesn't fit all. In the United States, each Repair Cafe can draw customers from up to a dozen different towns. In order to be embraced and supported, every Repair Cafe must be a grassroots effort, grown from within its own community, to meet its customers' unique needs. As we say, "Repairs by experts who are also your neighbors."

There is no one right way to start and manage a Repair Cafe, but this chapter will provide advice, tried-and-true "best practices," and suggestions gathered from organizers and their volunteers from across the United States and in Toronto, Canada. You'll learn how to attract volunteers and keep them coming back, as well as what kinds of tools and equipment they might need in order to offer a variety of repairs. You'll learn what type of location is ideal and how to set it up so coaches and guests can work together safely. You'll learn how to attract partners and sponsors to help promote your events and defray expenses.

If you'd like to start a community-based repair event, begin by visiting an existing cafe, clinic, or collective. To search for a location near you, check the organization's website, Facebook page, or blog. Expect to devote a couple of hours to wandering from table to table to observe what types of items people bring to be repaired, and to witness the interaction between the public and all the volunteers — friendly greeters, traffic flow managers, and repair coaches. Better yet, bring something that needs to be fixed so you can experience the process firsthand, from check-in to check-out.

Finding Volunteers

Look for Curious, Busy, Friendly People

People who want to start cafes of their own always ask existing Repair Cafe organizers, "How do you find volunteers?" The brief answer is look for active, friendly, helpful people in your own community who already volunteer for any type of activity, or the handy folks others call when they need something repaired. Here are some hints for where to look for such people and how to connect with them.

People who volunteer to help others fix things tend to have been curious kids who took things apart for fun, often to the dismay of their parents. Others grew up in handy, frugal households where repairing things was a way of life. Many other volunteers learned on the job or are self-taught. They all like the idea, as Warwick, New York, repair coach Tom Bonita says, "of keeping useful things useful and out of landfills." They like a challenge, enjoy learning new things, like sharing what they know, and feel a need to give back to their community.

Do you know the old adage, "Want something done? Look for a busy person"? It's true. Employed or retired, repair people are often engaged in multiple activities. Many of our repair coaches also volunteer at the local food pantry, with the PTA, as EMTs or in the Ambulance Corps or Red Cross, and with many other advocacy, networking, political, business, and social organizations. Across the USA, volunteers come from every walk of life and bring every skill set imaginable, including Airbnb hosts, artists, attorneys, authors, bakers, beekeepers, business owners, carpenters, chemists, career counselors, contractors, craftspeople, dads, electricians, engineers, firemen, grandparents, graphic designers, ham radio operators, homemakers, lawyers, locksmiths, massage therapists, mechanics, media producers, military veterans, moms, museum curators, musicians, nurses, pastors, plumbers, police investigators, professional organizers, psychotherapists, real estate agents, salespeople, teachers, students, school principals, seamstresses, social workers, television producers, tool- and diemakers, town board members — anybody! — everybody! — YOU!

Technical skills are important, but good repair coaches have other qualities as well: they are outgoing and friendly, good at listening and communicating, and curious. You want people who won't be discouraged if they can't fix the problem that day with the limited time, tools, or supplies available.

Some people volunteer to fix things at more than one event in more than one town. Others only have time to give to one location. Don't staff your events by poaching volunteers from another Repair Cafe, Fixit Clinic, or Fixers Collective. Organizers work hard to find and keep friendly, compatible, skilled coaches. Organizers and volunteers also work hard to promote their events in order to attract and keep a steady audience. Respect that.

As you are "staffing up" your Repair Cafe, consider the following tried-and-true tactics:

Talk It Up

Think of the search for volunteers as a passport to parts of your community you might not have known otherwise. Look for friendly folks with significant repair skills. Ask family, friends, neighbors, co-workers — anyone and everyone you know — to recommend handy men and women, especially those who have successfully fixed items for them. Professionals who have their own repair, carpentry, contractor, or sewing businesses often volunteer at repair events as a way to network and promote their services to a wider audience.

Offer to Speak

Tell the Repair Cafe story. Business, social, service, and civic clubs and organizations are often looking for speakers. Contact the organizers of these groups in your town and ask to speak or present a PowerPoint program about your repair event. Always end your talk by asking people to raise their hands if they're interested in volunteering; then ask them to add their contact information to a signup sheet. (Be sure to bring pen and paper for this!) Leave behind your contact information with the organizer or the group's secretary.

Get It in Print

Write a press release and calendar listing that include the who, what, when, where, how, and why of your repair event. State that you're looking for volunteers, include your contact information, and submit the release to local newspapers and magazines; radio and TV stations; the city/county tourism office; the city, village, town, and county recycling/ solid waste management team; the mayor, town supervisor, and city hall staff; houses of worship; and schools, colleges, and universities. Post your press release on social media. Follow up with each recipient by phone or in person to make sure that your press release was received, then ask when it will run.

Post flyers, announcing the search for volunteers, in a variety of locations that get lots of traffic: public bulletin boards in banks, post offices, grocery stores, coffee shops, pizzerias, libraries, real estate offices, gas stations, hair and nail salons, laundromats, fabric, yarn, craft and art supply stores, hardware stores, thrift and reuse stores, and other local businesses, and at bus stops and farmers' markets. Email the flyer to everyone you know; ask them to share it with all their contacts and on social media.

ALL DECKED OUT IN BUTTONS

Eager to promote her Repair Cafe more widely in her Connecticut community, Elizabeth Huebner snagged a booth at the annual Willimantic Downtown Country Fair to introduce her neighbors to the concept. Knowing that the space would be too small for volunteers to store supplies and use tools to make actual repairs, she planned to use the booth to teach people how to sew on a button — a task many people no longer learn. Thinking that "it would be cool to have a project where people could actually use their new-found skill," she decided to make a cloth banner onto which her students could spell out the words *Repair Cafe* in buttons.

continued on next page

The project's first step was to solicit flat, white buttons. Two businesses and two senior centers agreed to act as collection points for community donations. Once the buttons were in hand, the fair booth became a "hive of activity." Little ones were very interested in the button stash and in learning how to thread the needle, tie a knot, then sew on the button they'd chosen. People who had sewing skills were happy to sit and chat while sewing on a button or two or ten. Sometimes as many as fifteen people — grandmothers, dads, young adults, little kids — all gathered around, sewing. The letters weren't completely finished at the fair, of course, so Elizabeth organized a Chat and Sew party, open to any and all. Finally, the project was complete, and after "the technical aspects of readability and hangability" were solved, the button banner welcomed people to the next Repair Cafe at Willimantic's First Congregational Church. "About fifty people helped with sewing; many more, with advice, ideas, supplies, and moral support. This project brought together people of all ages and backgrounds who didn't know each other before, all the while sewing buttons on a banner, of all things!"

A Picture Is Worth a Thousand Words

I saw it advertised in our local paper, stopped by with a lamp that needed to be repaired, and stayed to volunteer ever since!

— Jen Picard, Pittsfield, Massachusetts

Elizabeth recalls: *I had only three coaches signed up two weeks before the scheduled launch of my county's first Repair Cafe, to be held in Warwick, New York. I wanted at least ten fixers to cover the basic repair categories — digital devices, lamps, vacuums, clocks and other small electrical/mechanical items, clothing, textiles and stuffed toys, knives and scissors, jewelry, ceramics, wooden chairs, and small tables. Knowing that elected officials often promote nonprofit ventures that benefit the whole community, I called Mayor Newhard and asked if he'd make himself available for a photo shoot in front of our planned venue, a community center. "Like the newspaper photos of you holding a big pair of fake scissors pretending to cut a ribbon stretched across the door of a new store," I suggested. Mr. Mayor agreed, told me to call the Chamber of Commerce ("They'll arrange everything"), and suggested asking the three coaches to each hold an example of the type of item — lamp, laptop, wooden toy — they were going to fix.*

The day of the photo shoot arrived. The director of the local Chamber of Commerce had arranged for photographers from two local newspapers to be there, and for the mayor, deputy mayor, town supervisor, chamber members, and other dignitaries to show up. The coaches held items to be fixed and I held a sign with the Hudson Valley Repair Cafe logo. After the photo ran in the papers, my phone rang off the hook with people offering to volunteer or calling to learn about what kinds of items might be fixed at the Repair Cafe.

If you plan a similar photo shoot, be sure to use the photos to promote future events and in any materials used to appeal for additional volunteers. Also, ask the city, town, and village clerk, the department of public works, and the county recycling department to post the photos on their websites with repair event dates, the location, and the organizer's contact information.

At the Movies

Many movie theaters and drive-ins are happy to promote local businesses and seasonal community events. Contact the owners to ask if they'll do the same for your all-volunteer, not-for-profit repair event. Last year, before Warwick's summer Repair Cafe, one of the new volunteers, a retired chief financial officer, talked the operator of a drive-in movie theatre into handing a Repair Cafe flyer to the driver of every car that drove through the gate on Fourth of July weekend. That added up to fifteen hundred people over the three-day weekend. It was great advertising, to an audience that might not have been reached through more traditional means, for the cost of printing the flyers. You might also ask the owners of movie theaters located in high-traffic urban neighborhoods if they would show still photos or videos of Repair Cafe activities, with date and location details, on the big screen, along with other trailers, prior to the scheduled movie.

Finding the Right Location

Repair Cafes can be found in all sorts of venues, but the ideal setting is a rent-free space on a main street in a walkable neighborhood a short distance from public transportation. Look for public and commercial spaces associated with your partners or sponsors, as well as locations such as libraries, houses of worship, art centers, craft and farmers' markets, church halls, community centers, holiday gift markets, co-working spaces, historic houses, makerspaces, museums, school gyms and cafeterias, fire department houses, senior centers, theaters, village and town halls, parking lots, and so on. No matter who organizes or sponsors the event, the people associated with the venue (librarians, faith community members, museum staff, etc.) should be educated about how this community outreach will benefit their group: it's a way to bring people through the door who might otherwise never come, and the Repair Cafe organizers can offer a network of volunteers who can help get the word out.

Ease of access is important. If volunteers and customers must drive to the venue, there should be adequate low-cost or free parking within easy walking distance of the Repair Cafe. Keep in mind that people must carry items that need fixing in and out of the location, and coaches will need to transport tools, sewing machines, bike stands, and bulky boxes stuffed with supplies and equipment. The refreshment team must tote coffee and tea-making gear, as well as food and serveware. Look for a location that has a level entryway and wide double doors. Curbs, stairs, and elevators can be hard to negotiate for a person in a wheelchair or someone carrying a fragile floor lamp while holding a toddler by the hand.

Inside, the ideal space consists of one large, open room with lots of natural light, wheelchair accessible bathrooms, a water fountain, and a kitchen (so long as it, too, is free) — all on the same floor. The setup should allow for easy flow of people and objects. You'll need enough space, next to multiple electrical outlets, to erect six to twelve tables, each six feet long and three feet wide, with chairs for coaches on one side and for visitors on the other. Arrange the tables in such a way that people carrying large or fragile items can walk around them without bumping into other folks. You'll also need additional chairs to seat all the people waiting to be helped. If you haven't got access to a kitchen, you can set up a table near an electrical outlet for brewing coffee and tea and serving snacks. Access to Wi-Fi allows coaches to look up man-ufacturers' product information, find where to buy parts, and access how-to videos on YouTube and other sites.

Organizers should also be aware of the spatial and sensory vari-ables that matter to repair coaches with autism and other NDs. In order to be comfortable and productive, they need to work in a space that is not close to another workspace and is not too bright or too loud. (Not right next to the folks repairing vacuum cleaners, for exam-ple.) And if you celebrate each repair with bells, horns, or cheers, you may need to suspend that practice around these volunteers. As much as organizers love to post pictures of their events, some neurodivergent repair coaches (and others) will opt out of publicity photos.

How to Organize Volunteers

> I don't repair anything....I "greet patrons" and direct them to the appropriate tables. So, in a way I'm learning to "tin-ker" by deciding what expert may be able to fix what.
>
> — Misha Harnick, New Paltz, New York

Once your Repair Cafe is up and running, you will likely find yourself with a small army of eager volunteers who come together regularly to bring broken items back to life. It's a lot of activity, and someone needs to coordinate it. You can start by identifying the volunteer roles your Repair Cafe will need. This section is adapted from the handy master volunteer list put together by Repair Cafe Toronto, Canada. Consider the tasks that best suit your cafe's needs, which might change over time.

Greeters

- Guide and assist visitors in finding their way around the cafe.
- Escort visitors to the correct repair area.
- Introduce visitors to the waiting list monitors.
- Provide directions to the washrooms, refreshments, and exits.
- Chat with waiting visitors.

Registration Team

- Welcome visitors and explain how the Repair Cafe process works.
- Describe the waiting list process.
- Inspect items for safety.
- Review waiver forms.

Waiting List (Monitors)

- Welcome and match each visitor with a repair coach based on their item.
- Invite each visitor to sit, and explain how the waiting list works.
- When able, provide visitors with an estimated wait time.
- Remind waiting visitors of the refreshment area.
- Monitor fixing activities to identify when a repair coach becomes available.

Repair Coach

A repair coach invites a visitor to choose one of three options:

- Repair coach does the repair, and the visitor watches.
- Repair coach and visitor conduct the repair together.
- Visitor does the repair, and the repair coach helps.

Categories of repair coaches include those who work with small appliances, furniture, computers, electronics, clothing, jewelry, book and paper repairs, garden tools, and bicycles.

Volunteer Coordinator

- Manage all volunteer communications.
- Recruit new volunteers.
- Maintain volunteer list.
- Manage and coordinate volunteers.
- Engage with volunteers and gather feedback.

Setup and Packup Crew

- Set up and pack up registration, refreshments, photo booth and lunch areas, signage, power cords, work mats, etc.
- Clean and reconfigure the space as it was upon arrival, including tables and chairs, whiteboards, floors.

Refreshment Captain

- Set up the refreshment area and the volunteer lunch area.
- Ensure all refreshment materials are arranged.
- Inform volunteers when lunch is served.
- Ensure the refreshment area remains tidy during the event.
- Clean up at the end of the event.

FIXED Photographer and Event Photographer

- Invite visitors to have their pictures taken with the FIXED sign (which indicates their items have been fixed).
- Inform visitors that pictures will be posted online.
- Set up and take down the photo booth area.
- Take photographs of cafe activities.

Waste Management Consultant

- Provide advice about proper disposal of nonrepairable items and hazardous materials.
- Promote improved waste management strategies.

Additional Volunteer Activities

- Collect event data and analyze results.

- Develop and maintain membership and subscription lists.
- Interview visitors to gather their perceptions and testimonials.

Marketing and Communication

- Create promotional materials, such as flyers, signage, and T-shirts.
- Maintain and develop website and social media accounts.
- Promote events through social media platforms.
- Talk to the media and community partners.
- Take photos and videos of the repair process and fixed items.

Organizing Committee

- Plan, organize, and carry out events and activities.
- Set objectives and develop short- and long-term strategies.
- Evaluate program outcomes.
- Review volunteer recruitment and retention efforts.
- Establish community partnerships.
- Maintain expense reporting and budgeting.

Choosing the Right Equipment

The Right Tools

Organizers can't run a Repair Cafe without tools and other materials for making repairs on-site. Here are some suggestions for what you will need and who should provide it.

We recommend that repair organizers establish a relationship with their local hardware store owner. A hardware store that has been in business for a generation or more is part of the "soul" of your town or neighborhood. Big box stores have made them an endangered species, and we delight in sending Repair Cafe customers to the local store to purchase parts that our coaches have identified as necessary to complete the job. We also remind our Repair Cafe visitors that the people who work at the local stores, especially those who have been there for years, are a reliable source of advice, day in and day out. All this strengthens local resistance to our throwaway culture. Make sure that your local hardware store understands such benefits of community repair, and that what you are doing will help, not hurt, their business. The hardware store will likely be willing to display your flyer and talk up the Repair Cafe.

We tell first-time coaches to "bring a small selection of tools you find most useful." We also say that if they need a tool they don't have, they'll likely find it somewhere among the tools the other coaches have brought. Tool sharing is part of the collaborative spirit among our fixers, and conscientiously returning borrowed tools builds bonds of mutual respect. A list of useful tools includes safety and magnifying glasses, multisocket power strips to provide protection against electrical power surges, a high-intensity or magnification light, a long extension cord (outlets are often far apart and used by many people), a sewing machine, thread, yarn, buttons, fabric for patches, and a sturdy, height-adjustable, floor-standing, bike repair workstand. In addition, many Repair Cafes stock and sell a limited supply of lamp and bike parts — ideally purchased from a neighborhood store at a discount. The customers pay what the Repair Cafe paid for them. At the Warwick, New York, Repair Cafe, FixIt Bob Berkowitz, who runs a handyman business, shops for and maintains the inventory of lamp supplies for use by all the small electrics coaches. Some of the parts are donated by customers who bring a socket or switch to complete their repair but learn, after talking to the coach, that they actually need another type, which is often available in our lamp supply box. Bob recommends that only one person be responsible for inventorying the parts after each event, so that he or she will know what to buy prior to the next event. See appendix 2 for Bob's recommended list of lamp parts to keep handy, as well as more basic supplies that can be used by all the coaches.

Donations Gratefully Accepted

Repair Cafes are free, as are all repairs provided by coaches. No one is paid — not the organizer and not the volunteers, no matter what their role. Tipping the repair coaches is actively discouraged. Yet we do have expenses — for flyers, signs, and other promotional materials; office and repair supplies; insurance; and refreshments. There are different ways to cover these costs. A common practice is to place one large donation jar in a prominent spot near the entrance/exit and another on the beverage and snack table. Some Repair Cafes add a sign suggesting a five-dollar donation. Others leave the amount up to the grateful visitor. Either way, send the signal by "seeding" your donation jar with several greenbacks before you open the doors. All receipts for purchases made by volunteers are turned in to the organizer for reimbursement, that very day, from the donation jar. Many Repair Cafes gratefully accept donations of tools, repair materials, and snacks and baked goods in addition to cash. Some, especially those located in houses of worship, also encourage donations of nonperishable items for the local food pantry.

Signage

Post several signs (printed on both sides) along the street, in the nearest parking lots, and near the building entrance to identify your location. You'll need a variety of signs to transform a generic space into a welcoming room, as well as to indicate repair stations for textiles, small electrics, jewelry, and so on. Sign templates with logos are included in the Repair Cafe manual, but cafes are encouraged to be creative and design their own logos. For example, Michele, organizer of the Repair Cafe held in Green Ossining, New York, hosted a lunch party where friends and soon-to-be coaches had fun pasting images cut from magazines onto the backs of plastic real-estate signs to create new signs.

Welcome people with posters printed with clever quotes, such as "worry never fixes anything" and "I couldn't repair your brakes so I made your horn louder." Many of the inspiring sentiments expressed throughout this book would be good for this purpose. Hang these around the room or display them on easels for a festive look.

Many cafes keep a "Fixed!" sign at the check-in/check-out table, and customers whose items were successfully repaired are invited to have a photo taken holding their item and the "Fixed!" sign to promote the cafe. Share these photos on social media, and include them with follow-up reports and press releases.

Satisfied customers always ask the date of the next event. Place a sign listing all event dates and locations for the current year on or near the entrance and exit tables. Encourage visitors to snap a photo of the sign with their phones or jot down the details.

Welcome Table

Whether you call it the welcome table, the check-in/check-out table, or the entrance table, it's an important place. Here you'll want to supply a box of name badges for all the volunteers. A reusable nametag is less wasteful than the peel-and-stick, self-adhesive type. This table can also stock notebooks or forms where attendees can register their thanks and comments, job tickets, house rules and liability disclaimer forms, a stock of pens, pencils, scissors, tape, push pins, and other office supplies, a basket or box to collect returned job tickets and other forms, and a donation jar.

Cafe Table

At minimum, most repair events provide free hot coffee, tea, milk, and sugar, with iced tea and/or lemonade in the summer. Many also offer fruit, baked goods, and other snacks to the public. Some organizers and volunteers solicit donations from their favorite sandwich shops, delis, pizzerias, and other food establishments. Other cafes benefit from donations of coffee, day-old bagels, and other baked goods from local stores. And some coaches like to bake cookies and other sweets as well as patch jeans or rewire lamps.

For the cafe table, you'll need a coffee percolator, an electric tea-kettle or large thermos filled with steaming hot water, a tablecloth that can be wiped clean, napkins and plates — ideally eco-friendly (compostable or made with recycled materials)— reusable bowls, baskets, platters, tongs, and other serving utensils, and a garbage can for non-recyclables. Some locations offer all the refreshments to both the public and the volunteers at no charge. Others place a jar on the table with a sign inviting donations. "Seed" the donation jar with several greenbacks before you open the doors.

Storage

Most coaches prefer to bring in and take home their own tools, equipment, and supplies for each event. However, all the communal supplies and signs need to be safely stored between repair events. Some host locations provide secure storage for items packed in lidded boxes and bins; others do not. Try to divide the items to be stored and the responsibility for maintaining stock levels among several people so no one person gets stuck with shopping, packing, storing, and toting everything.

Follow the Rules

There are only two rules for Repair Cafes: (1) repairs are free, and (2) it's not a drop-off service. Beyond that, every community gets to organize their events in the ways that work best for them.

Safety First and "On Call"

Safety is always a priority. It's mostly a matter of common sense and paying attention to what's going on around you. Repair coaches tend to have both skills. Most Repair Cafes decline to work on large, noisy, smelly, gasoline or propane-powered engines and other mechanical devices. The noise is disruptive, the fumes are unpleasant, and the use of gasoline or propane indoors is a potential fire hazard. However, the Repair Cafe in New Paltz, New York, does offer welding repairs done outside, weather permitting, in a vacant parking lot by a welding contractor who has served residential, industrial, and commercial clients for over twenty-five years. He even drives his rig to five different Repair Cafes on both sides of the Hudson River.

Even if they don't operate a repair business, most coaches know to check their tools and equipment to make sure that they are safe to use and to tape extension cords to the floor to prevent accidents.

But the organizer should check too, as well as provide safety glasses and remind people to use them. If you're going to offer bike repairs, always attach the bike to a repair workshop stand, designed for the purpose, even when the owner swears that he'll hold it. Children of all ages, accompanied by adults, are always welcome at Repair Cafes. For their own protection, older kids seeking volunteer community service hours should always be paired with adult mentors. "Shadowing" an experienced coach before attempting to make repairs is a smart way for prospective volunteers of all ages to determine if the Repair Cafe is a good fit for their enthusiasm and skill level. Organizers should prepare themselves to be "on call," ready to solve unanticipated problems and answer questions from volunteers and the public during the entire event, from setup to pack-up. Organizers will also need to be available to respond to inquiries from the press and municipal officials, as well as to jot down the wonderful stories told by both owners of and fixers of the quirky, antique, unique items brought in for repairs. That doesn't usually leave time to make repairs or pick up pizza for the volunteers' lunch.

Ours Is Not a Drop-Off Service

Greeters sometimes need to explain, especially to people who have never experienced a repair event, that ours is not a drop-off service. Rather, a Repair Cafe is a place where people will find tools and can fix their broken things with the help of skilled volunteer coaches. Even when guests aren't ready or able to attempt the repair project hands-on, they are expected to watch the process and hopefully learn something useful.

Repair organizers report that people often do want to learn how to fix things, and volunteers are more than happy to teach them. One Repair Cafe coach has very arthritic hands. Some doubted that he would be effective, but his deficiency is his asset. Sometimes, this coach needs the owner to hold or turn an item so that he can work on it. Other times, when his hands won't cooperate, he supervises the owners while giving them step-by-step instructions and the confidence to make their own repairs. "This often creates a deeper connection between the volunteer and the participant, which in turn creates a feeling of community and connection," says Lauren Gross, a Repair Cafe co-organizer in Portland, Oregon.

Two Items per Person

In order to serve as many people as possible and shorten the wait time, many Repair Cafes limit the number of items that people may bring to be repaired. Most organizers allow two items per person, although some will accept more if the coaches aren't busy. Lorraine, organizer of a Repair Cafe in Maplewood, New Jersey, has a policy that if multiple lamps needing lengthy repair are brought in by one person, the customer is directed to go to the end of the line after the first repair in order to give the next person in line a chance to be served. Some cafes use a take-a-number system — you arrive at the reception table, take a numbered ticket, and wait for your turn. Other cafes have a more elaborate traffic flow system. Jen Picard, who volunteers at the Repair Cafe held in Pittsfield, Massachusetts, describes their process: "Each person receives a number that matches their sheet, which tells us their name and basic information along with the item(s) that need to be repaired. The number is printed on a brightly colored piece of cardboard so that each person is taken in order. This way if the seamstresses or other volunteers are busy, each person is treated fairly and goes to the next available repairer." Some locations, like Repair Cafe NC, in North Carolina's Research Triangle, offer web-based workshop registration prior to the event. The Rodeo City Repair Cafe, in Ellensburg, Washington, also invites people to fill out an online repair reservation form in advance of their event. Organizer Don Shriner says, "The biggest benefit is since many parts have to be ordered, we can help folks locate and bring their replacement parts with them and avoid return visits."

The Customer Isn't Always Right

Repair Cafe customers don't always follow the rules. Sometimes it's because they don't know the rules, and sometimes they just want things to go their way. Whatever the case, Repair Cafe volunteers can gently point out that in a Repair Cafe, the rules are there for a reason. The customer is not always right.

Some people bring in more than the number of items allowed or things that coaches feel are too complicated, dirty, or unsafe to repair. Many house rules state that coaches have the right to refuse to repair any object they don't want to work on. One experienced sewing coach who runs her own business cautions new coaches not to take on intricate jobs like alterations, hemming clothing or curtains, or tailoring. These tasks require prep work — measuring, pinning, and ironing — before sewing. Unless the customer is prepared to take the item home to prep it before the next cafe, such jobs take a lot of time. That is frustrating to others waiting their turn for a simple, quick repair. Sometimes a coach who has a special area of expertise has a family emergency and isn't available as advertised, and the visitor seeking that expertise is annoyed. Usually a gentle reminder that we're all volunteers trying to serve as many people as possible, in the best way possible, with the resources at hand, is enough to defuse the situation.

Not Everything Needs to Be
or Can Be Fixed — and That's Okay

> No repair needed — just needs new bulbs
> — Note scribbled on Repair Cafe job ticket

Often, items brought in for repair aren't really broken; the owner simply needs to be taught how to use it as designed or shown a clever work-around. New Paltz Repair Cafe jewelry coach Renee Lee Rosenberg reports that she and fellow coach Barbara Lane have begun to give visitors advice about where they can purchase supplies and how to repair their jewelry at home. One woman who fixed her necklace at home sent a photo of her fix to the jewelry team. "It looked better than how we would've fixed it. We were thrilled, and so was she." Sometimes, despite the repair coach's best efforts, an item can't be fixed — there's not enough time, the right tools or special parts aren't available, or the design makes it impossible to remove the back. Sometimes the repair needs to be referred to the manufacturer or a repair professional. Most visitors appreciate the effort anyway, saying, "Well, now I know what's really wrong with it. Thanks for trying." Coaches, even those who don't run their own fix-it or mending business, sometimes offer to take an item home with them to complete the repair. Organizers shouldn't encourage that; you don't want your coaches to burn out. But neither is it your job to talk them out of it. That said, many coaches have reported that the person they helped for free is now a regular, paying customer for their professional services.

Liability

People who want to start a Repair Cafe often ask how to prevent accidents and what to do if a customer's beloved object is damaged by a repair coach or another customer. "What happens if one of the coaches works on a lamp and the owner takes it home, plugs it in, and sets his house on fire?" Well, first of all, that's never happened. Second, there are some sensible precautions that can be implemented, and the house rules should be read and acknowledged by everyone seeking the services of a repair coach.

When people sign in at the welcome table with their items, they "opt-in" with their signature, indicating that they have read and agree to the house rules. The rules state that the organizers, sponsors, and repair persons are not liable for any physical damage or loss resulting from work performed at the Repair Cafe, and that persons making repairs offer no guarantees and are not liable if objects repaired at the cafe turn out not to work properly at home. The welcome team also reminds people checking in that for everyone's safety they are always responsible for their own items, and cautions them not to park a fragile object on a chair, for example, then walk away for a cup of coffee.

Appendix 4 is a sample of Repair Cafe house rules. These particular

house rules serve as a waiver document for all of the Hudson Valley/
Catskills Repair Cafes. The language is derived from text provided by
the Repair Café International Foundation. Founder Martine Postma
points out that the text contains a generic disclaimer of liability, but
that it is "highly advisable to have a local lawyer or legal expert check
the validity and enforceability of the warranty and liability clauses in
the house rules document."

Insurance

More than forty Repair Cafes are held in the Hudson Valley/Catskills,
New York, area, located in churches and community centers, libraries,
and town halls and sponsored by both private and public groups. In
nearly all our locations, we've found that the host venue's general liability policy has been deemed adequate to cover our event. Libraries
and churches especially need the approval of their board, and an attorney often sits on the board that has approved the program. Repair
Cafes are program events that take place under the umbrella of the
sponsor organization. We have no separate legal or tax status. If the location where you would like to hold a Repair Cafe requires insurance,
be aware that there are many different types of insurance, with different price tags, that vary by state. Consult a local insurance agent and
possibly a lawyer before you open the doors to your repair event. At
the beginning of every Repair Cafe, organizers must remind coaches,
for their own protection, not to work on any item until and unless the
customer has signed the liability waiver/house rules form. It's a good
idea to appoint a member of the greeters' team to circulate the room
frequently to make sure that all guests have signed their house rules
form, including the liability waiver.

Beyond the Basics

In addition to the basic repair categories, many events offer more creative opportunities to learn, play, and fix what's wrong. Here are some
of the most popular activities.

Kids Take It Apart Table

An adult-supervised Kids Take It Apart Table, stocked with small screwdrivers and donated items deemed by experienced coaches to be beyond repair (VCRs, cassette recorders, portable radios, printers, and cameras are popular), offers kids an opportunity to "see what's inside" and learn while they play. Putting things back together is not required!

Tinkerbell Station

The Repair Cafe in Vancouver, Canada, offers a Tinkerbell Station designed to encourage girls to tinker. In addition to providing things to safely take apart, girls and boys are also encouraged to repair broken items and use broken tools and other items to make their own creations.

Photo Restoration, Wordsmithing, Listening Corner, and Massage Therapy

In addition to the standard repair categories, the Repair Cafe held at the United Methodist Church in New Paltz, New York, offers photo restoration, "wordsmithing," a listening corner, and massage therapy. After a career at IBM, Don Grice volunteers to digitally repair damaged photographs. One family brought him a pile of old pictures that had been torn in half long ago to fit into a Bible for safekeeping. "Taking images of each half and digitally restitching them provided new family memories that they didn't even know existed." Vernon Benjamin, author of a two-volume history of the Hudson River Valley, has been a writer all his life, "fifteen years in local journalism and thirty or more in public service." Vern sits next to Don and "fixes sentences (résumés, cover letters, and other writing projects) for free.... I can read people well when working with them on language and am inspired by the small miracles I see when I help someone find their voice and bring it out, seemingly all on their own."

In addition to helping clients in their private practices, friends, and colleagues, Vallerie Legeay and Leah Stukes provide therapeutic massage for the U.S. Military Academy track-and-field and cross-country teams and, every August, for the athletes at the U.S. Tennis Open Tournament. And they volunteer their time to Repair Cafes. Val says, "I have the sense that we can help repair the tissue and fabric of community, and it starts with people! Too often we throw ourselves away. Ourselves and others." Leah and Val offer ten-minute chair massages, for neck, shoulders, and backs, at different events. "I can't repair a bike, but I can bring the power of touch to people. Everyone in the community can be of value to each other," Leah says. "At the end of a Repair Cafe day," Val adds, "I find myself satisfied — and tired!"

Jo Gangemi, a practicing psychotherapist, approached the organizer of the Repair Cafe to suggest that active listening is a reparative and restorative act. "People have a hunger to feel heard. Too often the person who appears to be listening is really listening to what's going on in his own head and preparing a response to what you're saying. Listening is an art, one that is crucial to really connecting with each other." Gangemi invites people who have brought broken items to be mended to heal themselves by sitting at her table and talking about whatever is on their minds for five minutes. "Have a seat. Tell me what you'd like to talk about. I'm happy to listen."

Se Habla Español, Book Restoration, DIY Glue Station

The Repair Cafe held at the Clinton Avenue United Methodist Church in Kingston, New York, has a "Soul Repairer" who takes time to talk, as well as a bilingual advocate who can help Spanish-speakers negotiate difficulties with school, banks, and government offices. In addition, this cafe offers the services of a book restorer, who can also "handle ceramics and other things that require glue and patience." At the Repair Cafe in Green Ossining, New York, a designated sticky-stuff coach advises visitors how to fix heirloom and everyday broken bits. "A woman came with a whole box of odd and assorted items that needed to be glued," recalled organizer Michele. "She spent most of the day working under the tutelage of the repair coach and left with a box full of repaired items, a new sense of know-how, and a very grateful heart."

Healthy and Green Living Tips and Services

Several Repair Cafes have featured a dietitian from a local hospital who provided information about healthy snacks and dispenses samples. Other medical professionals have checked attendees' blood pressure and cholesterol levels. Sponsors and representatives from organizations promoting green products, technologies, and community activities — like composting, solar energy, home energy audits, and free clothing swaps — often set up tables at Repair Cafes to present information. Some cafes even have expert gardeners on hand to diagnose houseplant problems and offer advice on growing herbs and vegetables.

Library Table and Free to Take Table

A library table stocked with DIY and how-to books is always popular, and you can also provide up-to-date information, courtesy of your municipal recycling station, about where to donate/recycle/dispose of unwanted items. Consider setting up a Free to Take Table for clean, small items in good repair; this is especially popular right after Christmas or in the spring when people are cleaning out basements and attics.

Musical Instrument Repairs and Live Music

Some Repair Cafes offer setup and repairs to stringed musical instruments such as guitars and mandolins. Other locations, especially those with a piano, flute, or guitar-playing volunteer, offer live music.

How Often to Hold Your Event

The frequency of your events will be determined by how often you can book the venue and how often your volunteers can make themselves available. Happy volunteers are key to the success of your event. You want to make sure that you don't overwork them. Some locations host their events only two or three times a year. One team gathers once a month, but in different locations so that they can reach a variety of communities. Another group holds events once a month, and they also hold monthly organizational meetings and a volunteer group breakfast on event days. Another Repair Cafe hosts events every Sunday from 10 AM to 4 PM. In order to reach families that are busy with kids' weekend activities, one organizer hosts events on weekday evenings for two hours in a variety of locations. The Warwick, New York, team concluded that "we can be cheerful volunteers if our cafe is the third Saturday of every *other* month."

After Your Event

> Our friendship extends well beyond the Repair Cafe. Most volunteers were strangers before and now are reliable friends.
> — Don Shriner, Organizer, Rodeo City Repair Cafe, Ellensburg, Washington

Happy volunteers come back and often invite their family, friends, and co-workers to volunteer too. So it pays to show volunteers that you appreciate their efforts. Phone them. Write thank-you notes. Following every event, email volunteers a follow-up report, ideally with a couple of photos, listing how many people attended, from how many locations, what items they brought, how many items were repaired, and how many couldn't be fixed and why not.

Highlight any special stories, and share public comments and photos. Email a version of the follow-up report, along with photos, to the sponsor/partner organizations, the mayor and/or town supervisor, the county recycling or solid waste management coordinator, and local media. Encourage all of these individuals and organizations to visit your next event. Lobby elected officials to present a certificate of appreciation to all the volunteers for their efforts to keep useful items out of the landfill while strengthening community connections.

In between events, host a casual potluck picnic or party, and encourage volunteers to bring along a spouse, partner, or friend. Volunteers say that they appreciate this opportunity to visit with fellow volunteers because they're usually too busy to chat with folks working in other "departments" during the repair event. At your party, invite volunteers to take turns holding a designated "talking tool" — a wrench or screwdriver — and tell a tale about something funny or significant that they observed at a repair event.

Finding Partners and Sponsors

[
We mostly partner with tool libraries and reuse centers... venues that share similar values.

— Lauren Gross, Co-organizer,
Repair PDX, Portland, Oregon
]

As you think about starting a Repair Cafe in your town, consider how partners and sponsors can help your efforts by offering a free location, legal and tax advice, insurance, financial support, publicity, and/or networking opportunities to help you find volunteers. The diversity of resources available to support you is astonishing. Contact sources in several of the categories listed below to find multiple partners, sponsors, and volunteers who can help make your efforts a success.

Local Government Officials and Programs

Contact your elected representatives and local government. When Dära Salk, a community outreach director for Ameya Pawar, an alderman in Chicago's Ward 47, read a newspaper article about a Repair Cafe, she approached her boss about getting one started. Pawar, who believes in the importance of creating strong communities for all, included Repair Cafe information in his weekly email newsletter and posted flyers in his office window during his two terms in office. The 47th Ward Repair Cafe officially registered with the Repair Café International Foundation in 2013 and continues to meet at the Conrad Sulzer Regional Library, the second busiest in Chicago, the second Saturday of each month. In Clackamas County, Oregon, the local government pays the rent for the Wichita Center for Family and Community, where the Milwaukie Repair Fair is held, and provides funds for supplies and snacks for volunteers. Another Repair Cafe enjoys the sponsorship of both the village government and the local recreation and parks department, in addition to a coffee shop and a hardware store. The Repair Cafe in Palo Alto, California, received donations of new tools and a supplies trailer from GreenWaste, the city's contractor for waste and recycle collection, transportation, and processing services.

Libraries

Today's libraries provide hands-on learning opportunities in addition to books and are ideal partners for creating and sustaining Repair Cafes. In the spring of 2018, for example, Wendy Mahaney of Sustainable Saratoga contacted the Saratoga Springs, New York, Public Library, which was in the process of completing the Green Business Partnership Certification program, to explore how the two organizations might partner. Through social media, email blasts, word of mouth, and good old-fashioned posters, both organizations reached out to the community to find items that needed repair as well as coaches willing to volunteer their time. In Wellfleet, Massachusetts, the Wellfleet Recycling Committee partners with the local library to host a Fixit

Clinic. The Wellfleet Public Library is also home to Boomerang Bags Cape Cod, a community of volunteers who gather at the library, twice a month to sew reusable bags from clean, donated textiles. The cloth bags are distributed to the community for free, as an alternative to single-use shopping and tote bags. The Albert Wisner Public Library in Warwick, New York, named "Best Small Library in America" by *Library Journal* in 2016, hosted repair demos — basic textile mending (hand and machine) techniques, a bike safety check-over clinic, and a workshop on how to sharpen knives, scissors, and hand tools using a whetstone, taught by Repair Cafe volunteers. California's Berkeley Public Library, North Branch, has established STEM-oriented Fixit Clinics as a regular event.

Religious Institutions and Other Faith-Based Organizations

Perhaps a local church, mosque, synagogue, or temple would be willing to host your Repair Cafe or other reuse/repair event. Faith-based fraternal organizations such as the Knights of Columbus are also a potential source of volunteers. Synagogues often require youngsters preparing for their bar mitzvah or bat mitzvah, the Jewish coming-of-age rituals, to perform community service, as do churches instructing students on the rites of confirmation. GreenFaith, "a coalition for the environment that works with houses of worship, religious schools, and people of all faiths to help them become better environmental stewards," reminds us that people of many traditions see "repairing — making whole" as integral to their mission to act as good stewards to respect and protect the environment and share resources. The Green Muslims of New Jersey aim to educate people about the importance of environmental stewardship, or "going green," in the Islamic faith, and to implement strategies to solve problems regarding waste and overconsumption. Quaker Earthcare Witness is a North American network of Friends who are "taking Spirit-led action to address the ecological and social crises of the world, emphasizing Quaker process and testimonies."

Civic Clubs and Service Clubs

Libraries often host crafts and sewing clubs, another good place to look for skilled coaches. Newcomers Clubs are a resource for people wishing to meet others and enjoy social, civic, and charitable activities. Your local Chamber of Commerce can often provide a list of local organizations and their contact information. Local branches of national organizations such as the Independent Order of Oddfellows, Elks, Lions, Kiwanis, and Rotary clubs offer businesspeople and community leaders a chance to conduct business, socialize, and organize community service projects. These can all be places to find volunteers and participants.

Schools, Colleges, and Universities

Centers of higher learning see the benefits of repair skills too. The City of Gresham, Oregon, and the Coalition of Gresham Neighborhood Associations sponsor a Repair Cafe three times a year at Mt. Hood Community College. The Office of Campus Sustainability at SUNY (State University of New York) in New Paltz hosts a Repair Cafe each semester, with repair talent drawn from faculty, staff, and students — a rare opportunity to bring those three parts of the college community together.

Members of the campus undergraduate chapter of the Society of Women Engineers at the Francis College of Engineering in Lowell, Massachusetts, hosted a Repair Cafe for the campus and community. Linda Barrington, the college's engineering service-learning coordinator, described it this way: "Our twist is having women engineering students learn the hands-on skills to become experts, building their confidence to persist in the male dominated culture of engineering."

Retirees and Senior Associations

Retirees and seniors often feel isolated or without purpose when they no longer have a job to go to every morning. Such feelings can be even worse for those who have lost a spouse or have moved to a new community, without an existing network of family, friends, and co-workers. A recent study in *AARP* magazine reported, "When it comes to your health, loneliness may be as bad as smoking and worse than obesity.... Researchers also found that people with stronger social relationships had a fifty percent increased likelihood of survival than those whose relationships were weaker.... Maintaining a social life isn't just good fun — it's good for you."

Repair Cafes, clinics, and collectives, especially those held in senior centers located in housing complexes or town or village halls, provide a regularly scheduled event, in a location open to people of all ages and lifestyles, for retirees and seniors to share their organizational and technical skills while interacting with others who value their expertise. Plus, they say it's fun! Some counties, in conjunction with the public library system, publish a senior resource guide that lists senior social groups and retiree clubs, another potential source for volunteers.

Historical Societies

Historical societies and historic houses, farms, and museums, with their emphasis on preserving the past and presenting repairs as living history, offer partnership opportunities. "I can't fix the world's problems, and I don't focus on that," says Dawn Elliott, site manager at Locust Lawn Historic House and Farm, where she also organizes a Repair Cafe and mends textiles. Dawn, who sometimes wields her needle at the New Paltz Repair Cafe, says, "I help turtles cross the street; I darn socks."

Earth-Friendly and Reuse Events

Many cities recognize National Reuse Day on October 20. Earth Day is always celebrated on April 22, followed by Arbor Day, which falls on the last Friday in April. National events such as these and local events — like seasonal volunteer cleanups of roads, rivers, and parks; reuse events such as free community swaps; and end-of-the-school-year "green" locker cleanouts to salvage reusable supplies — are ready-made opportunities to promote your repair event to like-minded people.

Michele, a homemaker, mom, teacher's assistant, and Repair Cafe organizer from Ossining, New York, displayed a poster at a farmers' market, and by the end of the day, she had collected a skeleton crew of expert repair coaches. When Michele displayed her poster at the town's Earth Day Festival, which attracted nearly one hundred vendors promoting sustainable ideas, activities, and products, "more volunteers signed up," she says, "and we were ready to set a date for our first event!"

Climate Smart Communities, Climate Action Coalitions, and Transition Towns

In New York State, the Climate Smart Communities (CSC) program helps local governments take action to reduce greenhouse gas emissions and adapt to a changing climate. Organizing an ongoing repair program is an "action item" for CSC communities, which aim to mitigate and adapt to climate change at the local level. Points are awarded for each action item, which can qualify towns for funding. In LaGrange, New York, the Climate Action Coalition organizes the town's repair event. Transition US, a nonprofit organization that seeks to equip people and communities with the skills to make the transition from fossil fuels to a sustainable future, sponsors Repair Cafes and Fixit Clinics in more than twenty towns in the United States.

Green Clubs, Businesses, and Nonprofit Organizations

National and local environmental, ecological, and sustainability clubs and organizations such as the National Audubon Society, Riverkeeper, Youth Against Plastic Pollution, Mass Green Network, rural lands foundations, land trusts, and preservation alliances are natural partners.

One Hudson Valley Repair Cafe enjoys the support of the Dutchess County Soil and Water Conservation District, as well as the Climate Action Coalition. The Sierra Club, Lower Hudson Group, cosponsors Repair Cafes held in Westchester, Rockland, and Putnam counties in New York by providing publicity. Sustainable Warwick sponsors a Repair Cafe because it exemplifies the organization's goals: "It enables people to reuse items instead of tossing them in the landfill and buying new ones, which would require new materials and energy to produce."

Look for "green" 501(c)(3) nonprofit organizations such as the Scrap Exchange of Durham, North Carolina, a creative reuse center whose mission is to promote creativity, environmental awareness, and community through reuse. The Scrap Exchange operates a retail store where local residents purchase donated materials — anything from bolts of fabric to a manufacturing overrun of bottle caps — for use in activities ranging from art projects to home repair. The Scrap Exchange hosts Repair Cafe workshops organized and staffed by Repair Cafe NC, headed by Don Fick, which also runs bimonthly events in nearby Cary, North Carolina.

Fablabs, Hackerspaces, and Makerspaces

Fablabs, hackerspaces, and makerspaces — the community-based, not always for profit, DIY spaces where people gather to create, repurpose, and learn to tinker — are similar to Repair Cafes, Fixit Clinics, and Fixers Collectives. In Phoenixville, Pennsylvania, high school student Tyler Bernotas, whose grandfather taught him to repair things with whatever was at hand, convinced the owner of a local makerspace to partner with him to hold their town's first Repair Cafe. When the makerspace was no longer available, Tyler moved his cafe to the town's Technical College High School, a public school specializing in career and technical education for students in grades nine through twelve that is also a partner for economic and workforce development.

Vita Wells, founder of the Culture of Repair Project in Berkeley and Oakland, California, has been collaborating with maker educators to develop strategies for integrating maker-centered education in K-12 schools. Among their goals are encouraging hands-on learning and critical thinking and teaching youth to repair rather than "reflexively trash and repurchase."

TimeBanks

A TimeBank is a community-based skill-sharing system. Members earn credit for every hour spent helping someone with a task. Everyone's time is equal, whether it's been spent doing something as complex as writing a will or as simple as walking a dog. "The vision and values of Repair Cafes fit our core values," says Micaela Salatino, project director of the Long Beach, California, Time Exchange. "[This includes] sharing of skills and helping each other out, the passing on of skills, the intergenerational aspects and gathering people from all walks of life on a common cause."

Habitat for Humanity ReStores, Thrift and Reuse Centers

Habitat ReStores, independently owned reuse stores operated by local Habitat for Humanity organizations, accept donations of household items and building materials to be resold to the public at a fraction of the retail price. While the New River Valley TimeBank, based in Christiansburg, Virginia, held a Repair Cafe at their local Habitat ReStore in October of 2017, students from Myers-Lawson School of Construction at Virginia Tech provided household tips at a Sustainability Exposition, held in the ReStore's parking lot. LaGrange, New York, Repair Cafe organizer John Sommer, who volunteers at a nearby Habitat ReStore, saves key parts from damaged donated items so they can be used to make repairs to other damaged items, which in turn can go back on the floor for sale. Recently, he used a salvaged spindle to match the finish on a damaged chair brought to his Repair Cafe. Finger Lakes ReUse, with two centers located in Ithaca, New York, provides a convenient and affordable way to donate, purchase, and reuse home goods, furniture, electronics, clothing, books, and building materials. The organization has returned more than 2,059,000 items back into use, with a $2.1 million budget, thirty-eight living wage employees, sixty regular volunteers, and hundreds of other volunteers and supporters. Finger Lakes ReUse hosts the Ithaca Fixers Collective every Saturday afternoon from three to five o'clock.

Where to Get More Information

There is no one right way to set up and run a repair event, and there are many helpful guides. Some are free; others ask for a donation. The Repair Café International Foundation in Amsterdam offers a digital starter kit, with practical advice based on years of experience to help you through all the stages of setting up and promoting your own Repair Cafe. Vita Wells, who spearheaded a Fixit Clinic and Repair Cafe in Berkeley, California, also recommends these sources:

- The Restart Party Kit and supporting material, from the Restart Project: therestartproject.org
- "Start a Clinic," from Fixit Clinic: fixitclinic.blogspot.com
- "Host a Fix-It Clinic: A Comprehensive Guide," from the City of Austin, Texas: austintexas.gov (search fixitclinic)
- The digital starter kit from the Repair Café International Foundation in Amsterdam: repaircafe.org

CHAPTER EIGHT

Adventures in Repair

People today don't have the skills to do repairs, but it's not rocket science. I enjoy a better quality of life because I repair.
— Jim Rouleau, Repair Cafe, Bolton, Massachusetts

Elizabeth recalls: *I vividly remember the Christmas when I was five years old. My dad, a U.S. Air Force officer, had recently moved our family from Florida to Colorado. I'd never seen snow before, and I couldn't wait to see all the new toys that I'd told Santa I wanted when I'd sat on his lap at the on-base "exchange" store. I raced down the stairs to the living room in my mom-made pajamas — repurposed from a mom-made Halloween costume — and spotted a blonde Bonnie Braids doll dressed in a white, lacy, crocheted skating outfit topped off with a ski cap. She was perched on a little, crayon-yellow, wooden bed fitted with red-and-white-striped sheets and a matching pillow. Also tucked under the decorated tree's branches was a panda bear sporting a red plaid vest and matching bow tie. I was thrilled! But then, just as suddenly, I remembered that the doll, bear, and bed were not new. My dad had made the doll bed using wood salvaged from an old ammunition box a couple of summers ago. And I'd recently spied my mother crocheting something white and lacy while watching TV. And hadn't she just sewn herself a red plaid skirt? Didn't she always save fabric scraps to patch or decorate clothes? At the time, I was shocked and disappointed, as only a kid could be, but now I applaud my parents' thrift and creativity.*

Some people are lucky enough to live in families where repair is a way of life. As Jennifer Ferris, co-organizer of the Repair Cafe in Saratoga Springs, New York, says of her childhood, "Tools were a part of the daily routine. Fixing this, improving that, composting and only buying what you need." Today, many people who can afford to throw out their broken or torn things and buy new ones prefer to repair them — because it's sensible and satisfying. And it can be fun.

If you didn't have the opportunity to learn repair skills at home or on the job, or if you would like to improve your technique, here is some practical, hands-on, how-to advice from repair coaches, in their own words, about how to fix some of the items most often brought to their tables at repair events. There is no one right way to repair anything, but these tips and tricks should help you get started on your own adventures in repair. Power to the people! You might start by learning how to use a multimeter — it measures volts, amps (current), and ohms (resistance) in a circuit — to help you troubleshoot problems with lamps and other small appliances that need electricity to operate.

How to Use a Multimeter to Diagnose Electrical Appliances

By Ken Winterling, volunteer at Repair Cafes in Mamakating, Middletown, Montgomery, Newburgh, Pine Bush, and Warwick, New York

Ken has been repairing all sorts of things since he was a child. His dad repaired things for family, friends, and neighbors, and he taught Ken how things work, how to use tools, and how very satisfying it is to fix something rather than toss it. Ken only recently learned about Repair Cafes. "It seemed like a perfect fit," he says. "I volunteer to repair items for people I don't know for the same reason I helped people I didn't know when I was a volunteer EMT. It's a great way to use my skills and talents. It's fun to meet and help your neighbors and create a positive impact on the environment, all at the same time." Many of his small appliance repairs start by instructing visitors seated at his table how and why to use a multimeter.

The multimeter, one of the best tools for electrical troubleshooting, measures volts, amps (current), and ohms (resistance) in a circuit. When repairing appliances you will mostly be measuring volts and resistance, so this guide concentrates on those measurements. This basic instruction on how to use a multimeter also explains what all those confusing meter symbols mean. It is not comprehensive.

There are two basic types of multimeter, the VOM (volt-ohm-milliammeter) and the DMM (digital multimeter). The VOM type is older and uses an analog moving needle gauge to display measurements. The newer device, the DMM, uses a digital display to show what is happening in the circuit. Either will work for testing appliances, but the DMM's digital display is easier to read for most people.

To measure volts, amps, or ohms, you need to set the meter to the proper type of measurement and the correct range within that type. For example, to test if power is reaching the socket on a table lamp, you would need to set the meter to AC (alternating current) and the range to a voltage higher than 120, the U.S. household voltage.

Meters come in two selector types: manual ranging and autoranging. Almost all VOMs are manual ranging, while DMMs come in both manual and autoranging. With a manual ranging meter, you must use a dial to select the type of measurement, such as AC, then the range, such as 200, being careful to pick a range that is higher than the expected measurement. Selecting a lower value or incorrect measurement type could destroy the meter. Autoranging meters are easier to use because they only require the operator to set the measurement type, such as AC.

When using a meter for repairs, you must know the type of voltage — AC or DC (direct current) — and the approximate amplitude of that voltage so you can set the meter properly. For example, in the table lamp example above, we expected 120VAC (volts AC) because it was plugged into a wall socket. If you were repairing a toy, you would check what type of battery it used. If, for example, it had three AA cells, you would know that the toy ran on 4.5VDC (volts DC), since batteries are DC devices. The resistance (ohms) function of the meter is used to check for continuity. In appliance repair, this is most often used to check the integrity of power cords, fuses, thermostats, etc. You want a meter that uses common batteries such as 9V, AA, or AAA.

There are many multimeter tutorials on the internet. I can recommend three short tutorials on YouTube:

- "The Best Multimeter Tutorial (HD)"
- "How to Use a Multimeter for Beginners: Part 1 — Voltage Measurement/Multimeter Tutorial"
- "Collin's Lab: Multimeters #Adafruit"

How to Repair a Table Lamp

By FixIt Bob Berkowitz,
volunteer at the Repair Cafe in Warwick, New York

As a kid, Bob worked with his father, a licensed master electrician, on job sites, and there he was exposed to all the construction trades. During high school, he worked weekends in the maintenance department for a major commercial baker, and upon graduation Bob attended college and earned an associate degree in heating and refrigeration technology. Then Bob joined the U.S. Navy "Seabees" construction battalion, where he received advanced training in the operation and maintenance of nuclear reactors at remote military sites. At these sites, he had to repair what was broken

with the materials at hand — per the Seabee motto, "Can Do." After re-
tirement from a management position at a utilities company, Berkowitz
opened a handyman business specializing in small home repairs. When
asked why he volunteers at the Repair Cafe, Bob says, "It's in my blood to
make myself available to friends and colleagues."

Lamps are the most common item brought in for repairs throughout
the United States. Many lamp owners don't really know what's wrong,
and so we'll see vague descriptions on the job tickets, like "Socket?,"
"Contact not working," or simply "Doesn't come on." The first step in
any repair is to identify the problem. Replace the bulb with one that
you know is good, and then plug the lamp into an outlet that you
know is working. If it still doesn't work, unplug the lamp and inspect
the lamp and power cord. Examine the power cord for brittleness,
signs of fraying, or broken wires (dogs and cats love to chew on them),

especially where the wire connects to the plug or enters the lamp at the base. Check the lamp socket. If it is the twist type, can you feel it twist and click? Or does it just continue to twist? If it's the push type, do you feel some resistance when you push it? Or does it just slide easily? If it is a pull chain type, do you feel some resistance and a click when you pull the chain? Or does it pull with ease? In general, if the socket has a switch and the switch operates with some resistance and a pronounced click, the socket could be okay.

An inexpensive digital multimeter is an asset in troubleshooting all types of electrical problems, and one function of the meter is continuity testing. Use a continuity tester when performing your initial inspection. The tester will confirm that the power cord is not broken or that the socket is functioning properly.

How to Replace a Lamp Socket

1. Remove the shade and the harp (the hardware to which the shade is attached) by lifting the ferrules at the bottom of each leg. Squeeze the legs together in order to release them. Remove the harp.

2. Snap off the socket shell from the socket shell cap. Squeeze the area marked "PRESS," and pull it up to remove it. If the shell does not snap apart easily, slip a small screwdriver between the shell and the shell cap and pry it up.

3. Pull out the socket to expose enough wiring to allow the installation of a new socket.

4. Loosen the screws securing the wires, noting which wire was removed from the brass screw (hot) and which wire was removed from the silver screw (neutral).

5. Install the new socket in the reverse order, making sure to attach the power cord wires to the proper terminals. Note: The lamp power supply cord is normally not color-coded, but the wires can easily be identified. The hot wire insulation is smooth to the touch; the neutral wire has ribs extruded on the insulation that you can see and feel.

How to Replace the Power Cord

1. Follow steps 1–4 above.
2. Remove the wire through the base of the lamp.
3. Install the new wire in the reverse order.
4. Wire the new plug as you wired the socket: smooth insulation wire to the brass screw (hot) and the ribbed insulated wire to the silver screw (neutral).

Lamp repair materials are relatively inexpensive. I recommend that you replace both the socket and the power supply cord at the same time. In some cases, replacing the power supply cord is more involved, necessitating the complete disassembly of the lamp. In that case, replacing just the socket should do the job so long as the power cord is in good condition. Work completed, your lamp should be as good as new, if not better.

How to Repair a Vacuum Cleaner

By Ken Winterling, volunteer at Repair Cafes in Mamakating, Middletown, Montgomery, Newburgh, Pine Bush, and Warwick, New York

Ken, who wrote the section on how to use a multimeter that appears earlier in this chapter, has worked as a service technician, applications engineer, and network analyst working on voice and data networks. He's held an amateur ham radio license for fifty years, and he is regularly asked to repair various electronic, electric, and mechanical items for family members. "Unfortunately, there are few places that repair items anymore. Those that do have charges that are out of proportion when compared to the cost of a new item. As a result, many people throw out a damaged item and buy a new one when a simple repair could have saved it."

Repair Cafe coaches see almost as many vacuum cleaners as lamps. Many of the machines are much-loved older models that "suddenly stopped working." Frequently, the problem is that the owner doesn't know how to clean or lubricate the machine. Or how to straighten the bent prongs on the plug or replace the belt. Vacuum cleaners come in various forms — canister, upright, stick, and hand-held; some plug into a power source, others are "cordless" and powered by an internal rechargeable battery. The first step to correcting what's wrong with your vacuum cleaner is to observe what is or isn't happening.

Diagnostic Process

Regardless of the type of vacuum cleaner, the repair process begins with diagnosis: identifying what doesn't work as well as what does work. Does the machine turn on; do you hear the motor running? Does it make unusual noises? Do you notice the smell of burning rubber or other unusual odors? Is there suction at the end of the hose? Is the beater bar turning? Is the dust bag/collector cup full? Is the filter (or filters) dirty? Answers to these questions help guide you to the source of the problem. After you check/correct each item in the list below, try using the machine to see if the problem has been corrected. If not, continue down the list of possibilities. A continuity tester or inexpensive digital multimeter is helpful for assessing electrical problems and checking fuses.

1. Is the motor running but making a squealing sound? If a loud screeching/squealing sound is coming from the motor, it is likely that the motor shaft bearings need to be oiled. See "Opening the Motor Housing" below.

2. Is the motor not running? Assuming a corded vacuum cleaner is turned on and the controls are set properly, a common cause for the motor not running is that the machine is not plugged into a working outlet. Is it plugged into an outlet controlled by a wall switch that is turned off? Check the outlet using a lamp or another device you know is working. Move the power cord to a working outlet.

3. Check the prongs on the plug. Are they straight, bent, missing? If bent, use pliers to straighten them. If it is a three-wire grounded plug, be sure the ground pin is firmly attached.

4. If the outlet and plug are good, then check the cord. You are

looking for cracks, brittle/stiff sections, frayed wires, and crushed areas, which could happen if the cord was caught in a closed door, etc. This can sever a wire inside the cord without being visible on the outside. Damage to a cord often occurs at the plug and where it enters the machine.

5. Aside from bent prongs that can be straightened, if any of the above issues are discovered, then power cord replacement is indicated. I do not recommend patching/splicing the cord since it is normally under stress from being dragged around during use as well as occasionally getting caught on things, like furniture, while vacuuming. See item 9 on power cord replacement, below.

6. If the vacuum cleaner is cordless and the motor won't run, it may be that the battery needs to be recharged. Some machines have a light or display to indicate the state of the battery charge and/or that the charger is recharging the battery. Unfortunately, some machines do not have an indicator, which makes troubleshooting more difficult. Use a DMM (digital multimeter) to check the voltage from the charger. Also check the charger cable and plug as advised above.

7. A dead battery is another possibility. Open the case and use a DMM to check the battery voltage at its terminals. Then, with the charger connected to the battery, plug in the charger and see if the voltage increases. If the voltage increases, then the charger is working. If the voltage does not increase, it may indicate a dead battery. See "Opening the Motor Housing" below.

8. Another reason for any vacuum cleaner motor to stop running is an activated thermal motor protection switch. If the motor overheats due to a full dust bag/cup or clogged suction hose, the thermal protection switch disconnects the motor power until the switch cools and closes again. Several manufacturers advise unplugging the machine and waiting forty-five minutes before plugging in the machine again and trying to use the vacuum cleaner. It is also possible that the thermal switch has failed and left the motor disconnected from the power cord. To check the switch you have to open the case. See "Opening the Motor Housing" below.

9. Power cord replacement is specific to each vacuum cleaner, but once you get the housing open, with most models it is easy to determine how the power cord is connected. For safety's sake, purchase a replacement cord from the manufacturer. See "Opening the Motor Housing" below. (Note: Always grasp the plug, not the cord, to remove a cord or charger from a socket in the house or car. Pulling the cord to remove the plug will lead to failure at the joint where the wire meets the plug. It can cause wires to fray, start a fire, or shock you.)

10. Is the motor not running even though the power cord appears to be okay, the power switch is on, and the machine is plugged into a working outlet? In this case, you'll need to open the motor housing and check the internal wiring. See "Opening the Motor Housing" below.

11. Is there no suction or weak suction? Suction problems can be caused by a clog in the hose, extension wand, or floor nozzle; an open suction control vent on the hose handle (not all vacuums have one); a cut(s) in the hose; a full dust bag/cup; or a clogged filter(s). Check the following: Is the dust bag/cup full? Is the bag firmly attached to the short tube? Are there any holes, cuts, or tears in the bag? Is the dust cup cracked or the gasket damaged?

    Empty/replace the cup or replace the bag as indicated. Check the filter(s) (some vacuum cleaners have more than one filter), and clean/replace the filter(s) as recommended by the manufacturer. If there is still no suction, remove all attachments from the machine and turn it on. Place your hand over the suction port; if you feel strong suction, it is likely that a blockage exists in the hose or extension wand. See "Clearing Blockages" below. If you feel weak suction or none at all, look into the suction port. If you find an obstruction, remove it if you can. If you can't see an obstruction, you'll need to open the vacuum cleaner motor housing. See "Opening the Motor Housing" below.

Clearing Blockages

To clear a blockage from an extension wand or hose, disconnect it from the machine, and then look into it to see if it is blocked. If the blockage is near either end, grab it by hand, or try using a bent coat hanger or stiff wire to retrieve it. Be careful not to puncture the hose. If the blockage in the hose is past a place where you can see or grab it, place the hose flat on the floor in a straight line. Use a broom or mop handle that easily fits inside the hose to push the blockage toward the other end. If the hose is longer than the broom/mop handle, try compressing the hose toward the end where you inserted the handle. You can also try attaching the hose to the exhaust port on the vacuum, if it has one. Or use your shop vacuum, if you have one. Do this *outside* so you don't spew dust and dirt in the house.

Another possible blockage location is the floor nozzle, both powered and unpowered. In the case of the powered floor nozzle, check that the beater bar is not covered in debris. Remove any debris wrapped around the beater bar. Check to see if the beater bar is freely rotating and turns when the power switch is turned on. If it does not turn, check that the drive belt is in place. Reseat or replace the belt as necessary.

Opening the Motor Housing

There are several circumstances in which you will have to open the motor housing: if you need to replace the power cord; if the vacuum cleaner itself has no suction, and you can't see an obstruction; if the motor is making squealing sounds; or if you need to check/replace the battery in a cordless vacuum cleaner. Most vacuum cleaners have visible screws that you remove to separate the sections. Sometimes, however, a screw(s) will be under a name plate or otherwise hidden from view. Try removing the visible screws and separating the case. Make note of the screw size in each location as some might be longer or wider than others.

If the case won't come apart, see where it seems to be stuck and look for a name plate, label, or other item possibly covering a screw. These plates and other items that might be covering screws are usually held in place by plastic clips, so be gentle when prying them off. Labels are usually affixed with adhesive. You can usually pry them off very slowly. You can also search the internet for a YouTube video about your model.

Once the housing is open, perform any or all of the tasks that necessitated opening the case:

1. Look for and remove an obstruction in the vacuum path.
2. Apply a few drops of light machine oil to the motor shaft bearings.
3. Check the power cord, switch, and motor wiring connections.
4. Check continuity.
5. Check the thermal switch; it should be closed when cool.
6. Check/replace battery in a cordless vacuum cleaner.

How to Fix a Sewing Machine

By Ken Fix It Boscher, volunteer at Repair Cafes in Esopus, Gardiner, Kingston, LaGrange, New Paltz, and Rosendale, New York

Ken Fix It remembers taking apart old radios and other appliances when he was six or seven years old before moving on to bicycles, lawn mowers, and cars. He had to work on his first car because he couldn't afford to get it fixed by a professional. Second car, too. All the cars, actually. He ended up working as a professional auto mechanic for about a decade and credits that experience with enhancing his troubleshooting and diagnostic skills. Later, Ken operated huge factory machinery, and he fixed and operated computers. These days, he says, "I fix stuff, mostly houses." Ken volunteers regularly at Repair Cafes. "I picture a square with all four points connected, and a couple words at each corner: 'To learn,' 'To teach,' 'To fix,' and 'To help.' Maybe that's why I keep showing up."

Sometimes the Repair Cafe feels like a cross between *Antiques Roadshow* and the Island of Misfit Toys! Sewing machines, when they work properly, are assemblages of spinning and oscillating parts that perform a function that seems almost magical. They loop one piece of thread around another, locking them together so stitched seams don't unravel the way they do in a *Looney Tunes* cartoon.

At the Repair Cafe, I see quite a few sewing machines, mostly older, simpler ones that have been sitting around for a few years. The usual complaint is that they run very slowly or not at all. Others, especially the ones with fancy switch options, can have a host of problems best left to a professional sewing machine mechanic.

Simple sewing machines that run very slowly usually respond well to a good oiling. This involves adding a drop of oil to all the oil holes and everything that slides back and forth. Take off the top cover, turn on the machine, and look for a long spinning shaft that runs the length of the machine. At the ends of the shaft you'll see a square metal thing, called a *pillow block*, with a small hole on the top. That is the oil hole.

The pillow block is designed to locate the main shaft of the machine and allow it to spin freely. The bearing surfaces in the pillow blocks, called *bushings*, are made of a porous bronze metal designed to accept and hold oil. But certain oils oxidize and get gunky after long exposure to air.

The solution is to add a light oil and let it de-gunkify and flush out the old oil. Air tool oil, light machine oil, even automatic transmission fluid — a gear lube with many different additives, some of which are detergents — are good to use. I use Tri-Flow, a light, low-gunk lube available at bike stores. I don't recommend WD-40. It's light, but it's not a lubricant.

Occasionally, a machine is really stuck and the motor alone won't turn it. In this case, gently rock the wheel on the end, back and forth, where the belt goes around. Once everything is turning, run it for a full minute, varying the speed. Then, run it at full speed for a good fifteen seconds. I have heard machines speed up dramatically with this method, going from barely groaning around to whirring merrily, like sewing machines are supposed to do! Sewing machines work great when they work, and it's usually pretty easy to get them to work.

How to Patch a Hole

By Raheli Harper, volunteer at the Repair Cafe in Warwick, New York

Raheli Harper is a self-described stay-at-home mother, fiber artist, and homesteader who teaches visible mending classes and writes for Dirt *magazine. She believes that sewing gets less respect than other handicrafts because it's traditionally been done by women working at home, hidden from the world. Hand sewing, which once provided everyone's clothing and many tools, is now "dismissed or seen as a kid's craft."*

Raheli's grandmother taught her to knit at age eight, and by the time she was in elementary school, she was stitching her doll's clothes. Inspired by her mother's creative "designer" patches on worn jeans, Raheli appreciates clothes that have a story: "Lots of people brag, 'I got this on sale!' That's their clothing story. When I mend my clothes, the story is more personal."

Raheli volunteers to repair clothes and textiles using a sewing machine or hand stitching. She has repaired Velcro on shoes, seams in shirts and skirts, and an endless supply of jeans with holes. She calls the Repair Cafe "a place where people can come together to admire each other's handiwork, instead of our consumer choices."

Our culture assumes that all goods are disposable and replaceable, but it takes so little to keep a shirt or pair of jeans usable — just a needle, some thread, and a bit of patience.

What You Will Need

You will need embroidery sewing needles (with a big eye), button/craft thread, a fabric patch, pins, standard thread for basting, and chalk or a disappearing ink pen. Your patch should be a piece of fabric similar in weight to the item you are mending. A button-down shirt can be patched with quilting fabric, but the ripped knee in your jeans will need a heavier piece of fabric, like denim or twill.

Good to Know

- Additional basic sewing techniques can be found on YouTube and in the book *Mend It Better: Creative Patching, Darning, and Stitching* by Kristin M. Roach.

- Basting, or tacking down with loose stitches, will take just a few minutes and keep your patch secured while you work. Once you're done basting, you can remove the pins so you can work without getting poked. When I skip this step, the pins always slide loose, and I am forced to work very carefully while sitting at a table. Basting allows me to lounge on the couch while I work or to carry mending projects in my bag without losing the patches.
- When I place my patch on the inside of the garment, I don't bother finishing the edges of the patch. They will unravel a little over time, but the stitching ensures that it doesn't go too far.

Instructions

1. Lay the garment on a flat surface and smooth out the ripped area so it is as flat as possible. If the hole is in the knee area, the cloth may be stretched out by use; just do the best you can to lay it flat.

2. Measure the area you will need for your patch by adding one inch above and one inch below the hole. So, for example, a rip that is three inches across and half an inch high will need a patch that is five inches wide by two and a half inches high. If the fabric around the hole is worn thin, your patch will need to extend beyond that so it can be stitched to strong fabric.

3. Turn the garment inside out and lay the patch over the hole, double-checking to make sure it covers the whole rip and extends into stable fabric. Pin the patch to the fabric, being sure you don't pin through the back of the garment.

4. Using an embroidery needle, thread a color that contrasts with the color of the fabric, and baste the patch in place. Baste using half-inch to one-inch stitches, making sure to secure as much of the patch as possible, around the rip and right up to the edges.

5. Remove pins. Turn the garment right side out. Thread your needle with button/craft thread, and knot the end; do not double the thread. Use chalk or a disappearing ink pen to mark the center line of the patch (vertical, horizontal, or diagonal is your choice), then mark parallel lines from the center line to the edges of your patch. The lines should be about a half inch apart.

6. Begin stitching on the center line, starting at one edge, aiming for quarter-inch long stitches or slightly shorter.

7. When you get to the end of the first row, end with the needle inside the pant leg. Bring the needle back up at the beginning of the next line of stitching. Repeat this process, stitching along each of your marked lines.

8. When you have four inches of thread left on the needle, stitch through the same spot three times in a row; this will make a secure knot (or used your preferred method for making a knot). End with your needle inside the pant leg, cut your thread, and start a new one.

9. If you begin at the center line and stitch the lines moving toward the left edge of the patch, eventually you will arrive at the left edge and you will need to end your thread with a knot, cut the thread, and move toward the right side of the patch. Begin again on the line marked to the right of the center line, and continue stitching the lines marked to the right.

10. Cut your basting threads and pull them out.

11. Wear your mends with pride!

How to Repair a Torn Teddy Bear

By Joan Bono, volunteer at the Repair Cafe in Warwick, New York

Joan Bono is a stained-glass artist who learned how to make teddy bears at a class held at her local fabric shop years ago. Today, she has a business creating custom teddy bears from a pattern designed by her daughter-in-law, Terie. One of Joan's specialties is creating memorial teddy bears for people after the death of a loved one. Each bear is crafted from the material of the loved one's fur coat, which might otherwise have been discarded. Bono even crafts a scarf for the bear, cutting the coat's silk lining in a way that highlights the original owner's monogrammed initials.

Recruited to volunteer by a friend and fellow sewing coach, Deanne, Joan wields her needle to restore battered but beloved soft toys at Warwick's

Repair Cafe. "Just seeing the smile on a child's face when I can repair their favorite buddy makes my day. I believe in the Repair Cafe concept, fixing not dumping. Above all, my fellow fixers are a happy, enthusiastic bunch of fun people to be with!"

Teddy bears suffer many of the same traumas experienced by dolls and other soft toys made of fiber. Because children and dogs love to carry teddies around by an arm, leg, or one ear, reattaching a torn limb or ear is a common task.

What You Will Need

- A pair of small microtip scissors, five inches long, or embroidery scissors
- Straight pins
- A seam ripper
- A thin, straight, two-inch-long hand-sewing needle
- Standard 100 percent polyester thread the same color as the bear
- Embroidery thread in the same color as the bear's nose and mouth

Instructions

Ears

If the ear has been lost or is too damaged to replace, fashion a head-band or a bow to camouflage the absence. If you have the detached ear, turn the raw edge under one-eighth of an inch. Use straight pins to attach the ear to the bear's head, carefully lining up the detached ear so that the position is symmetrical with that of the opposite, attached ear.

Thread the needle with doubled polyester thread. Knot the thread. Tack the ear to the head with loose stitches to hold it in place. Remove the pins. Pinch the back of the ear to give it dimension and make it look more real. Sew the pinch in place at the ear's base. Using overhand stitches, sew the ear to the bear's head at the turned-under raw edge.

Eyes

If the bear is to be played with by a child, not just displayed, don't replace the original detached button eyes. Buttons can be easily swallowed. Rather, replace both buttons with safety lock-in eyes, which can be purchased at fabric or craft stores.

First, use a seam ripper to open a seam at the back or side of the bear's head. Remove stuffing as necessary. Push the safety lock eye from the front of the fabric into the opened head at the position of the original eye. If the hole supporting the eye is too big, a few stitches with matching thread will close the hole and support the eye snuggly. Then attach the safety lock into the head; it will be concealed when the stuffing is inserted into the head. Attach the washer on the inside of the fabric head. Replace the stuffing. Use a needle and thread to make slip stitches to close the seam at the back or side of the bear's head.

Nose and Mouth

Use embroidery thread to fill in the damaged outline of the nose with tight, flat "satin" stitches. Create a mouth by sewing an upside-down Y under the nose.

Fluff the Fur

When repairs are complete, use a sewing needle to carefully pick or lift the bear's "fur" out of the seams, taking care not to disturb any stitches. This is tedious work, but if it's done carefully, the seams will be nearly invisible, giving the bear a nice finished look.

How to Fix a Broken Zipper

By Deanne Singer, volunteer at the Repair Cafe in Warwick, New York

After Deanne Singer retired from teaching marketing to advanced-placement high school students, she looked for something creative to do. In addition to volunteering for the Warwick Friendly Visitor Program, the Warwick Valley Gardeners Club, and Too Good to Toss, an annual free community swap, Singer started her own custom baking business and another business offering alterations, mending, tailoring, and custom sewing.

Three years ago, Deanne, aka "the Zipper Lady," was one of the very first to volunteer for Orange County's first Repair Cafe. "It's an awesome opportunity to move beyond self and make the world a better place. Everyone benefits. It's a win-win event at no cost to the town. And it's a pleasure to work with the other women in the sewing area. We're all so compatible, sharing ideas and supplies but with different areas of expertise."

There are two types of zippers: open-end zippers, used on outerwear like jackets, and closed-end zippers, used on skirts, pants, and jeans. Zippers have only a few parts — teeth, slide, pull, top and bottom stops, and the box at the bottom of open-end zippers. The good news is that 80 percent of broken zippers do not need to be replaced completely!

Open-End Zippers

Start by evaluating the problem. The easiest predicament to fix is a broken pull tab, the part on the slider that you grab to make the zipper go up and down. A broken pull tab can be replaced easily and quickly with a bent paper clip, a keyring, a shoelace, or any other object that you can slip onto the slider.

The next thing to examine is the slider. Held under tension and repeatedly forced up and down, it might have lost its connection to the teeth. Most often, the problem is evident because the zipper opens both above and below the slider. Sliders expand with use and lose connection with the teeth. It's easy to fix this problem, too. Use pliers to apply gentle pressure to both sides of the slider to compress it back to its original size so that it reconnects with the zipper's teeth.

Be careful! If you apply too much pressure, the slider will break, and you'll have to replace it. If that happens, be sure to replace the slider with another slider exactly the same size. The size is usually printed on the back of the slider. Purchase a new one at a fabric store, or take a slider from an old garment that you no longer wear and are ready to discard.

With the proper-size slider in hand, your next task is to put the slider back on the teeth. If your jacket has an open-end zipper, you will only have to attach the slider to one side. Remove the stop at the top, put the new slider on, then replace the stop. If you didn't manage to save the old stop or it is broken, you can use thread to create a stop in its place. Simply hand-stitch a horizontal line between the last two teeth of the zipper tape to stop the slider from slipping off.

If the zipper is missing teeth, or if the bottom box (the part used to engage the zipper on outerwear) is worn or missing, you must purchase a new zipper. Always take the garment, with the old zipper intact, to the store with you. Zippers come in an array of colors, lengths, and types, including metal, plastic, and nylon. It's best to replicate the original one installed by the manufacturer. Carefully remove the old zipper and note how it was sewn into the garment. Then sew in the new zipper.

For more information on replacing a zipper, look for online instructions specific to the type of zipper you are replacing and its use. There are all types of zippers and many, many videos.

Closed-End Zippers

Closed-end zippers are commonly used in pants, skirts, and jeans. Again, evaluate the problem. Is it a problem with the pull tab or slider? If so, follow the directions above. If teeth are missing near the bottom, the zipper can be salvaged. Remove the bottom stop, reinstall the slider above the missing teeth, then use needle and thread to hand-stitch a new stop so that the zipper does not come in contact with the missing teeth. This can also be done by removing the top stop. If you have salvaged the bottom stop, it can be moved up, to just above the missing teeth to stop the zipper's progress. Unfortunately, if the missing teeth are at the top of the zipper, you will need to purchase a new one.

How to Do a Simple Wooden Chair Repair

By Naomi Aubain, volunteer at the Repair Cafe in New Paltz, New York

Naomi grew up in a family with a lifestyle that was frugal and rich in the arts. Her grandmother was a seamstress who passed her skills and passion along to her daughter and granddaughters. Her mother, an art teacher and painter, tackled house renovations at a time when women could not get a legal permit to do that kind of work. Naomi grew up thinking that women could do anything and discovered that she liked working with her hands. She has worked as a cabinetmaker, a commercial artist, a baker, and a graphic design manager. Now Naomi fixes furniture for a living and enjoys sharing her skills with other like-minded people at the Repair Cafe in New Paltz, New York. "The community energy is so strong when people get together to keep a family heirloom going for another fifty years....It is very satisfying to make people happy and help make the world a little better. I am constantly surprised at how curious people are in the repair process. It helps to remind me to make it a teachable moment."

Wobbly wooden chairs make frequent appearances at Repair Cafes. They're often part of a dining room set that was inherited, or purchased secondhand, or found sitting on a curb. The cause of the wobble is sometimes unintentional misuse — there's something about teenagers that makes them want to rock back on the chair's two back legs! Sadly, there's no quicker way to destroy a beloved chair.

Loose Chair Joints

The first thing that usually compromises a well-used wooden chair is the joints. The old glue dries out, the wood loses moisture and shrinks, and the up-and-down stresses cause the joints to work loose. Sometimes the problem is caused by missing screws or nails, and simply replacing these can be a big help. Tightening loose screws is also a common remedy. But if these issues are not the problem, the chair needs to be reglued.

First Steps for Regluing

In order to understand the extent of the damage, examine the whole chair. Look for loose arms, legs, dowels, and supports; recessed nails or screws; and cracks in the wood. Once you have identified all the problem areas, you can focus on making the repairs.

You'll need to separate all the loose joints and clean out as much of the old glue as possible. Use a mallet to encourage loose joints to separate, ideally one with a rubber end to prevent damage to the furniture. If you do not have one of these specialty mallets, tape about four layers of cardboard onto the working end of a regular hammer. To check if a joint still has a good glue hold, strike the area with a few sharp blows. Try not to be over-zealous on the "good" joints as they could still have lots of life left.

Cleaning the Joints

After you have taken the chair as far apart as it wants to go, clean out the old glue. Use a flat rasp on the dowel-shaped tenon end of the joint. Rough sandpaper or a sharp chisel can also be used. It is harder to get into the hole or slot part (the "mortise") of the joint to clean it out. If it is accessible, a chisel is the best tool to loosen the glue at the bottom, while a round rasp works best on the sides. A rolled-up piece of rough sandpaper can also be used on the sides of the hole.

Gluing the Chair

Once the joints are clean, it is time to glue the chair back together. Make sure that all the joints are free of old glue and any other residue. Dry-fit the joints before putting any glue on them to make sure they go together well. Prepare the work area so glue drips can be easily cleaned up. You will also need a wet rag or cellulose sponge to remove excess glue. Yellow carpenter's glue designed for wood repairs works best, such as Titebond Original Wood Glue. The yellow wood glue is water soluble, which makes for easy cleanup, and it can be coaxed apart if more repairs are needed later. Do not use the type of glue that expands while it dries (like some Gorilla brand glues). Other types of glue that cannot be reversed, like epoxy, will limit your options down the road.

Apply a liberal amount of glue to the tenon and a moderate amount inside the mortise joint. You don't want too much at the bottom of the mortise, as it will keep the tenon from going all the way in. Also apply glue onto the "shoulders" of the tenon. Basically, put glue wherever the wooden pieces will touch each other in the joint. One of the most common reasons for joint failure is not enough glue. A small straw or popsicle stick is very helpful for getting glue all around the inside of the mortise.

Assemble the glue-ready joints, and use the mallet to make sure they close up as much as possible. Apply woodworking clamps with as much pressure as you can. Use scrap wood or cardboard under the clamp heads to protect the furniture.

If you do not have traditional woodworking clamps, here are a few options:

- Use a rope and screwdriver to make a tourniquet around the glued area.
- Ask your local bicycle shop for an old tire inner tube. Cut off the air valve, and wrap the tube around the glued area, tightening it as much as possible.
- Bungee cords, a commercial version of the inner tube but with hooks, also work well.

Clean off any excess glue with a damp rag, making sure to get it all. It is much easier to clean up glue when it's wet than it is to scrape it off later. Let the glue set as recommended on the label, usually at least thirty minutes. Wait another twenty-four hours before using the chair. If screws were previously used to keep the joints together, they can be put back into the same holes. Add a toothpick to the inside of the hole before putting the screw back in, as that will give it more "bite" and hold it in place better. Do not put nails back, as they don't do much for the joint and make it harder to repair later.

Congratulations! Your chair is ready for another thirty years of use. Enjoy your well-earned sit-down.

How to Repair a Bike

By Roger Bergman, volunteer at the Repair Café in Warwick, New York

For forty-nine years, Roger owned a shop that sold, rented, and repaired brand-name bicycles on New York City's Upper East Side. He says that he learned his trade "mostly by trial and error, as well as in conversation with those more skillful than I." Roger was trained and certified by numerous top-end bicycle and parts manufacturers, including Campagnolo, Mavic, RockShox, Shimano, and Trek. His store's service department repaired all brands and types of bicycles; the staff prided themselves on being able to complete most repairs while the customer waited. Roger brings this same sensibility to his work as a repair coach. "I see too much in the marketplace that is designed not to be repaired. It hurts me to see a bicycle — or any object — that does not have adjusting screws or a way to access the works. There is real satisfaction in fixing something that is broken. [That is why] I have spent twenty minutes repairing a small object, such as a bicycle bell, that costs only two dollars wholesale....The satisfaction of making something work is wonderful."

Look, Look, and Look Again!

In addition to running a shop, I also organized bike tours in the city and farther afield. For safety's sake, I recommend a bike tune-up every thousand miles or every six months. The first rule for bike repair is to take a very good look at the bicycle. If your bike is making noise, look carefully while you turn the wheels, pedals, and chain separately to see whether something is dragging on a moving part. Look all over — underneath, around the back, behind a decorative cover, really all over — using a flashlight if necessary. If you see a broken wire, trace it in both directions to see what it does. On bicycles, most parts do exactly what they seem to do. A wire that connects the brake lever to the brake calipers probably transmits the brake power when you squeeze the lever. If that brake isn't working and you find a broken wire, you may have diagnosed the problem just by looking. If you have access to a working duplicate of the item needing repair, look at the working one too. The front brake may be a duplicate of the rear brake, so look at both and compare the broken one to the working one.

Continue to look even when you think you have found the problem. If you are fixing a bicycle's flat tire, first look for something sharp that punctured your inner tube. But don't stop there! Keep looking for other sharp objects stuck elsewhere in the same tire. Search for cuts in the tire and places where the rubber is worn so thin that small sharp objects will penetrate it easily.

Stay Organized

The second rule of bike repair is to stay organized. We can't always select the time and place for bike repair, but we can certainly stay organized. Always line up the parts as you remove them, so you will know the correct order in which to put them back. Many parts seem to have reversible orientation, but they might not. Lay the parts out carefully, in the order that you remove them, and you will have a fighting chance to get everything back in the right place.

Be Very Skeptical of Online Repair Videos

There are tons of bike repair videos, many produced by the Park Tool Company and other manufacturers, as well as retail bike shops and home mechanics. But rule three is to be very skeptical of online repair videos. They are often either way too general and therefore unhelpful, or way too specific and therefore irrelevant. Many videos will say, "Replace if worn out" and "Ensure bolt is tight." But how is the first-time home mechanic supposed to know when something is worn out, or when the bolt is tight enough?

My definition of "worn out" is "shouldn't be reused." If you are repairing your bike at home, rather than on the road in a remote location, and you see a part that should be round but has some small gouges in it, you must answer several questions: (1) Would this part be dangerous to reuse? (2) Do I want to make this repair again when the symptom gets more annoying? (3) Do I want to ride this bike until I can find a replacement part? (4) If the part is expensive, does the bike merit the cost? (5) Will continued use of this worn part damage other bike parts? (6) Is this one of those bike parts, such as some brands of chain rivet, that are *not* designed to be removed and then reinstalled?

How tight is "tight"? Most threaded fasteners have turning resistance that remains constant as you turn, until the resistance gets harder and harder, which keeps the fastener securely in place. Turn it too hard, and you've damaged the fastener or the work, or both. The trick is to stop someplace in the middle of the increasing resistance: not at the top, not at the bottom, but in the Goldilocks zone where it's "just right." Technical mechanics use a torque wrench, which measures how much turning force they are applying. Charts are readily available on the internet to indicate the desired turning force value for parts, and many modern bike parts have torque values printed right on them! Get used to the nomenclature — newton meters (nm) and inch-pounds (in.-lb.) — and practice using torque tools to learn, for example, what 5 nm feels like. I also suggest that you experiment with disposable parts to overtorque them intentionally (gasp!). Know that small bolts are more easily destroyed than large ones and that different metals behave differently. You will begin to appreciate both the use of torque tools and the art of not using them.

Professional Bike Technicians Deserve Respect

Rule four is to respect the retail bike shop, a place that supports your local community and where a responsible and caring technician must deal with numerous models and variations that change frequently. The average repair shop will have parts and experience to fix a thirty-year-old bike, a department store BSO ("bicycle-shaped object"), or a newly produced multi-thousand-dollar road bike, all in just twenty-four hours. I do advocate for DIY repairs, but I sincerely respect the job done by a professional.

Quick Tips for Troubled Digital Devices

By Gabrielle Griffis, co-organizer of the Fixit Clinic
on Cape Cod, Massachusetts

Gabrielle is the outreach coordinator for the Wellfleet Public Library located on Cape Cod, Massachusetts. In this capacity, she organizes community programs, such as the Fixit Clinic, and offers regular tech assistance to library patrons. She grew up in a household with her parents and four older siblings. Her maternal grandfather, a first-generation American, was an inveterate fixer and tinkerer. He took things apart at the kitchen table, and he taught Gabrielle's mother how to care for bicycles and cars. Gabrielle's father, a technician by trade, routinely repaired household items, including electronics. When Gabrielle bought her first laptop, she understood that she was responsible for its maintenance, but she didn't know that the diagnostic and hands-on skills she picked up around the kitchen table would one day serve her so well in her career. "Helping people with problems on all kinds of devices — tablets, smartphones, and laptops — is now part of my job. Repairing is an act of resistance; it's recognition that the Earth's ecological systems are finite, fragile, and should be respected."

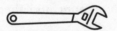

People often bring their laptops or tablets to repair events with the complaint that they "run slow." A variety of problems, including slow processing speed, can be solved across a range of electronic devices by doing a system reboot. Whether it's a smartphone, laptop, or tablet, turning a device off will reset a lot of malfunctioning programs. This is especially true if a device has been used and left on for a number of days. The logic of the reboot can also be applied to the practice of refreshing or restarting programs. Often a nonresponsive or lagging program, such as a word processor or internet browser, can be fixed simply by exiting and restarting the software, without having to turn the device completely off. In the same way, when third-party email servers have issues with incoming or outgoing mail, many times a quick solution will be to delete the account and add it back onto the device.

Another major fix for many device problems is to ensure that the operating system or software is up-to-date by checking the general settings. Wi-Fi issues, cloud storage problems, and disorganized text conversations magically resolve after an update. This is another reason why reboots solve so many problems; they're necessary to finalize updates.

When things go awry on a device with no obvious explanation, check the machine for buttons that may have been inadvertently switched "on" or "off." Sometimes a silent switch or Airplane Mode button can interfere with internet connectivity and other functions.

First Steps in Device Repair

1. Turn the device off and on.
2. Exit and restart applications.
3. Check for accidentally turned-on buttons (like Airplane Mode or the ring/silent switch).
4. Check to see if the operating system or software is up-to-date and compatible.
5. Uninstall and reinstall the program.
6. Log out or erase the account and then add the account or log back in.

In certain cases, slow programs can be attributed to mechanical issues, especially with regard to temperature. Cold temperatures can drain a battery, while hot temperatures can fry a motherboard, and God forbid coffee is spilled on the keyboard! In some instances, laptops can run for months, if not years, after sustaining liquid damage, and then suddenly stop working. With issues regarding mechanical malfunction, small problems can cascade into big problems. A displaced tracking pad can lead to a strained cable, which can affect the circuit board and even break it. That's why it's best to fix the smaller issue before it turns into a larger and more costly one.

Conversely, sometimes a seemingly large problem can turn out to be a small one. For example, a charging port that stops working on a smartphone could be the result of accumulated dust or debris. Gentle removal of dirt particles can save you from having to buy a new phone.

It's important to consider how a device is being used, looking at the complexity and number of tasks being run at the same time. Video processing requires more RAM (random access memory) than using a basic calculator. Knowing your device's capabilities can help you avoid or solve a lot of problems. For instance, while updates are typically a necessary part of operating system maintenance, completely updating an operating system can make a device run slower. And in some cases, it will make running older applications impossible.

Questions to Ask When Troubleshooting

- Is there anything physically wrong with the device?
- Has the device been exposed to extreme temperatures? Is it too hot? Too cold?
- Has anything happened to the device in the past that could be affecting it now?
- Do I have background programs running? Have I turned the device off?
- How will an update affect the device? Will it run faster? Slower? Is the update compatible with other software?
- What is the device's history? Is it refurbished?

It's good to remember that although smartphones, tablets, and laptops can share many of the same functions, no two devices are used in exactly the same way. Everything from the type of applications to battery-charging habits impact what's going on. We all have programs and patterns of use that determine how well our device runs. Being mindful of storage and system memory can help you better determine what's happening when things go wrong.

One solution for slow devices or internet browsers is to periodically clear cookies and the cache. These features can make an internet browser run faster in the short term, but over time they can have the opposite effect. Clearing the cache can be one of many things that frees up space on a smartphone with limited storage. The size of a phone's storage space can be determined by going to its general settings.

Tips for Freeing Up Storage and Making a Device Run Faster

- Delete or transfer large files such as videos and other media.
- Clear the internet browser's cache, browsing history, and cookies.
- Clean out voicemail, old text conversations, and call history.
- Look in storage for applications using excessive space, and delete unnecessary apps.

Adware is another problem on smartphones and laptops that many people can fix themselves. Unlike malware or spyware, adware can usually be disabled or erased by going to a program's settings, the application itself, or the internet browser's settings. Adware typically starts when a new application, such as a game or a toolbar, is installed on a device. When persistent and consistent advertisements for getaway vacations, get-rich-quick schemes, or dragon fantasy games infiltrate a screen, there's a good chance it's adware.

Given the accelerated rate at which technology is changing and the sheer number of devices and their uses, staying current can be a real challenge. For many folks who did not grow up with or have access to these devices, navigating them can be really anxiety provoking. Computer phobia, like math phobia, is very real! It's important to remember what a privilege it is to use technology; not everyone can afford these wonders. We should always take the best care of our devices and remember what it costs to make them and what a gift it is to use them.

by Martine Postma,
Director of Repair Café International Foundation

When I started the very first Repair Cafe in October 2009, I had no idea that ten years later, there would be a worldwide movement of passionate volunteers, each of them promoting repair in their own communities. Still, this is exactly what happened. Apparently people worldwide are ready for change, ready to say goodbye to our throwaway society and move toward a more sustainable way of living, with less waste and more care — for products, for the environment, and for each other.

As director of Repair Café International Foundation, I have seen the network grow — starting in Amsterdam and spreading from there to Belgium, Germany, France, and beyond, now reaching as far as the United States, Canada, Australia, and even India and Japan. In the United States there are now more than a hundred Repair Cafe locations. And this is just the beginning! As John Wackman and Elizabeth Knight have pointed out in this book, there is room for a Repair Cafe or similar initiative in every community across the United States — across the world, really — because community repair meetings are useful, and they're fun. They bring people together and prevent waste. And in our busy lives they slow people down and connect them with their inner sense of what is right. When you sit down and take the time

to make a repair, you realize that this is a normal thing to do. You become aware that the normal reaction when something breaks is not "I need to get a new one" but "I need to fix this" or "I need to have this repaired."

Since 2009 I have done a lot of thinking about how we got here, how we arrived in a situation where throwing away instead of repairing is considered to be the default, where consequently we create huge amounts of waste and use up the world's natural resources much too fast by creating new products every day. I have also been thinking about what we can do to turn this around. The community repair movement has an important role to play here, in putting repairability on the agenda, creating public debate, and showing — one repair at a time — that there is a solution, that a sustainable way of living, without unnecessary waste, is within reach.

Establishing more Repair Cafes and similar initiatives is part of that solution. But it's not the only solution. Products break every day, whereas Repair Cafes — run by volunteers — are usually open only once or twice a month. This naturally limits their impact. To really be able to compete with cheap new products that are available every-where, every day, repair needs to be available in every community on a daily basis too.

In a genuine repair society, people should *always* be able to go somewhere for a repair, and they should have a choice: making the repair themselves, repairing their item together with a volunteer, or bringing their item to a professional repairer and paying for the repair. All of these options should be available for everyone, every day, just like new products are.

In 2019, Repair Café International Foundation and its partners in the Netherlands started to investigate this future scenario in an exper-iment with circular craft centers (*circulaire ambachtscentra* in Dutch). These are spaces where products can get a second life when they're broken or when the current owner wants to get rid of them. Circular craft centers are part of the Netherlands' strategy to become a fully equipped circular economy. In such an economy, resources are pre-served and can be used over and over again. That's quite a change from the current linear economy, based on perpetual extraction of raw mate-rials to create new products, which after a period of use are discarded as waste and burned or sent to a landfill.

Product reuse is the central focus of the circular craft centers, which should combine a variety of facilities that are now only available separately: a recycling center, a secondhand store, refurbishing and re-pair facilities, and maker facilities, where new products can be created from products that cannot be repaired anymore or from products for which there is no demand on the secondhand market. Circular craft centers should also provide teaching facilities, where young people can learn repair and maker skills, where school classes can visit for a practical course, and where people can attend workshops on various subjects. These centers could be vibrant hotspots, where visitors are inspired for reuse and see what huge possibilities there are after the first life of a product.

Circular craft centers will make repair more widely available and will definitely promote the benefits of repair and reuse among a much broader public. Still, not even circular craft centers can lead the way to a future without unnecessary waste. More is needed for that future to become a reality.

For even if it becomes possible to have a product repaired at any time, that doesn't mean that every product will be repairable. At this moment, for a great many products it's still true that newer models are less repairable than older ones. This aspect of planned obsolescence is a serious threat to the potential of the circular economy and should be addressed immediately.

It is vital that manufacturers start producing products to fit into the circular economy. These products should be repairable. It should be possible to disassemble them using normal tools, without causing damage to the casing. Also, spare parts should be widely available for longer periods and at affordable prices. And most importantly, manufacturers should share repair manuals openly, so that repairers — professionals *and* amateurs — will know where to look and what to do when the item needs fixing, instead of having to figure all this out for themselves.

This kind of measure will have to be enforced by law, since there is now no incentive for manufacturers to undertake them voluntarily. They can still make the best profit by selling new products, and their sales are still highest when products are not repairable.

Manufacturers will only change their business model when this is no longer the case, when lack of repairability limits the popularity of a product — when, for instance, an unrepairable product is more expensive than a repairable one. And this won't change by itself. At this point, consumers could use some help from governments in changing the rules of the game so that sustainable behavior is stimulated and unsustainable behavior is discouraged.

Governments will start implementing this kind of measure when the pressure from society becomes strong enough. In the past ten years, this pressure has increased enormously. When I started the first Repair Cafe in 2009, repairing was not really an item on the social agenda. There was no wide-reaching public debate about our throwaway society. To me, it seemed that no one really cared that we are polluting the

Earth with unnecessary waste, using up the world's commodity stocks, and losing exactly those skills that make us independent and enable us to solve our own problems. Now, ten years later, we have a worldwide repair movement, we have the means to collect and share repair data to serve as evidence that measures are needed, we have people standing up for their right to repair and reclaiming control over their possessions. All this increases the political pressure for measures that move us toward more sustainability and more repairability.

The bigger this movement gets, the louder its voice will sound, and the sooner it will reach its goal. Every local citizen around the world can contribute to this progress by helping the community repair movement to grow and to maintain this growth in the coming years. This means that people everywhere should start new Repair Cafes and similar initiatives, thus inspiring and empowering their community and inviting more people to speak up too.

For this ongoing growth it is also vital that existing Repair Cafes continue their work in the future. This requires that they appeal to younger generations too. In this area there is still much to be done. Many Repair Cafes are now populated by people over fifty, over sixty, over seventy years old. On the one hand, this is no more than logical: these people are the ones who still possess repair skills, who grew up at a time when repairing was mainstream, and who learned these skills from their parents and in school. These are also the people who have the time to spend as Repair Cafe volunteers or visitors.

On the other hand, the "seniority" of many Repair Cafes is a potential threat to the viability of the movement. Looking at it from the outside, young people might get the idea that repairing is something for old folks, something from the past. Clearly, this is not true. On the contrary — repairing is *especially* for young people. They are the ones reaching furthest into the future, which makes them the ones who will benefit the most from a sustainable, livable, unpolluted world.

Inspiring younger generations is still a challenge for the community repair movement. However, I am confident that we will manage. Repair Café International Foundation has created a Repair in the Classroom curriculum for primary schools. In this series of lessons,

Repair Cafe volunteers come into the classroom to teach basic repair skills and show the pupils how they can fix beloved but broken items that they have brought from home: a favorite toy, a backpack, their bicycle. The first experiences with these lessons are promising; kids are eager to work with their hands and to learn new techniques, especially when they themselves can benefit from the results. Someone just needs to show them and help them along.

This will be possible in more places, in more different ways, when repair becomes more widely available. This will further kindle people's enthusiasm for repair and for a sustainable lifestyle. New forms of repair initiatives could arise, as could new business models for repairable products.

The past ten years have taught me that it is impossible to predict exactly how things will develop and what the future will look like. However, I am sure that we are moving toward a more sustainable society, in which repair has an important position. The circumstances demand it. We simply must do it. So let's create such a society together, and let's make it fun too!

In this book, John Wackman and Elizabeth Knight have shown that a sustainable future is possible. They have pointed out that community repair fits into American society very well. This characteristic, combined with the huge size of the United States, makes the future for Repair Cafes and similar initiatives in this country very promising. It's this future that I look forward to.

Recommended Online Repair and Parts Resources

Whenever I need to fix something — or break it further while trying to fix it — I go to YouTube.
— Steve Jones-D'Agostino, Repair Cafe, Bolton, Massachusetts

Repair coaches never know what kinds of damaged items will be brought through the door at any repair event. Yet they say that they enjoy the challenges that present themselves and the opportunity to collaborate with others to solve problems. And they're not shy about looking for answers online. By this point, you may be inspired to try your hand at fixing. Or maybe you just can't get yourself and your beloved but broken item to a repair event. To get you started on the way to repair, this section offers a curated list of online sources recommended by our teams of volunteers.

Our volunteers suggest that you start your research by reading the product's owner's manual to help ensure that you understand the basics of how it's supposed to work. Ideally the manufacturer's service manual will provide detailed drawings and describe the recommended process for replacing parts, but this has become less common. All too often, only setup information is provided. An article in the *Wall Street Journal* in December 2018 told part of the story: "Instructions are not what — or where — they used to be." YouTube is the go-to site to that Repair Cafe fixperts across the country use when they're searching for information online. Next in popularity is Google, followed by iFixit, DuckDuckGo ("Mainly because it doesn't surveil me like Google does," explains one repair coach), GoodSearch, and Bluprint. Those who use YouTube like to use it for troubleshooting problems. One coach recommends watching "at least three demos to avoid an idiosyncratic fixer." Others use Google for information about a part, a component, an instructional manual, and "a method to fix."

Websites Recommended by Repair Coaches

- iFixit: The Free Repair Manual (ifixit.com) — Teardowns, repair guides, and answer forums appear for free on this site. "A real community affair, typical of the movement."
- Microsoft's community forum (answers.microsoft.com) — For instruction or troubleshooting.
- Appliance Parts (applianceparts.com) — For troubleshooting, appliance repairs, lawn equipment repairs, heating and cooling repairs, parts, and more.
- DIY Network (diynetwork.com/how-to/maintenance-and-repair): Tips and how-to instructions for common household repairs indoors and out.
- DoItYourself.com (doityourself.com): Information on home improvement and repairs for common problems.
- eReplacementParts.com (ereplacementparts.com) — For troubleshooting, excellent how-to videos, and parts. "They'll email documents pre-sale to help you figure out what's wrong and what you need."
- Family Handyman (familyhandyman.com) — Go to the site, then go to the pulldown menu and click on "How To & Repair."

- Repair Clinic (repairclinic.com) — Find parts for appliances, lawn and garden equipment, heating and cooling equipment, and more from the top brands in the industry.
- RepairPartsPlus (repairpartsplus.com) — iPhone parts, iPad parts, and cell phone parts.
- Sears Parts Direct (searspartsdirect.com/diy/repair-help) — "Step-by-step instructions and videos for repairing kitchen and laundry appliances, small appliances, lawn and garden equipment and more.... If you're not sure what the problem is, our descriptions of symptoms can help you pinpoint the solution."
- See Jane Drill (youtube.com/user/seejanedrill) — "The only DIY home improvement channel where a woman provides the instruction."
- TechNet (technet.microsoft.com) — For instruction or trouble-shooting.
- Bluprint (mybluprint.com) — For sewing and crafting classes.
- So Sew Easy (so-sew-easy.com) — A sewing blog with tips and tutorials for "new and improving sewers" that intends to "inspire, guide, and learn with you."

Lamp/Electrical Inventory and General Repair Cafe Supply Boxes

Lamp/Electrical Parts Suggested Startup Inventory

DESCRIPTION	QTY	MANUFACTURER
Lampholder/socket, 3 way, medium base, metal shell	6	Leviton 7090-PG or equivalent
Lampholder/socket, turn knob, medium base, metal shell	6	Leviton 10083-16 or equivalent
Lampholder/socket, push type, medium base, metal shell	6	Leviton 06098-PG or equivalent
Lampholder/socket, pull chain, medium base, metal shell	6	Leviton 19980-PG or equivalent
Lampholder/socket, 2 circuit, turn knob, medium base, metal shell	4	Leviton 70707-PG or equivalent
Switch, feed thru, inline, rocker, white	3	Leviton 5410-W or equivalent
Switch, feed thru, inline, rocker, brown	3	Leviton 5410 or equivalent

DESCRIPTION	QTY	MANUFACTURER
Switch, push button, SPST, on-off, wire leads	1	Gardner Bender GSW-24 or equivalent
Switch, rotary, SPST, on-off, wire leads	1	Gardner Bender GSW-61 or equivalent
Lamp wire, 18/2 SPT-1, white	100 feet	Southwire 49909503 or equivalent
Lamp wire, 18/2 SPT-1, brown	100 feet	Southwire 55680801 or equivalent
Plug, screw term, white, polarized, light duty	4	Leviton 101-WP or equivalent
Plug, screw term, brown, polarized, light duty	4	Leviton 101-P or equivalent
Plug, 15 amp, 2 wire, cord clamp	2	Leviton 115PR or equivalent
Plug, 15 amp, 3 wire, cord clamp	2	Leviton 515PV or equivalent
Socket, keyless, 2″, candelabra base	2	Satco 90-403 or equivalent
Socket, keyless, adjustable 3 1/4″ to 4 1/4″, candelabra base	2	Satco 90-402 or equivalent

Additional Electrical Supplies

Batteries: A small assortment of batteries may come in handy.

Glue: For quick repairs, Super Glue or epoxy. Ask your coaches for the specific products they'd recommend.

Bulbs: Have a regular light bulb and a 3-way bulb on hand for testing lamps brought in for repair. Often people do not bring in bulbs, or the bulbs they bring are no good.

Pricing: Price the repair parts in even dollar increments (for example, wire is $0.50/foot). This simplifies making change, and folks are happy to get their items repaired in one stop.

General Repair Supply Boxes

The event organizer should provide a box of basic supplies to be used by all. Ask your repair coaches to suggest additional items.

- Extension cords and surge bars
- 1 roll of duct tape to tape down extension cords
- 1 bottle each of carpenter's wood glue, single-use Super Glue, and epoxy glue
- 2 pairs of safety glasses
- 1 package of reusable shop towels
- 1 or 2 rolls of Carpenter Clamp Tape
- 1 roll of black electrical tape
- 1 package of sandpaper
- 1 package of assorted steel wool pads
- 1 can of WD-40
- 1 can of 3-in-One oil
- 1 bottle of rubbing alcohol
- 1 box of cotton swabs (Q-tips)
- 1 bag of cotton balls
- 1 box of toothpicks
- Basic first aid kit

APPENDIX THREE

Sample Repair Cafe
and Fixit Clinic Flyers and Forms

WELCOME!

&

OUR HOUSE RULES

▶ If you offer items for repair, you do so at your own risk. We invite you to watch & learn! Note that Repair Café is not a drop-off service.

▶ The persons making repairs offer no guarantee and may only be able to offer advice. Limit 2 items per person please.

▶ The organizers of Gardiner Repair Café, the Gardiner Library, and the repair coaches are not liable for any damage or loss resulting from work performed at the Repair Café.

<u>This is an all-volunteer community service project</u>

THANK YOU!

Rosewood Repair Café

Thursday August 10, 6-8pm

@Rosewood Initiative

16126 SE Stark St, Portland, OR 97233

Bring your broken items to be repaired for **FREE** by skilled volunteers. Items accepted include bikes, small appliances, electronics, and items needing mending or sewing.

<u>Not Accepted:</u> Televisions, Microwaves, or Small Engines.

¿Tiene usted cosas rotas que necesitan ser arregladas? ¡Únase a nosotros para este evento de reparación gratuito! Si usted desea más información en español acerca de nuestro evento de reparación, por favor llame al 503-618-2297.

У вас есть поломанные вещи, которые нуждаются в ремонте? Присоединяйтесь к нам в этом мероприятии бесплатного ремонта. Для получения дополнительной информации на русском языке пожалуйста звоните 503-618-2469.

www.repairpdx.org
Facebook: @RepairPDX
repairpdx@gmail.com
repaircafegresham@gmail.com
503-618-2694

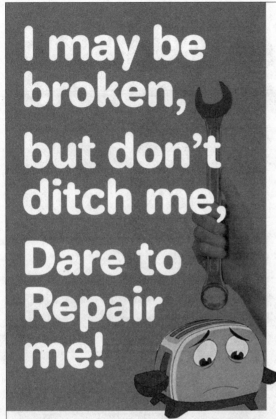

I may be broken, but don't ditch me, Dare to Repair me!

JOIN US AT AN UPCOMING EVENT

Dare to
RЦPAIR
Cafe

SATURDAY OCTOBER 19
9:00AM-12:00PM
Bennett Community School Campus
2885 Main Street
Buffalo, NY 14214

SATURDAY NOVEMBER 16
10:00AM-1:00PM
Herman Badillo Bilingual Academy
315 Carolina Street
Buffalo, NY 14201

SATURDAY DECEMBER 14
9:00AM-12:00PM
Southside Elementary School
430 Southside Pkwy
Buffalo, NY 14210

The **Dare to Repair Cafe** is a community event where individuals can bring broken items (lamps, small electronics, vacuums, toys, etc.) to the repair cafe and have volunteer "fixers" try to repair the item alongside them *for free!*

We're reducing waste by connecting those with a need to those with the know-how. Save money and help save the planet in the process!

Note: Repairs are not guaranteed and all participants will be required to sign a waiver. Replacement parts are limited, so bring 'em if ya got 'em!

PARTNERS IN REPAIR:
City of Buffalo Department of Recycling, The Tool Library, The CoLab, Knowledgefire, Preservation Buffalo Niagara, The Foundry, Valu Home Centers, NYS Department of Environmental Conservation, Friends of Reinstein Woods, UB Sustainability, Buffalo Promise Neighborhood, Say Yes Buffalo/BPS Community Schools, ISEP, Buffalo Museum of Science

thetoollibrary.org/daretorepair

#daretorepair
#fixitdontditchit

CALL FOR VOLUNTEERS!

Are you a tinkerer? Have fixing skills? Volunteer to be a Fix-It Coach!

FIXIT CLINIC

SATURDAY, JANUARY 11ᵀᴴ, 2020 2-5PM

Fix-It Clinic is an all-ages repair activity to try and fix broken household items rather than throw them "away". As a Fix-It Coach you will help participants disassemble, troubleshoot, and possibly FIX broken things. *Examples of items: household appliances, clothing and fabric, sewing machines, lamps, electronics, computers and phones, toys and wooden items, jewelry.*

For more information please contact Jed Foley at: wellfleetjed@gmail.com

  Wellfleet Public Library *(508) 349 – 0310* 55 W. Main Street, Wellfleet, MA 02667

Sponsored by Wellfleet Recycling Committee, Wellfleet Public Library, Boomerang Bags Cape Cod

REPAIR CAFÉ
N E W B U R G H

12PM–4PM   GRIT WORKS   115 BROADWAY NEWBURGH

OCTOBER 19TH 2019

COME VISIT OUR REPAIR COACHES AND GET YOUR ITEMS FIXED

FUNDING FOR
THIS PROJECT
WAS PROVIDED
IN PART BY:

AWESOME
FOUNDATION
NEWBURGH

CALL: 845.432.4033
FIND US ON FACEBOOK: NEWBURGH REPAIR CAFÉ

FREE
EVENT

GRIT WORKS
Co-working space in the heart of Newburgh

IMPACT!
INC.

NEWBURGH FREE ACADEMY
P›TECH

Get Ready to Repair!

Learn basic D.I.Y. skills at the Time Bank Skill Share Fair! Get simple fixes from Repair Café gurus hosted by Transition Howard County.

*Questions about time banking? Visit **Columbia.Timebanks.org** or call 410-884-6121. **Register your broken item at TransitionHoCo.org.***

FREE and OPEN to the public!
Saturday, November 16 · 1-4pm
East Columbia 50+ Center
6600 Cradlerock Way, Columbia

Learn a skill   Fix it fast   Connect with the sharing economy

Repair Café Fix-It Fair

1-4pm ..... Bring your broken items: Small appliances, bicycles, computers/devices, furniture/wood, clothing/sewing, jewelry, lamps, and more.

Time Bank Skill Share Fair

1pm ..... Lamp Repair 101

1:30pm ..... T-Shirt Bags

2pm ..... Origami: Let's Make a Bird

2:30pm ..... Intro to Holistic Healing

3pm ..... Koudi Quiltmaking

3:30pm ..... Ask a Fixer: Simple D.I.Y. Repair Hints

NEW 1-4pm ..... Tech Basics: Individual Consultations About Software

Time Bank Project Tables

1-4pm ..... Koudi quiltmaking; origami; plastic bag sleeping mats; T-shirt bags — bring your old T-shirts!; recycling basics

Sample House Rules (Long Form) and Job Ticket

For their safety, children must be accompanied by an adult or seated at the Kids Take It Apart Table.

Visitors are always responsible for their own items. The Repair Cafe team can't be held responsible for any unattended items.

All work carried out in the Repair Cafe is performed free of charge, on a voluntary basis, by the repair persons (AKA Repair Coaches) at hand.

Visitors carry out the repairs themselves whenever possible, but Repair Coaches can help.

If you offer items for repair, you do so at your own risk.

The organizers, sponsors, and any and all event co-sponsors of Repair Cafe Warwick, the Warwick Senior Center, Community2gether, Sustainable Warwick, Wickham Works, repair persons, and any and all volunteers, are not liable for any physical damage or loss resulting from work performed at the Repair Cafe.

Persons making repairs offer no guarantees and are not liable if objects repaired in the Repair Cafe turn out not to work properly at home.

Use of new materials supplied by the Repair Coaches such as leads, plugs, fuses, bike parts, etc., will be paid for separately.

Repair Coaches are entitled to refuse to repair certain objects at their discretion.

Repair Coaches are not obliged to reassemble disassembled appliances and other items that cannot be repaired.

Visitors to the Repair Cafe are solely responsible for the tidy removal of items that could not be repaired.

To cut down on unnecessary waiting times, during busy periods, a maximum of TWO items per person, including knives, scissors, and tools, will be examined.

Visitors will join the back of the line if they want to have a third item examined by a Repair Coach.

The Repair Cafe is free, but we do have expenses. A voluntary donation is greatly appreciated.

I HAVE READ AND AGREE TO THE HOUSE RULES.
SIGNATURE _____

Sample Job Ticket

Name _____ Email and/or Phone# _____

Repair Café HUDSON VALLEY

Town you are from _____ First time? Yes ☐ No ☐

OK to use your photo for Repair Café promotion? Yes ☐ No ☐

ITEM #1 for repair	ITEM #2 for repair
Item _____	Item _____
What's wrong? _____	What's wrong? _____
Fixed? Yes ☐ No ☐ Why not? _____	Fixed? Yes ☐ No ☐ Why not? _____
Helped by Date	Helped by Date

APPENDIX FIVE

Sample Letter to New Coaches

Thank you for your interest in volunteering to be a Repair Coach. As you know, the Repair Cafe is an all-volunteer, free community event, and no one involved receives any compensation. What's involved?

There are really two levels to being a Repair Coach. One is technical: your repair knowledge and ability to troubleshoot what can be done to fix the "beloved but broken" item a person brings to your table. The other is interpersonal and involves communicating and even some teaching.

A good Repair Coach is:

- A curious troubleshooter
- A good listener
- Interested in helping make the repair...but won't be frustrated if that isn't reasonable or possible

You will be in good company. There is a remarkable range of skills and talents in our community. I expect you will meet and make some good friends here. You'll likely collaborate on some of the repairs you undertake. No one expects you to know everything, so feel free to ask another coach to take a look. Two heads are better than one in this business, and it's more fun! Everyone is sharing, teaching, and learning — on both sides of the table.

We have worktables for our eight "core" categories of repair: Mechanical, Electrical & Electronic; Things Made of Wood; Clothing & Textiles; Jewelry, Dolls & Stuffed Animals; Digital Devices. Many Repair Cafes also offer bicycle repair, knife and tool blade sharpening, and even metal welding.

A common question has to do with tools. We recommend that you bring a few tools that you like and find particularly useful for your repair category. Tools are also often shared among our repair coaches. Some of the guys and gals bring a pretty good selection, so if you haven't got something, ask around to see who else might have just what you need to complete the repair. We have a "general supply box" of things for your safety and use: a basic first aid kit, protective eye goggles, heavy-duty paper towels, cloth rags, sandpaper, wood shims, heavy-duty rubber bands, "clamp tape," carpenter's wood glue and epoxys, rubbing alcohol, Q-tips, WD-40, contact cleaner, and a box-tray of screws and nails in a variety of sizes. (See Appendix 2 for a complete suggested list.)

At Repair Cafe we only "stock" basic lamp parts: sockets (several types), plugs, and wire (white and brown). It is a great help to customers to be able to identify the exact parts needed for their repairs; we love to send our customers to the local hardware store with a broken part or part description to say: "Repair Cafe sent me!" We value our relationship with our local hardware stores.

Some of our coaches are also true professionals who run repair businesses. We invite them to display their business cards. People sometimes bring items that cannot be reasonably fixed within the scope of the Repair Cafe (i.e., parts are needed or it would take too much time). These cases are your judgment call, and you can invite people to bring their items to you on another day at your normal rate of compensation.

A note about liability — every person who brings an item to you for repair will have signed this statement: *If you offer items for repair, you do so at your own risk. Neither the organizers of the Repair Cafe, the sponsors, nor the repair persons are liable for any physical damage or loss resulting from work performed at the Repair Cafe. Persons making repairs offer no guarantees.*

Once you've had the experience of fixing things for people you don't even know, we hope you'll want to come back for more! We have found that the level of gratification is very high on both sides of the table. Our goal is to run the Repair Cafe in a way that makes you feel appreciated and keeps you happy. We honor your knowledge and value your time.

The Repair Cafe is "open" for three or four hours — times vary at each community. It's good to arrive a half hour to twenty minutes ahead of opening to help set up your workstation. But you are not obligated to stay for the whole time if your schedule doesn't permit it. We say: come when you can, leave when you must.

Lastly, you will see that we put out a donation jar. The donated money, typically about one hundred dollars per event, goes for pizza (snacks and beverages are always free of charge to volunteers) and miscellaneous expenses, with the balance donated to the host organization, food pantry, or other local charity.

Please don't hesitate to call or email me with any questions. Our website calendar is always up-to-date at repaircafexxx.org. We invite you to like and follow our Facebook page: Repair Café–XXX. We are also active on Instagram.

Best,

[Organizer's name, email address, and phone number]

List of Recommended Items for Kids Take It Apart Table

J im Harper, a senior project manager for an engineering website, volunteers with sons Able (eight) and Eli (five) to man Warwick's Kids Take It Apart Table. Jim recommends the following list of items as particularly educationally appropriate for kids to take apart with adult supervision. Their component parts provide real learning opportunities if you are lucky enough to have an adult who understands and can describe how the parts make the product work. Note: all items you bring to the table should be "take-apartable" by removing screws; it's not safe for kids to try to pry things apart. You'll need to supply several screwdrivers of various sizes, including extra small. Jim also recommends using a battery pack to allow you to power an item and to show the kids the parts working (or partially working), without plugging it in to a wall socket (which would not be safe).

- LCD projectors (there is an awesome array of optics in older projectors)
- Overhead projectors (convex and fresnel lenses)
- Personal cassette players or tape decks (small motors, tape heads, switches)
- Analog or digital cameras (lenses, mechanical shutters, servos)
- Portable radios (digital and analog tuners, dials, and speakers)

- Remote-control toys (wheels, motors, servos, radio sets)
- Wind-up toys (gears, springs)
- Scanners and all-in-one printers (motors, gears, proximity sensors, light bars)
- Mechanical or electronic scales (springs, LEDs, rack-and-pinion gears, strain gauge sensors)
- Analog desk phones (speaker, microphone, mechanical dial, number pad, buttons)
- VCRs (motors, video heads)
- Audio speakers (speakers, magnets)
- Sewing machines (motors, gears, wheels, switches, springs)
- Mechanical typewriters (springs, gears, letter keys)
- Kitchen countertop appliances (mechanical parts, electromagnetic motors)

The following items are not recommended for the Kids Take It Apart Table: cell phones, computers, monitors, tube/CRT/flat panel TVs.

Acknowledgments

I n 2018, literary agent Deirdre Mullane brought some items to the Repair Cafe in Beacon, New York. She sat down at John's woodworking table and said, "I've been watching what goes on here. I think it's wonderful, and I think there's a book in this." She recognized that repair is about social change, and we couldn't have found a better shepherd for what turned out to be a rather massive undertaking. We are grateful for Deidre's encouragement, enthusiasm, and knowledge of the publishing industry.

To be paired with the right publisher was just as important. Jason Gardner, executive editor at New World Library, recognized the significance of this movement and championed this book. We are thankful for the attention and professionalism, as well as the support of the whole New World Library publishing team — especially Kristen Cashman, Tracy Cunningham, Tona Pearce Myers, and Monique Muhlenkamp — and copyeditor Patricia Heinicke.

Our book grew out of months and months of research, interviews, and communications with more than one hundred people across the U.S., Canada, and the world who are also committed to the repair revolution. We're indebted to everyone who took the time to share their stories, insights, and resources. We've done our very best to accurately report what they told us.

John Wackman

When Elizabeth and I undertook this book, we knew we wanted to include as many voices as possible and represent repair initiatives in every part of the United States. We wrote a questionnaire and sent it to every Repair Cafe in the country, a long list of Fixit Clinics, and as many Tool Libraries as we could find, with this message: "Here's the way we see it: This is our book and YOUR book. We ask you to share this questionnaire with all of your fixers and menders, your welcome table team, coffee makers, and brownie bakers — anyone and everyone who shows up to build community and keep things out of the landfill."

We are grateful to everyone who responded.

Thanks to the repair organizers who have shared so much. They include Ray Pfau in Bolton, Massachusetts; Don Fick in North Carolina's Research Triangle; Don Shriner in Ellensburg, Washington; Jeanette Nakada and Larry James in Lincoln, Nebraska.

Thanks to all the places and partners who have championed community repair: the churches, libraries, town and village halls, and community and senior centers.

To Pastor Better Sohm and Margaret Howe at New Paltz United Methodist Church, who in a heartbeat said, "Yes, please! We'd love to have that here." I am so grateful to all our dedicated repair coaches and volunteers in New Paltz, where this all started for me, including those who were the first core group: Ken Fix It, Wolf Bravo, Felicia Casey, Helen Karsten, Dawn Elliott, Barbara Lane, Leah Stukes, Renee Rosenberg, Rob Greene, Frank Burnham, and Patrick Murphy.

The grassroots organizers who helped get repair off the ground in the Hudson Valley: the New Paltz Climate Action Coalition, especially Ann and Dan Guenther, Miriam Strouse, and Kimiko Link; Kingston Transition, especially Gai and Dimitri Galitzine; and Woodstock Transition, especially Caroline and Kirk Ritchey.

For bringing the books in: the Mid-Hudson Library System and my local bookstore, Inquiring Minds (thank you, Rebekkah and Jai).

To our colleagues in the Right to Repair movement: Gay Gordon-Byrne, Nathan Proctor, Kyle Wiens, and Peter Mui.

The staff of the New York State Department of Environmental Conservation: Amy Bloomfield, Terry Laibach, and Dazzle Eckblad.

To the Omega Institute in Rhinebeck, New York, and Laura Weiland for welcoming our work.

To the incredible group of educators at the RISD Museum in Providence, Rhode Island. Their exhibition *Repair and Design Futures* widened our understanding of everything repair can mean.

To the Good Work Institute, which deepened my understanding of the economic and social challenges the repair revolution aspires to address and introduced me to so many others doing good work.

This book is focused on repair in the United States. We have not been able to write much about the incredible global movement of repairers we have corresponded with, primarily through the portal of Instagram and the Restart Project. (Hello, Purna in Bengaluru, Fern in Toronto, Pierre in Paris, Ugo in London!) We'd love to see others write books about the repair revolution from the cultural perspective of every continent.

To my brother, Chris, and sister, Anne, with whom I shared memories of our mom and dad.

And finally, thank you to my darling companion, Holly.

Elizabeth Knight

I would like to thank Eleanor Nicholson Knight, my mother, for inviting me and my sister, Amy, to help her set up the library on the U.S. Air Force Base in Taranto, Italy. Mom didn't mind when we girls wandered off to read a book instead of shelve it.

I would like to thank my husband, Roger Moss, because whenever I say, "I think this community needs…," he always says, "Go do it!" and shows up to help.

I would like to thank my friend Deanne Singer, who always says, "You can do it," followed by "And you know, *we* could do…"

I would like to thank my friend Sharon Halper, who says, "We're not obligated to save the world, but we each must help the person at the end of our hand."

I'd like to thank Jerry Fischetti, who was the first person to raise his hand and volunteer to be a repair coach. Jerry celebrated his eighty-eighth birthday fixing things for many people he didn't even know at Orange County, New York's very first Repair Cafe.

I would like to thank Sustainable Warwick and Community2gether for sponsoring our Repair Cafe, now in its fourth year of community service.

I would like to thank all the cheerful, dedicated, talented, generous volunteers, from at least nine different towns and two states, who have enriched my life by their example. You give me hope and make me laugh.

I'd like to thank the hundreds of people who have walked through the Warwick Senior Center doors and trusted us with their beloved but broken items and their stories about what those things mean to them. Now they matter to me too.

Notes

Introduction

p. 2   *"Convenience decides everything":* Evan Williams, cofounder of Twitter, quoted in Tim Wu, "The Tyranny of Convenience," *New York Times*, February 18, 2018.

p. 2   *one of the greatest sources of human enjoyment:* Edith Hall, *Aristotle's Way*, p. 27, 33, and Nicomachean Ethics 10.7. I am grateful to Christopher C. Raymond, assistant professor of philosophy at Vassar College for his perspective on Aristotle's view of how knowledge contributes to well-being.

p. 2   *"All over the world, people are pooling their resources":* Northeast Recycling Council newsletter, "Repair Cafés — Is There One in Your Neighborhood?" February 18, 2014, nerc.org/news-and-updates/blog/nerc-blog/2014/02/18/repair-caf%C3%A9sis-there-one-in-your-neighborhood.

p. 3   *"The idea is exquisitely simple":* NBC Sunday Today, "Repairing Things, Restoring Hearts," April 16, 2017.

p. 4   *"In Europe, we throw out so many things":* Martine Postma, quoted in Sally McGrane, "An Effort to Bury a Throwaway Culture One Repair at a Time," *New York Times*, May 8, 2012.

p. 5   *The Dutch Ministry of the Environment decided to fund:* Information about the formative days of the Repair Café Foundation are from an interview with Martine Postma and Judy Sijlbing recorded and transcribed by JW, Amsterdam, Holland, July 10, 2018.

p. 5   *The idea is eminently replicable:* Information about the first four Repair Cafes in the United States is from organizational records provided by Repair Café Foundation International.

p. 11   *which, according to the calculation method used by a British researcher:* "One Repair Can Prevent 24 Kilos of CO_2 Emissions" [in Dutch], Repair Café International Foundation website, January 21, 2019, https://repaircafe.org /een-reparatie-kan-24-kilo-co2-uitstoot-voorkomen.

p. 12   *"The value of the Repair Cafe":* William McDonough, "*New York Times* Features 'Repair Cafe' in the Netherlands, inspired by Cradle to Cradle," William McDonough + Partners website, May 31, 2012, https://mcdonoughpartners .com/new-york-times-features-repair-cafe-in-the-netherlands-inspired-by -cradle-to-cradle.

p. 12   *"It's very much a sign of the times":* Evelien H. Tonkens, quoted in Sally McGrane, "An Effort to Bury a Throwaway Culture One Repair at a Time," *New York Times*, May 8, 2012.

p. 13   *"see their own community in the midst of cooperation":* The "signal we send" statement was written by John Wackman and Martine Postma, inspired, in part, by an editorial printed in the *New Paltz Times* on January 29, 2015, written by Paul Brown titled "Repairing New Paltz." In the editorial, Paul referred to "a basic lack of problem-solving and decision-making skills" on the part of the town and village's elected officials. Of his experience attending his local Repair Cafe, he wrote: "Although I was of course thrilled that the vacuum cleaner was repaired, that success turned out to be just a small part of what made the experience so much fun. Equally important was the sense of community spirit, the camaraderie and the laughter. And in the midst of all this cooperation, conviviality and downright decency, goals were achieved and positive outcomes realized." Paul Brown, "Repairing New Paltz," *Hudson Valley One*, February 4, 2015, https://hudsonvalleyone.com /2015/02/04/repairing-new-paltz.

p. 16   *"Economic development has created persistent assaults on the global ecosystem":* Susan Strasser, *Waste and Want*, p. 16.

p. 16   *"Ours is not the task of fixing the entire world all at once":* Clarissa Pinkola Estés, "Letter to a Young Activist in Troubled Times," *Resilience Circles*, March 10, 2011, https://localcircles.org/2011/03/10/letter-to-a-young-activist -during-troubled-times-by-clarissa-pinkola-estes.

Chapter 1: The Community Repair Experience

p. 19   *The museum, housed in a home built in 1907:* The Museum of American Heritage, www.moah.org.

p. 27   *"I explained to the mother what I did and why":* Bob Berkowitz, written response to our questionnaire, 2019.

p. 27   *Winterling got an education one morning:* Ken Winterling, written response to our questionnaire, 2019.

p. 27   *"Sometimes the challenge is not how to fix an item":* Naomi Aubain, written response to our questionnaire, 2019.

p. 28   *Charles Goedeke, a retired electrical engineer and organizer of a Repair Cafe:* Charles Goedeke, written response to our questionnaire, 2019.

p. 30   *"Last week my paper shredder refused":* Robin Romeo, written in a Facebook comment following her visit to the Repair Cafe in New Paltz, New York, in July 2019.

p. 30   *"I always tell people when they get a sewing machine":* Jackie Carter, quoted in the Moscow, Idaho, *Daily News*, October 15, 2018.

p. 31   *Mario Fernandez, one of the organization's outreach workers, told Rich:* Elizabeth was present at two of the three bike deliveries accepted by Mario between May and September 2017–2019 and recalls this story.

p. 32   *fondly remembers "hanging out under my family's dining room table":* Michele S., written response to our questionnaire, 2019.

p. 32   *"Our boys never complain about going to the RC":* Raheli Harper, recorded and transcribed interview with EK, text confirmed by Raheli via email, June 27, 2019.

p. 33   *"The Repair Cafe is one part of why I moved my family":* Regina Shaw, written response to our questionnaire, 2019.

p. 34   *A boy who wanted to fix a part on his game console:* Tom Treat, written response to our questionnaire, 2019.

p. 34   *"My youngest son is on the autism spectrum":* Colleen M. Johnston, written response to our questionnaire, 2019.

p. 36   *"I love to experience the singular joy of repairing":* Steve Carras, written response to our questionnaire, 2019.

p. 36   *"My definition of local is planet Earth":* Heidi Spinella, written response to our questionnaire, 2019.

p. 36   *Back during Warwick's very first Repair Cafe:* Edwin Winstanley, as recalled by EK in a follow-up report emailed to RC volunteers, including Winstanley, December 9, 2016.

p. 39   *"More than once a parent has come in":* Dära Salk, written response to our questionnaire, 2019.

p. 39   *he uses the same management skills as a volunteer:* Dan Barkevich, written response to our questionnaire, 2019.

p. 40   *As a kid, he learned to sew patches on his Cub Scout uniform:* Jonathan Ment, written response to our questionnaire, 2019.

p. 40   *"Everything that comes in here has had a life":* Cathe' Linton, as recalled by EK in a follow-up report emailed to RC volunteers, including Linton, July 17, 2017.

p. 41   *an older woman rushes in, clutching a braided silver chain:* Susanne O'Brien, as recalled by EK in a follow-up report emailed to RC volunteers, including O'Brien, December 9, 2016.

p. 41   *"Once, a young woman presented me with a bracelet":* Barbara Lane, written response to our questionnaire, 2019.

p. 41   *"When I fix something for someone, even just a lamp":* Larry James, written response to our questionnaire, 2019.

p. 42   *On a Wednesday evening at the Fixers Collective:* Vincent Lai, Emily Forman, Joe Holdner, and David Kline, Fixers Collective, Brooklyn, New York. From a conversation recorded by JW at Brooklyn Commons on April 4, 2019.

p. 43   *"It's nice to know that with the news":* Ethan Bele, as recalled by EK, September 16, 2017.

Chapter 2: The Road to Sustainability

p. 45   *"Every decently-made object":* Kevin McCloud, *43 Principles of Home,* Principle 30. The quote accompanies the "Materials Science" exhibition at the Chicago Public Library, which is where I found it.

p. 45   *In southwestern Pennsylvania, an archeological site called Meadowcroft Rock-shelter:* Information collected by JW during visit to the site on June 1, 2019.

p. 45   *"We cannot exist without tools":* Lucy Johnson, professor emeritus, Department of Anthropology, Vassar College, from her course syllabus for "Tools and Human Behavior." Used with author's permission.

p. 46   *Archeologists have found "drilled holes on each side of a crack":* Stanley South, "Archeological Evidence of Pottery Repairing."

p. 46   *"to drill the nation's first commercial oil well":* American Oil and Gas Historical Society website, AOGHS.org editors, "First American Oil Well." Also, Bud Pelaghi, historian of the Venango Museum of Art, Science & Industry, Oil City, Pennsylvania, phone interview with JW, October 19, 2019.

p. 47   *In 1733, Ben Franklin published the first edition:* "Poor Richard's Almanack," Ben Franklin Historical Society website, www.benjamin-franklin-history.org/poor-richards-almanac.

p. 47   *"Herein lies one of the strangest of American beliefs":* Eric Sloane, *Return to Taos,* 36.

p. 48   *"It is easy to see that a greater self-reliance":* Ralph Waldo Emerson, *Essays, Poems, Addresses,* 138.

p. 48   *"There is a close intellectual lineage":* Andrew L Yarrow, *Thrift: The History of an American Cultural Movement,* p. 160. Yarrow's chapter "From Thrift to Sustainability" offers a full and insightful analysis of that lineage.

p. 48   *"All repairing must be done by hand":* Susan Strasser, *Waste and Want,* p. 10. Strasser cites her source: Charles Godfrey Leland, *A Manual of Mending and Repairing, with Diagrams,* published in New York by Dodd, Mead in 1896.

p. 49   *"University of the Wilderness":* John Muir, *The Story of My Boyhood and Youth,* p. 287.

p. 50   *"When we try to pick out anything by itself"*: John Muir, *My First Summer in the Sierra*, p. 110. See also sierraclub.org, "The John Muir Exhibit," which points out how often Muir's words have been paraphrased and misquoted.

p. 50   *Aldo Leopold entered the University of Wisconsin:* The Aldo Leopold Foundation website, aldoleopold.org.

p. 50   *"All ethics so far evolved rest upon a single premise"*: Aldo Leopold, *A Sand County Almanac*, p. 203.

p. 50   *"man-made changes are of a different order"*: Aldo Leopold, *A Sand County Almanac*, p. 218.

p. 51   *"People everywhere are today disobeying the law of obsolescence"*: Bernard London, "Ending the Depression through Planned Obsolescence" [pamphlet], Hathi Trust Digital Library, https://babel.hathitrust.org/cgi/pt?id=wu.89097035273&view=1up&seq=9#.

p. 51   *"Though the policy was not implemented at that time"*: Giles Slade, *Made to Break*, 81.

p. 52   *"Why is it prohibited?" asked the Savage:* Aldous Huxley, *Brave New World*, p. 262.

p. 52   *by 1943, about one-third of all the vegetables:* Stuart A. Kallen, *The War at Home*, pp. 43–44.

p. 52   *"Eat what you can, and can what you can't"*: William L. O'Neill, *A Democracy at War*, p. 137.

p. 53   *"The American economy's ultimate purpose is to produce"*: Raymond Saulnier, chairman of President Eisenhower's Council of Economic Advisors, January 27, 1959, Congressional Hearing before the Joint Economic Committee.

p. 53   *In 1863, in their home in Sterling:* "Butterick History," Butterick-McCall website, n.d., butterick.mccall.com/our-company/butterick-history.

p. 54   Popular Mechanics *began publishing in 1902: Popular Mechanics* website, https://www.popularmechanics.com/about/a45/about-us.

p. 54   *Frank Szenher, a Repair Café volunteer:* Frank Szenher, written account emailed to JW, March 11, 2018.

p. 55   *"We are as gods and might as well get good at it"*: Stewart Brand, *The Whole Earth Catalog*, Statement of Purpose, p. 2.

p. 55   *"The Whole Earth Catalog was one of the bibles"*: Steve Jobs, Stanford University commencement speech, June 12, 2005. Text on the Stanford University website, https://news.stanford.edu/2005/06/14/jobs-061505.

p. 55   For a twenty-first-century version of *The Whole Earth Catalog*, see "Cool Tools: A Catalog of Possibilities" created by Kevin Kelly, cool-tools.org.

p. 56   *"This would be my biggest, scariest project by far"*: Andrew Willner, written account emailed to JW, August 21, 2019.

p. 57   *social psychologists try to track how changes:* E.J. Milner-Gulland, "Interactions between Human Behaviour and Ecological Systems," Philosophical

Transactions/Royal Publishing Society, cited in PubMed Central, U.S. Library of Medicine, January 19, 2012, https://www.ncbi.nlm.nih.gov/pmc/articles/PMC3223800.

p. 57   *The American public has generally balanced protection:* Jeffrey M. Jones, "Americans' Identification as Environmentalists Down to 42%," Gallup, April 22, 2016, https://news.gallup.com/poll/190916/americans-identification-environmentalists-down.aspx.

p. 57   *"With the possible exception of China":* Andrew Yarrow, *Thrift*, p. 136.

p. 58   *the desire to own something a little newer:* Brooks Stevens, quoted in Giles Slade, *Made to Break*, p. 153.

p. 58   *the volume of waste generated in the United States rose five times faster:* Beth Porter, *Reduce, Reuse, Reimagine*, p. 25.

p. 58   *sustainability is the subject of a broad debate or "discourse":* John Dryzek, *The Politics of the Earth*, p. 7–8. "A discourse is a shared way of apprehending the world."

p. 58   *"the sustainable society envisioned by so many":* Jeremy L. Caradonna, *Sustainability: A History*, p. 254.

p. 59   *"It smelled like a septic tank":* Tim Folger, "The Cuyahoga River Caught Fire 50 Years Ago. It Inspired a Movement," *National Geographic*, June 21, 2019.

p. 59   *"Build an extraordinary boat and people would come":* Betsy Garthwaite, "Restoring Clearwater," *Wooden Boat*, p. 3.

p. 60   *"Sailing down my dirty stream":* words and music by Pete Seeger, first recorded on *God Bless the Grass*, Smithsonian Folkways Recordings, 1964. Lyrics have been quoted in many publications, including David Schuyler, *Embattled River*, p. 57.

p. 60   *"If towns up and down the river start putting in waterfront parks":* Pete Seeger, quoted in David Schuyler, *Embattled River*, p. 60.

p. 61   *"The great privilege of the Americans is to be able to have repairable mistakes":* Alexis de Tocqueville, *Democracy in America*, vol. 1, part 2, chap. 6, p. 222.

p. 61   *the recycling industry has largely been an export business:* Katherine Wei, "Plastic Waste Piles Up as China's Ban Goes into Effect," *Sierra*, February 3, 2018, sierraclub.org/sierra/plastic-waste-piles-china-s-ban-goes-effect.

p. 61   *the results of a social marketing study conducted at Boston University:* Shankar Vedantam, "Why Recycling Options Lead People to Waste More," *Hidden Brain*, NPR, June 2, 2017, www.npr.org/2017/06/02/531173499/why-recycling-options-lead-people-to-waste-more.

p. 61   *The conference title was "Keeping Cool":* Conference materials for the twenty-eighth annual NYS Recycling Conference, "Keeping Cool in an Age of Climate Change: Impacts of Materials Management," New York State Department of Environmental Conservation, Cooperstown, New York, November 7–9, 2017.

p. 62   *Five years earlier, China had instituted its Green Fence rules:* Brad Plumer,
"China Doesn't Even Want to Buy Our Garbage Anymore," May 9, 2013,
www.washingtonpost.com/news/wonk/wp/2013/05/09/chinas-crackdown-on
-trash-could-make-it-harder-for-u-s-cities-to-recycle.

p. 62   *"There was a lot of uncertainty in the room":* Dan Lilkas-Rain, transcribed
telephone interview with JW, March 18, 2019.

p. 62   *"We are in a crisis moment in the recycling movement":* Fiona Ma, quoted in
"As Costs Surge, Cities' Recycling Becomes Refuse," Michael Corkery, *New
York Times,* March 17, 2019.

p. 62   *The Chinese standard has proven to be impossible:* Rob Cole, "Increased China
0.5 Per Cent Contamination Limit a 'Very Challenging Target,'" Resource.
com, November 21, 2017, resource.co/article/increased-china-05-cent
-contamination-limit-very-challenging-target-12253.

p. 62   *"I think the Chinese have done us a tremendous favor":* Neil Seldman, recorded and transcribed telephone interview with JW, May 23, 2019.

p. 63   *To prove his point, Seldman offers this analysis:* Neil Seldman, email to
JW, October 21, 2019.

p. 63   *The operation realizes a "quadruple bottom line":* Saint Vincent de Paul
Society of Lane County (Oregon) website, svdp.us.

p. 64   *"Almost every municipality has an environmental street":* "Competition for
circular craft centers," Repair Café Foundation website, April 30, 2019.

p. 65   *The Post Landfill Action Network (PLAN) was started:* www.postlandfill.org.
Telephone and email exchange with Alex Freid, organization founder and
codirector, December 15–16, 2019.

p. 66   *"consumption time bomb" and "material intensity":* The World Economic
Forum, the Ellen MacArthur Foundation, and McKinsey & Company,
Towards the Circular Economy, vol. 2, *Opportunities for the Consumer Goods
Sector.*

p. 66   *the Institute of Earth, Ocean, and Atmospheric Sciences at Rutgers:* Stephen
Leahy, "Hidden Costs of Climate Change Running Hundreds of Billions a
Year," *National Geographic,* September 27, 2017, www.nationalgeographic.com
/news/2017/09/climate-change-costs-us-economy-billions-report/#close.

p. 66   *More than a hundred years ago, British economists recognized:* Sarah Gonzalez,
"Decades Ago, British Economist Created the Framework for a Carbon Tax,"
NPR Morning Edition "Planet Money," November 7, 2019, https://www
.npr.org/2019/11/07/777133401/decades-ago-british-economist-created-the
-framework-for-a-carbon-tax.

p. 67   *We just haven't chosen to use them:* See Mariana Mazzucato, *The Value of
Everything,* p. 132. "Consider a river polluted by industrial waste. When
the polluter pays to clean it up, the expenditure is treated as a cost which
reduces profits and GDP. But when the government pays another company

to clean up the river, the expenditure adds to GDP because paying workers adds value. If the cost of cleaning up pollution is borne by someone other than the polluter it is called an externality — the cost is 'outside' the polluter's profit-and-loss account — and increases GDP. Simon Kuznets argues that such a calculation should be balanced by the 'dis-service' that has been created by the pollution, and therefore that the cost of that 'dis-service' be taken out of the 'net' calculation of value added. But national accounts do not do that: instead they state that it is not 'appropriate' or 'analytically useful' for 'economic accounts to try to correct for presumed institutional failures of this kind by attributing costs to producers that society does not choose to recognize."

p. 67   *what biologist Garrett Hardin described as the "tragedy of the commons":* Garrett Hardin, "The Tragedy of the Commons," *Science* 162 (no. 3859), 1243–1248.

p. 67   *"We need to decouple growth from environmental impact":* Paul Polman, quoted in David Gelles, "To Drive Change, Look Past the Bottom Line," *New York Times*, September 1, 2019, www.nytimes.com/2019/08/29/business /paul-polman-unilever-corner-office.html.

p. 68   *"meeting the needs of the current generation":* United Nations, "Our Common Future," chapter 2, "Towards Sustainable Development," conclusion (no page number), http://www.un-documents.net/ocf-02.htm#I.

p. 68   *It must also be a "just transition":* Among many resources, see Movement Generation website, Justice and Ecology Project, https://movementgeneration .org/about/our-theory-of-change.

p. 68   *The economic model that is gaining the most momentum:* Kirsi Sormunen and Kimmo Tiilikainen, "The Circular Economy Enters the World Stage," *The Guardian*, June 6, 2017, www.theguardian.com/global-development -professionals-network/2017/jun/06/the-circular-economy-enters-the-world -stage-with-finland-leading-the-way.

p. 68   *"What is the entire system":* William McDonough and Michael Braungart, *Cradle to Cradle*, p. 82.

p. 68   *The 2014 report estimated the economic benefits:* The World Economic Forum, the Ellen MacArthur Foundation, and McKinsey & Company, *Towards the Circular Economy*, vol. 3, *Accelerating the Scale-up across Global Supply Chains*, report summary, January 24, 2014, www.ellenmacarthurfoundation.org/publi- cations/towards-the-circular-economy-vol-3-accelerating-the-scale-up-across- global-supply-chains.

p. 69   *The foundation's 2019 follow-up report:* The World Economic Forum, the Ellen MacArthur Foundation, and McKinsey & Company, *Completing the Picture: How the Circular Economy Tackles Climate Change*, September 2019, p. 12.

p. 70   *"Re-thinking how we manufacture industrial products":* International Re- source Panel, *Re-defining Value: The Manufacturing Revolution*, www.resource panel.org/reports/re-defining-value-manufacturing-revolution.

p. 70   *"A 2019 survey of U.S. business leaders"*: Article posted by ING Wholesale Banking, "How Circular Thinking Could Change U.S. Business Models" January 2020. www.ingwb.com/themes/americas-here-i-come-articles/how -circular-thinking-could-change-us-business-models. The full survey is available for download at this site.

p. 70   *"We do not know how the shift will come about"*: The World Economic Forum, the Ellen MacArthur Foundation, and McKinsey & Company, *Towards the Circular Economy*, vol. 1, *An Economic and Business Rationale for an Accelerated Transition*, executive summary, p. 11.

p. 70   *"It's hard work. The road to change has a lot of skeptics"*: Paul Polman, quoted in David Gelles, "To Drive Change, Look Past the Bottom Line," *New York Times*, September 1, 2019, www.nytimes.com/2019/08/29/business/paul-polman -unilever-corner-office.html. After stepping down from Unilever in 2018, Polman started Imagine, a consulting firm focused on environment and social responsibility ("Unleashing business to achieve our global goals"), https://imagine.one.

p. 71   *the typical electric drill is used for only twelve to thirteen minutes*: Rachel Botsman, "The Case for Collaborative Consumption," TED Talk, December 2010. See also Rachel Botsman, "The Currency of the New Economy Is Trust," TED Talk, September 2012.

p. 72   *"What if all the effort spent on recycling over the last fifty years"*: Joel Newman, "How Many R's Is Enough?," Repair Reflections blog post on Portland Repair Finder website, May 28, 2019, www.portlandrepairfinder.com/how-many -rs-is-enough.

p. 72   *The Manhattan Solid Waste Advisory Board and the Citizens Committee for New York City*: CitizensNYC.org, "Grantee Projects," 2019, www.citizensnyc .org/grantee-projects.

p. 72   *New York State made it a priority to significantly decrease*: NY State Department of Environmental Conservation, Division of Materials Management Solid Waste Plan Stakeholder Meeting, New Paltz, New York, February 28, 2019. Subsequent email correspondence with DEC staff, December 8–9, 2019.

p. 73   *"Repair economies don't regard material things as expendable"*: Katherine Wilson, "A 'Repair Economy' Might Fix More than Just Stuff — It Could Fix Us as Well," World Economic Forum website, June 18, 2019, www.weforum.org /agenda/2019/06/mending-hearts-how-a-repair-economy-creates-a-kinder -more-caring-community.

Chapter 3: The Wisdom of Repair

p. 75   *The* Oxford English Dictionary *takes the position that it is "impossible to attempt a complete record"*: *OED*, cited in "re-," Online Etymology Dictionary, www.etymonline.com/word/re-.

p. 76   *"Sorry," says Merriam-Webster, "it's too late to fix this problem":* "A Tale of Two 'Repairs,'" Word History blog, Merriam-Webster website, www.merriam -webster.com/words-at-play/a-tale-of-two-repairs.

p. 77   *"My experience of the world is that things left to themselves don't get right":* Thomas Henry Huxley, *Science and Education,* p. 439.

p. 78   *"Is it the imaginary nineteenth-century world":* Steven J. Jackson, "Rethinking Repair," chapter 11 in *Media Technologies,* p. 221.

p. 78   *"deep wonder and appreciation of the subtle arts of repair":* Steven Jackson, "Rethinking Repair," in *Media Technologies,* p. 222.

p. 78   *"Repair is a radical act of resistance to the unmaking of our environment":* These sentences are based on and build upon a portion of exhibition text written by Kate Irvin from *Repair and Design Futures* at the RISD Museum of Art, Rhode Island School of Design, October 5, 2018–June 30, 2019. Kate Irvin, exhibition curator. Her text reads: "Repair, a humble act born of necessity, expresses resistance to the unmaking of our world and the environment." Used by permission.

p. 81   *"an impulsive habit of material problem solving":* Katherine Wilson, *Tinkering,* p. 5.

p. 81   *"this ineffable thing called tinkering":* Katherine Wilson, *Tinkering,* p. 1.

p. 81   *"Despite its fascination with things and bits":* David Pescovitz, BoingBoing blogpost, "Alex Pang on Tinkering," May 29, 2009, https://boingboing.net /2009/05/29/alex-pang-on-tinkeri.html.

p. 81   *"Tinkering offers a way":* Alex Pang, quoted in BoingBoing blog post, "Alex Pang on Tinkering."

p. 82   *"It's the ability to look at things maybe two degrees off-center":* Tom Joscelyn, interview recorded and transcribed by JW, August 8, 2018.

p. 82   "Hey Dad, you want to tinker?": Erik Hoover, interview recorded and transcribed by JW, September 19, 2019.

p. 83   *Maintenance engineers offer a cost-benefit analysis they call the "iceberg model":* John Grant, "Maintenance — The Tip of the Iceberg," Festival of Maintenance website, June 18, 2019, https://festivalofmaintenance.org.uk/2019/06/18 /maintenance-the-tip-of-the-iceberg.

p. 84   *Festival of Maintenance is "a celebration of those who maintain different parts of our world":* Festival of Maintenance website, www.festivalofmaintenance .org.uk/about-us.

p. 84   *"In rich countries, as far as domestic equipment is concerned…repair no longer exists":* David Edgerton, *The Shock of the Old,* p. 81.

p. 84   *"We've been inspired by different practices elsewhere in the world":* Ugo Valauri, transcribed by JW from the video "Our Story, Our Community" on the Restart Project website, https://therestartproject.org/about.

p. 86   *"We live in a world of things":* Leonard Koren, *Wabi-Sabi for Artists, Designers, Poets & Philosophers,* p. 59.

p. 86   *"Beauty can be coaxed out of ugliness":* Leonard Koren, *Wabi-Sabi for Artists*, p. 51.

p. 86   *"The good things of the past were not so often* articles*":* Eric Sloane, *Diary of an Early American Boy, 1805*, p. viii.

p. 87   *events they call "The Timeless Art of Repair":* Also on display are "make-do's" from Locust Lawn's collection — everyday objects that have been ingeniously repaired — a broken porcelain dish reassembled with staples, for example. Once considered "orphans" of the antiques world, they are now collectible. See interior designer Andrew Baseman's blog "Past Imperfect: The Art of Inventive Repair."

p. 87   *"It should be more than just about making":* Alexander Langlands, *Craeft*, pp. 339–40.

p. 88   *"there's a critical link between symptoms of depression and key areas of the brain":* Kelly Lambert, *Lifting Depression,* pp. 6–7.

p. 88   *Britain's Health Ministry, in response to statistics:* Chris Smyth, "Doctors Urged to Offer More Gardening Courses and Fewer Pills," *Sunday Times,* July 23, 2018, www.thetimes.co.uk/article/doctors-urged-to-offer-more-gardening -courses-and-fewer-pills-to-treat-mental-health-problems-pn20xdjdz.

p. 88   *Men's Sheds is a prime example:* "What Is a Men's Shed?" Men's Sheds Association website, https://menssheds.org.uk/about/what-is-a-mens-shed.

p. 88   *"a hand-eye-head-heart-body coordination":* Alexander Langlands, *Craeft,* p. 22.

p. 89   *"It simply implies there is an intersection between mending and being mindful":* Katrina Rodabaugh, "Mendfulness and the Long Journey to Repair," *Made by Katrina* (blog), February 24, 2014, http://katrinarodabaugh.blogspot.com /2014/02/mendfulness-and-long-journey-to-repair.html.

p. 89   *"If your desire is a garment that is repairable":* Dawn Elliott, interview recorded and transcribed by JW, July 17, 2019.

p. 89   *"Mending embraces the fact that when we wear clothes":* Raheli Harper, response to author's questionnaire, 2019.

p. 90   *Lisa Z. Morgan, department head for apparel design at the Rhode Island School of Design, says:* Lisa Z. Morgan, interview recorded and transcribed by JW, February 16, 2019.

p. 91   *In Amsterdam in 2008, the artist collective Platform21:* "Platform21 = Repairing," https://www.platform21.nl/index.php.html.

p. 91   *Proteus Gowanus started its Fixers Collective:* Robin Lestere, "Proteus Gowanus: Communal Repairs," *Project for Public Spaces,* May 18, 2009, https://www.pps.org/article/proteus-gowanus-communal-repairs.

p. 91   *"Jan gave me a bag of LEGO":* Dispatchwork website, www.dispatchwork .info/92-khak-st-sulaymaniyah-amnasuraka-irak/.

p. 92   *agency is the ability of individuals to act on their intentions:* Nicki Lisa Cole, "How Scientists Define Human Agency," ThoughtCo, January 22, 2019, www.thoughtco.com/agency-definition-3026036.

p. 92   *Matthew Crawford considers the merits of "individual agency in a shared world":* Matthew B. Crawford, *Shop Class as Soulcraft*, p. 205.

p. 93   *The organizers titled her presentation "Repair Cafe":* Martine Postma's presentation can be viewed through the Omega Institute's online archives: https://vimeo.com/315997079/bac28befd1.

p. 94   *Luria saw that God filled the entire universe:* Irwin Kula, *Yearnings: Embracing the Sacred Messiness of Life,* p. 295.

p. 95   *"So often in religion we start with a stain or a sin or moral judgment":* Irwin Kula, telephone interview recorded and transcribed by JW, June 11, 2019.

p. 95   *"We see our separateness from each other as the cause of poverty, injustice, and suffering":* Irwin Kula, *Yearnings: Embracing the Sacred Messiness of Life,* p. 296.

p. 95   *"Broken shards are everywhere":* Irwin Kula, *Yearnings: Embracing the Sacred Messiness of Life,* pp. 296–97.

p. 95   *"Repair Cafe makes it okay and laudable":* Irwin Kula, telephone interview recorded and transcribed by JW, June 11, 2019.

p. 95   *"The metaphor is so rich":* Irwin Kula, telephone interview recorded and transcribed by JW, June 11, 2019.

p. 96   *"'Real isn't how you are made,' said the Skin Horse":* Margery Williams, *The Velveteen Rabbit.* The book was originally published by the George H. Doran Company in London in 1922. It is now an open-source book, available in the public domain.

Chapter 4: The Right to Repair

p. 97   *Crawford's stated approach was "an inquiry into the value of work":* Matthew B. Crawford, *Shop Class as Soulcraft*, p. 3.

p. 98   *Then Kyle came across the "repair manifesto":* Kyle Wiens, recorded and transcribed interview with JW, July 30, 2019.

p. 98   *"Before we came along and started doing this":* Kyle Wiens, recorded and transcribed interview with JW, July 30, 2019.

p. 100   *"Tossing things out instead of fixing them has far-reaching consequences":* Kyle Wiens and Gay Gordon-Byrne, "Why We Must Fight for the Right to Repair Our Electronics."

p. 100   *"When fixing items is actively discouraged by manufacturers":* Kate Lyons, "Can We Fix It? The Repair Cafes Waging War on Throwaway Culture," *The Guardian*, March 15, 2018, www.theguardian.com/world/2018/mar/15/can-we-fix-it-the-repair-cafes-waging-war-on-throwaway-culture?CMP=Share_Android App_Gmail.

p. 101   *In 2012, Massachusetts passed the Motor Vehicle Owners' Right to Repair Act:* Gabe Nelson, "Automakers Agree to 'Right to Repair' Deal," *Automotive*

News, January 25, 2014, www.autonews.com/article/20140125/RETAIL
05/301279936/automakers-agree-to-right-to-repair-deal.

p. 101   *"the spread of copyrighted software…embedded in everyday products…raises
particular concerns":* Introductory letter by Kayrn Temple Claggett, acting
register of copyrights and director, U.S. Copyright Office, in U.S. Copyright
Office, "Software-Enabled Consumer Products: A Report of the Register of
Copyrights," December 15, 2016, www.copyright.gov/policy/software/software
-full-report.pdf.

p. 101   *"complex and opaque language to frustrate reasonable user expectations":* U.S.
Copyright Office, "Software-Enabled Consumer Products: A Report of the
Register of Copyrights," December 15, 2016, p. 67.

p. 101   *"Can a company that sold you something use its patent on that product":*
"Why You Should Care about the Supreme Court Case on Toner Cartridges,"
Consumer Reports, May 3, 2018, www.consumerreports.org/consumerist/why-
you-should-care-about-the-supreme-court-case-on-toner-cartridges.

p. 102   *"The growing complexity of electronic devices means that people need help":*
"The Right to Repair" [editorial], *New York Times*, April 7, 2019.

p. 102   *Austin McConnell, a YouTube blogger in Springfield, Missouri:* Austin McConnell,
"Ink Cartridges Are a Scam," https://www.youtube.com/watch?v=AHX6tHd
QGiQ.

p. 102   *"The stay-at-home-mom community is huge and full of talent":* Jessa Jones,
iPad Rehab website, https://www.ipadrehab.com/index.cfm?Page=About.

p. 104   *"As the industry gets bigger, there's more and more money":* Kyle Wiens, recorded and transcribed telephone interview with JW, July 30, 2019.

p. 104   *Tech companies, by one estimate, are outspending other interests:* Margaret
Sessa-Hawkins, "In Fight over the Right to Repair Equipment, Farmers Are
Outspent 28-to-1," Maplight website, June 6, 2017, https://maplight.org
/?s=right+to+repair.

p. 104   *Gay Gordon-Byrne began her career buying, selling, and leasing large enterprise
computers:* Gay Gordon-Byrne, recorded and transcribed interview with JW,
Albany, New York, May 21, 2019.

p. 104   *"We saw right to repair as a strategic place":* Nathan Proctor, recorded and
transcribed interview with JW, Albany, New York, May 21, 2019.

p. 105   *"The big question is why it hasn't happened already":* Joe Morelle, press conference, recorded and transcribed by JW, May 1, 2018, Statehouse, Albany, New York.

p. 105   *"A company puts out sophisticated equipment and then says":* Elizabeth Warren
on *All In with Chris Hayes*, MSNBC, March 27, 2019.

p. 106   *A follow-up survey of more than one thousand registered voters:* Avery Wendell
and Mark White, "The Public Supports a Right to Repair," Data for Progress,
May 29, 2019, www.dataforprogress.org/blog/2019/5/29/right-to-repair-laws
-are-popular.

p. 106   *"Mrs. Warren has the right idea"*: "It's Your iPhone. Why Can't You Fix It Yourself?", *New York Times*, April 7, 2019, www.nytimes.com/2019/04/06 /opinion/sunday/right-to-repair-elizabeth-warren-antitrust.html?search ResultPosition=1.

p. 106   *"right-to-repair policy is a smart plan"*: Editorial board, "The Right to Repair: Companies Should Not Dictate Where Items Are Fixed," *Pittsburgh Post-Gazette*, April 15, 2019, www.post-gazette.com/opinion/editorials /2019/04/15/Right-to-repair-items-tools-farming-fixed-Elizabeth-Warren /stories/201904150020.

p. 106   *the Federal Trade Commission hosted "Nixing the Fix"*: Federal Trade Commission, "Nixing the Fix: A Workshop on Repair Restrictions."

p. 106   *The statutes discussed included the Magnuson-Moss Warranty Act of 1975*: At the July 16, 2019, FTC workshop, Commissioner Wilson characterized the act in her introductory comments to the hearing: "Magnuson-Moss prohibits companies from linking warranty coverage to the use of particular products and services unless the company provides those products or services for free." She went on to say, "In the last year the FTC sent warning letters to several businesses whose warranties appeared to violate the law. Notably, those businesses responded by adjusting their business practices." See Federal Trade Commission, "Nixing the Fix: A Workshop on Repair Restrictions."

p. 109   *"In the United States, more than 416,000 cellphones"*: The EPA estimate as reported by Charmaine Crutchfield in her article "Smartphone disposal poses security risks, experts warn," *USA Today*, November 10, 2014, www.usa today.com/story/news/nation/2014/11/10/smart-phone-security-risks/18798709/. This estimate was released by the EPA in the midst of the big tech changeover from cell phones to smart phones. The EPA has not revised this figure, but with more than 161 million new smartphones sold in the U.S. in 2019 and consumers upgrading to newer models on average every two years, this estimate has likely gone up.

p. 109   *In 1967, the Maytag Corporation of Newton, Iowa*: Susan Krashinsky, "The Maytag Man through the years," *Toronto Globe & Mail*, June 19, 2017, https://www.theglobeandmail.com/report-on-business/industry-news /marketing/the-maytag-man-through-the-years/article16247650.

p. 110   *"How do you change the material economy of the world?"*: Kyle Wiens, recorded and transcribed interview with JW, July 30, 2019.

p. 111   *"Once people start repairing, they start asking questions"*: Peter Mui, recorded and transcribed interview with JW, July 24, 2019.

p. 111   *New product releases are like catnip to tech hotshots*: For example, on the day the iPhone 10 was released in November 2017, Kyle and a team of iFixit experts flew from their home in San Luis Obispo, California, to Sydney,

Australia, to be first in line, in the earliest time zone, to get their hands on the new iPhone. Jason Koebler, the editor of *Motherboard*, accompanied Kyle and the iFixit team to Australia to cover the process, which he documented in a video titled *How iFixit Became the World's Best iPhone Teardown Team*.

p. 112   *"Getting students to think about the longevity of products":* Marty Rippens, quoted in Madeleine Gregory, "A New Generation of Students Is Teaching Us How to Reduce E-Waste," *Vice Motherboard*, August 23, 2019, www.vice.com /en_us/article/3kxqmv/a-new -generation-of-students-is-teaching-us-how-to-reduce-e-waste.

p. 112   *"I think of ourselves as an operating system to the repair world":* Kyle Wiens, recorded and transcribed interview with JW, July 30, 2019.

p. 113   *Motorola's partnering with iFixit to provide repair kits:* Vaughn Highfield, "Motorola Joins the Right to Repair Movement with DIY Repair Kits," October 24, 2018, www.alphr.com/motorola/1010086/motorola-ifixit-right-to -repair-movement-repair-kit.

p. 113   *In Portland, Oregon, an organization called Portland Repair Finder:* Portland Repair Finder, www.portlandrepairfinder.com. Its series of blog posts by Joel Newman and Molly Simas is excellent.

p. 113   *In New York City,* Sandra Goldmark: Fixup website, fixup.nyc

p. 114   *80 percent of the environmental impacts:* William McDonough and Michael Braungart, *Cradle to Cradle,* p. 91.

p. 115   *"Europe's 'take-make-use-throw' economy is costing consumers money":* Chloé Fayole and Stéphane Arditi, "We Need More Durable and Reparable Products to Build a Circular Economy," *Euractive,* https://www.euractiv.com /section/circular-economy/opinion/we-need-more-durable-and-reparable -products-to-build-a-circular-economy.

p. 115   *the European Commission considerably weakened the proposals:* "EU to Deny Citizens Longer-Lasting and Repairable Popular Consumer Products," November 29, 2018, https://eeb.org/eu-to-deny-citizens-longer-lasting-and -repairable-popular-consumer-products-media-brief.

p. 115   *"We are part of a growing movement":* "The Manchester Declaration," https://therestartproject.org/about/the-manchester-declaration.

p. 115   *The European Commission approved new rules for appliance manufacturers:* Roger Harrabin, "EU Brings in 'Right to Repair' Rules for Appliances," BBC News, October 1, 2019, www.bbc.com/news/business-49884827?n s_linkname=news_central&ns_source=twitter&ns_campaign=bbc_politics &ns_mchannel=social.

p. 115   *"When repair activities stay in the hands of a few firms":* Stephane Arditi, quoted in "EU Brings in 'Right to Repair' Rules for Appliances."

p. 116   *Individual European countries are adopting other kinds of repair-friendly policy:* Richard Orange, "Waste Not Want Not: Sweden to Give Tax Breaks for Repairs," *The Guardian*, September 19, 2016, www.theguardian.com /world/2016/sep/19/waste-not-want-not-sweden-tax-breaks-repairs.

p. 116   *The Open Repair Alliance is establishing an "open standard":* "Sharing Data on Repair, Open Repair Alliance," n.d., https://openrepair.org/open-standard.

Chapter 5: Repairing in Place

p. 119   *a "veritable repair shop" for our bodies and spirits:* Elizabeth Spelman, *Repair: The Impulse to Restore in a Fragile World,* p. 33.

p. 120   *single female homeowners outnumber single male:* Emmie Martin, "Twice as Many Single Women Are Buying Homes as Single Men," *Make It*, CNBC, May 11, 2018, www.cnbc.com/2018/05/11/single-women-account-for-twice-as -many-home-purchases-as-single-men.html.

p. 120   *breadwinning mothers are increasingly the norm:* Sarah Jane Glynn, "Bread-winning Mothers Are Increasingly the U.S. Norm," Center for American Progress, December 19, 2016, www.americanprogress.org/issues/women/reports /2016/12/19/295203/breadwinning-mothers-are-increasingly-the-u-s-norm.

p. 120   *"The towns were empty":* Dar Williams, recorded and transcribed telephone interview with JW, May 8, 2019.

p. 121   *"Well we're heading for a past that you can leave":* Dar Williams, "Bought and Sold," song written by Dar Williams (1997). Lyrics copyright BMG Rights Management. Used by permission.

p. 121   *She recalled a dinner in Charlottesville, Virginia:* Dar Williams, *What I Found in a Thousand Towns,* p. xi.

p. 123   *"Let's look at what Repair Cafe is doing":* Dar Williams, phone interview recorded and transcribed by JW, May 8, 2019.

p. 123   *"Communities thrive when there is a diverse range of equal voices":* Beth Macy, quoted by Dar Williams in *What I Found in a Thousand Towns*, p. 250.

p. 124   *"In this remote valley I felt a yearning for something":* Rob Hopkins, *The Transition Handbook*, p. 13.

p. 124   *"The following month we held our first Repair Cafe":* Therese Brummel, in Don Hall, ed., *10 Stories of Transition in the U.S.*, p. 22.

p. 124   *and the other strategies included in the 2019 book:* Don Hall, ed., *10 Stories of Transition in the U.S.*

p. 125   *"Social infrastructure influences seemingly mundane but actually consequential patterns":* Eric Klinenberg, *Palaces for the People*, p. 14.

p. 125   *a series of discussions initiated by the Sullivan County Human Rights Commission:* "Dialogue2Change," Human Rights Commission, Sullivan County website, n.d., http://sullivanny.us/Departments/Humanrights/Dialogue.

p. 125   *"It was just perfect for what we were trying to do":* Peggy Johansen, recorded and transcribed interview with JW, June 15, 2018.

p. 126   *Ray Kinsey hosts summertime Repair Cafes as part of his teen program:* Bonni McKeown, "Roy Kinsey, Rapper and Librarian," *Austin Weekly News*, April 29, 2019, https://www.austinweeklynews.com/News/Articles/4-29-2019 /Roy-Kinsey,-rapper-and-librarian-/Photos/64358/; and Bonni McKeown, "Local Group Offers Free Repairs for West Siders," *Austin Weekly News*, July 15, 2019, https://www.austinweeklynews.com/News/Articles/7-15-2019/Local -group-offers-free-repairs-for-West-Siders-.

p. 127   *"In library-speak, we catalog items and you can check them out":* Rebekkah Smith Aldrich, recorded and transcribed interview with JW, September 10, 2019.

p. 128   *"I want to create a space for self-directed learning":* Tessa Vierk, recorded and transcribed interview with JW, Chicago, Illinois, July 14, 2019.

p. 128   *"All people should have access to the things they need":* Jim Benton, recorded and transcribed interview with JW, Chicago, Illinois, July 14, 2019.

p. 128   *The "Great Tool Library Shout-Out":* Five posts on the Chicago Tool Library's Instagram page, January 11–16, 2019. Posted by Tessa Vierk.

p. 131   *In the last few years there has been an outcry in some quarters:* Tove Danovich, "Despite a Revamped Focus on Real-Life Skills, 'Home Ec' Classes Fade Away," *The Salt*, NPR.org, June 14, 2018, www.npr.org/sections/thesalt /2018/06/14/618329461/despite-a-revamped-focus-on-real-life-skills-home-ec -classes-fade-away?fbclid=IwAR2ZP5Wvlu_5mUwNtJam5nVnnaPOEQ6iR PJYgSDnBjljC2j2nZl_oAuOGOg. See also Celia Stall-Meadows, "Weaving Sustainability into Family and Consumer Sciences Education"; Michelle Yungblut (chief knowledge officer), *Bringing Back Shop Class,* Electronic Security Association blog, January 9, 2019, http://esaweb.org/News/bringing -back-shop-class.

p. 131   *"the real change will come when the learning of repair skills":* "Lack of Repair Knowledge Hinders Circular Economy," Repair Café Foundation website, posted April 3, 2019.

p. 132   *a curriculum called "Repair in the Classroom" has been developed:* Repair Café International Foundation, *Repair in the Classroom*, available in English, French, German, and Belgian, www.repaircafe.org.

p. 133   *"I fix things for people so they will tell a story":* Michael Whitney, written response to our questionnaire, 2019.

p. 133   *Culture of Repair is "working to transform our culture":* Vita Wells, Culture of Repair, www.cultureofrepair.org.

p. 134   *has a well-established maker-centered professional development program for teachers:* Agency by Design website, http://www.agencybydesign.org.

p. 134   *Shraddha Soparawala, a math teacher, created a class:* Shraddha Soparawala

(Sopar), "The Art of Repair: A Middle School Elective Class," *Agency by Design News,* March 17, 2019, www.abdoakland.org/news/2019/3/17/developing -a-repair-mindset-with-middle-school-students.

p. 134   *"I'm confident that the combination of the momentum behind Maker education":* Vita Wells, email exchange with JW, November 29, 2019.

p. 134   *the* Apollo 13 *spacecraft was fixed 248,655 miles from home:* "Apollo 13," NASA website, July 8, 2009, www.nasa.gov/mission_pages/apollo/missions/apollo13 .html. See also Stephen Cass, "Apollo 13, We Have a Solution," IEEE Spectrum website, April 1, 2005, https://spectrum.ieee.org/tech-history/space-age /apollo-13-we-have-a-solution.

p. 136   *Repair in the Museum:* All quotations in this section are from recorded and transcribed interviews with JW, RISD Museum of Art, Rhode Island School of Design, Providence, Rhode Island, February 16, 2019. Interviewees: Kate Irvin, Brian Goldberg, Anna Rose Keefe, Markus Berger, Lisa Z. Morgan.

p. 139   *The* Clearwater *is a 106-foot-long:* Betsy Garthwaite, "Restoring Clearwater," p. 3.

p. 140   *"sailing in the industrial sewer":* David Schuyler, *Embattled River,* p. 67.

p. 140   *The work was beautifully documented in the film:* Jon Bowermaster, executive producer, *Restoring the Clearwater* [documentary film], soundtrack transcription.

p. 141   *"the essential art of civilization is maintenance":* Pete Seeger, quoted in Betsy Garthwaite, "Restoring Clearwater," p. 4.

p. 141   *In the midst of these changes, a small private property:* Lynn Woods, "Sacred Space: Kingston Groups Hurrying to Buy Site of 250-Year-Old African Burial Ground," *Kingston Times,* February 21, 2018.

p. 142   *In 2019 the property was listed at auction:* Further information about land protection efforts for the Pine Street African Burial Ground came from email exchanges with Julia Farr, executive director, Kingston Land Trust, December 5, 2019.

p. 142   *legal scholar Katherine Franke makes the case for community land trusts:* Katherine Franke, *Repair: Redeeming the Promise of Abolition.* p. 131.

p. 142   *"Right over there on Pine Street is proof":* Micah Blumenthal, recorded and transcribed interview with JW, Kingston, New York, August 22, 2019.

Chapter 6: Repairing Is Caring

p. 144   *"In taking up repair....":* Brian Goldberg, critic at RISD Department of Architecture and project consultant to the "Repair and Design Futures" exhibition. Quote is from *Manual: A Journal About Art and Its Making,* Fall 2018, preface.

p. 144   *In the UK, the Restart project calls their events* parties: https://therestart project.org.

p. 144   *"This occasion and this meeting":* Anthony Man-Tu Lee, *The Japanese Tea Ceremony* (Brighton, UK: Ivy Press Limited, 1999), p. [46/33].

p. 145   *"Benedict's Rule is a foundational expression of the principle of hospitality":* Christine Valters Paintner, "Monks in Our Midst: Christine Valters Paintner on Hospitality," Monasteries of the Heart, https://www.monasteriesofthe heart.org/monks-our-midst/christine-valters-paintner-hospitality.

p. 145   *"Every color of the earth":* This Invitation to Communion was written by Bette Sohm, pastor of New Paltz United Methodist Church from 2010 to 2018. It is unique to this church and is cherished by its congregation (where coauthor John is a member). Pastor Sohm described her intention in writing it: "I have always been a person who has struggled with, and understands, being the outsider, the unwanted. This is the closest I could get to going out and taking each person by the hand, looking in their eyes, and saying, 'yes, even you are welcome.'"

p. 145   *the word's true first meaning is "from the root":* Robert Schnase, *Five Practices of Fruitful Congregations,* p. 21.

p. 146   *"It breathes in more life, brings in new stories":* Noah Hargett, director, ROSS Program, Beacon Housing Authority, recorded and transcribed phone interview with JW, November 14, 2019.

p. 146   *"This is the thing":* Teryl Mickens, email to JW, November 22, 2019.

p. 146   *"This is more than just an opportunity to fix broken things":* Jordan Scruggs, email to JW, November 19, 2018.

p. 147   *"Ever since I was a little girl," she says, "I loved my dad's workshop":* Jo Schilling, recorded and transcribed phone interview with JW, October 16, 2019.

p. 147   *"My Mom's and electrician's daughter":* "Electrician's Daughter," music and lyrics by Ken Lonnquist, copyright 1992. Used by permission. From the CD "Welcome 2 Kenland." kenlonnquist.com (Madison, Wisconsin). "One hell of a good songwriter and singer." — Pete Seeger.

p. 148   *"I can't stand to see them sent to a landfill":* Dave Panico, email to JW, November 5, 2018.

p. 149   *"The first year we did this, all the bikes got stolen":* Bill Shader, recorded and transcribed interview with JW, June 1, 2019.

p. 149   *a feature article titled "Pedal Power" that ran in their monthly lifestyle magazine:* Deana Carpenter, "Recycle a Bicycle," *Suburban Living,* June/July 2011.

p. 151   *"Pramageddon has truly been upon us over the last two weeks":* Repair Cafe Glasgow Instagram posts, and emails with Lauren Crilly, communications, events, and volunteer officer at Repair Cafe Glasgow, November 26–December 4, 2019.

p. 151   *community-made "welcome packs" to "forcibly displaced people arriving in Glasgow":* Ibid.

p. 152   *"Through a youth mentoring program":* Frank Szenher, email exchange with JW, March 11, 2019.

p. 152   *"autistics and other neurodivergents":* In response to our questions about language and autism, Leanne Scalli recommended this very helpful article: "Talking About Autism" written by Erin Bulluss, PhD, and Abby Sesterka. *Psychology Today*, October 1, 2019. www.psychologytoday.com/au/blog /insights-about-autism/201910/talking-about-autism. Arianna Reybitz adds: "I personally have no big hang-ups about the terminology. Everyone with autism is different. Some have more challenges with different things than others and that needs to be acknowledged." Email to JW, December 10, 2019.

p. 152   *Panda Méry is active with Restart:* Paul Méry, "About Spoons and Spudgers: Community Repair for Neurodivergents," *Restarters*, June 18, 2018, https://talk.restarters.net/t/about-spoons-and-spudgers-community-repair -for-neurodivergents/503.

p. 152   *In blog posts and podcasts, he relates:* "Neurodiversity and Mental Health," *Restart Radio*, Resonance 104.4 FM (London), October 11, 2017, https://the restartproject.org/podcast/neurodiversity-mental-health/?_ga=2.266 462158.1925059530.1567105161-506008652.1559663819. See also Jim Sinclair, "Being Autistic Together."

p. 154   *"I've always been really passionate about taking care of the planet":* Leanne Scalli, recorded and transcribed phone interview with JW, August 23, 2019.

p. 156   *One version, organized by Swap Positive, is called "free fashion & frugal fun":* Swap Positive blog, https://swappositive.wordpress.com/.

p. 156   *she wrote her master's thesis about both experiences:* Sarah Guldenbrein, "Convivial Clothing: Engagement with Decommodified Fashion in Portland, Oregon."

p. 157   *"Brands Taking Stands":* The name of a media forum that highlights stories and case studies of private companies taking leadership roles on a range of social and environmental issues. It was created by media company Triple Pundit to advance the business philosophy known as the "triple bottom line" in which equal priority is given to people, planet, and profits.

p. 157   *Philip Kotler and Christian Sarkar made a case for "brand activism":* Philip Kotler and Christian Sarkar, "Finally, Brand Activism!," *Marketing Journal*, January 9, 2017, www.marketingjournal.org/finally-brand-activism-philip -kotler-and-christian-sarkar.

p. 157   *"Brand purpose of this nature is a marathon":* Paul Alexander, "The Case for Brands Taking a Stand," *Wall Street Journal Online*, December 12, 2018, https://deloitte.wsj.com/cmo/2018/12/12/the-case-for-brands-taking-a-stand.

p. 158   *"fosters an unhealthy dissatisfaction with what one has":* Juliet B. Schor, *True Wealth*, p. 41.

p. 158   *"the scale of fast fashion is so massive":* Mark Liu, "For a True War on Waste the Fashion Industry Must Spend More on Research," The Conversation, August 15, 2017, https://theconversation.com/for-a-true-war-on-waste-the -fashion-industry-must-spend-more-on-research-78673.

p. 158   *"We're trying to take responsibility":* Eileen Fisher, quoted in "Eileen Fisher Wants Those Clothes Back When You're Done," *Washington Post*, August 31, 2018, www.washingtonpost.com/business/economy/eileen-fisher-wants -those-clothes-back-when-youre-done/2018/08/31/cd873aea-ac58-11e8-b1da -ff7faa680710_story.html.

p. 158   *It takes 713 gallons of water to make one cotton shirt:* World Resources Institute, quoted in Daisy Alioto, "Eileen Fisher's Westchester Factory Paves the Way to Sustainable Fashion."

p. 158   *it announced a recycling initiative that was a carbon copy of Eileen Fisher's:* H&M (Hennes & Mauritz AB), 2016 annual report.

p. 159   *"We realized that we need to share what we know":* Eileen Fisher, quoted in Daisy Alioto, "Eileen Fisher's Westchester Factory Paves the Way to Sustainable Fashion."

p. 159   *"with the "ambition to become 100% circular and renewable":* Robin Turk, "H&M Group and Ikea join to study recycled materials," *Fashion United*, https://fashionunited.in/news/fashion/h-m-group-and-ikea-join-to-study -recycled-materials/2019102223060.

p. 159   *"We work with different factories, and they may recommend our ideas":* Denise Neil, interview recorded and transcribed by JW, Bard College, October 1, 2019.

p. 159   *"Why is repair such a radical act?":* Rose Marcario, "Repair Is a Radical Act," Patagonia website, November 25, 2015, https://www.patagonia.com/blog/2015 /11/repair-is-a-radical-act.

Chapter 7: How Do I Get One of These in My Town?

p. 165   *Eager to promote her Repair Café more widely:* Elizabeth Huebner, written response to our questionnaire, 2019.

p. 169   *the handy master volunteer list put together by Repair Café Toronto:* "Volunteer Descriptions," Repair Cafe Toronto, http://repaircafetoronto.ca/volunteer -descriptions-pamphlet-2/, reprinted with permission. The "Greeters" section was moved to the beginning of the reprinted text; other minor changes were made for stylistic reasons.

p. 174   *Sign templates with logos are included in the Repair Café manual:* "Start Your Own," Repair Café website, https://repaircafe.org/en/start.

p. 178   *"Each person receives a number that matches their sheet":* Jen Picard, written response to our questionnaire, 2019.

p. 181   *it is "highly advisable to have a local lawyer or legal expert check":* Martine
         Postma, https://repaircafe.org/en/foundation.

p. 189   *GreenFaith, "a coalition for the environment":* Green Faith website,
         https://greenfaith.org/.

p. 189   *The Green Muslims of New Jersey aim to educate people:* Green Muslims of
         New Jersey website, http://greenmuslimsnj.blogspot.com/p/welcome.html.

p. 189   *Quaker Earthcare Witness is a North American network of Friends:*
         www.quakerearthcare.org.

p. 190   *"When it comes to your health, loneliness may be as bad as smoking":* AARP
         magazine, https://www.aarp.org/health/healthy-living/info-2018/loneliness
         -isolation-personal-stories.html.

p. 192   *"It enables people to reuse items instead of tossing them in the landfill":*
         Sustainable Warwick website, http://sustainablewarwick.org.

p. 192   *The Scrap Exchange operates a retail store:* See the Scrap Exchange website,
         https://scrapexchange.org/programs.

p. 193   *teaching youth to repair rather than "reflexively trash and repurchase":* Culture
         of Repair Project website, www.cultureofrepair.org.

p. 193   *"The vision and values of Repair Cafes fit our core values":* Micaela Salatino,
         written response to our questionnaire, 2019.

Bibliography

Books

Aldrich, Rebekkah Smith. *Sustainable Thinking: Ensuring Your Library's Future in an Uncertain World.* Chicago: ALA Editions, 2018.

Caradonna, Jeremy L. *Sustainability: A History.* Oxford: Oxford University Press, 2014.

Crawford, Matthew B. *Shop Class as Soulcraft: An Inquiry into the Value of Work.* New York: Penguin Books, 2009.

Dougherty, Dale, and Ariane Conrad. *Free to Make: How the Maker Movement Is Changing Our Schools, Our Jobs, and Our Minds.* Berkeley, CA: North Atlantic Books, 2016.

Dryzek, John. *The Politics of the Earth: Environmental Discourses.* London: Oxford University Press, 1997.

Edgerton, David. *The Shock of the Old: Technology and Global History since 1900.* New York: Oxford University Press, 2007.

Emerson, Ralph Waldo. *Essays, Poems, Addresses.* Roslyn, NY: Walter J. Black, 1969.

Franke, Katherine. *Repair: Redeeming the Promise of Abolition.* Chicago: Haymarket Books, 2019.

Grun, Bernard. *The Timetables of History.* New York: Simon and Schuster, 1975.

Hall, Don, ed. *10 Stories of Transition in the U.S.: Inspiring Examples of Community Resilience Building.* Sebastopol, CA: Transition US, 2019.

Hall, Edith. *Aristotle's Way.* London: Penguin Press, 2019.

Hardin, Garrett. *Exploring New Ethics for Survival: The Voyage of the Spaceship Beagle.* Baltimore: Penguin Books, 1973. First published 1972 by Viking Press (New York).

Hawken, Paul, ed. *Drawdown: The Most Comprehensive Plan Ever Proposed to Reverse Global Warming.* New York: Penguin Books, 2017.

Hopkins, Rob. *The Transition Handbook: From Oil Dependency to Local Resilience.* Devon, England: Green Books, 2008.

Huxley, Aldous. *Brave New World.* New York: Random House (The Modern Library edition), 1932.

Jackson, Steven J. (contributor). *Media Technologies: Essays on Communication, Materiality and Society.* Cambridge, MA: MIT Press, 2014. See esp. chap. 11, "Rethinking Repair."

Kallen, Stuart A. *The War at Home.* San Diego: Lucent Books, 2000.

Klinenberg, Eric. *Palaces for the People: How Social Infrastructure Can Help Fight Inequality, Polarization, and the Decline of Civic Life.* New York: Crown, 2018.

Koren, Leonard. *Wabi-Sabi for Artists, Designers, Poets & Philosophers.* Berkeley, CA: Stone Bridge Press, 1994.

Kula, Irwin. *Yearnings: Embracing the Sacred Messiness of Life.* New York: Hyperion, 2006.

Lambert, Kelly. *Lifting Depression: A Neuroscientist's Hands-on Approach to Activating Your Brain's Healing Power.* New York: Basic Books, 2010.

Langlands, Alexander. *Craeft: An Inquiry into the Origins and True Meaning of Traditional Crafts.* New York: W.W. Norton, 2018.

Leonard, Annie. *The Story of Stuff: The Impact of Overconsumption on the Planet, Our Communities, and Our Health, and How We Can Make It Better.* New York: Free Press, 2010.

Leopold, Aldo. *A Sand County Almanac.* New York: Oxford University Press, 1949.

Mazzucato, Mariana. *The Value of Everything: Making and Taking in the Global Economy.* New York: Public Affairs, Hachette Book Group, 2018.

McDonough, William, and Michael Braungart. *Cradle to Cradle: Remaking the Way We Make Things.* New York: North Point Press, 2002.

Muir, John. *My First Summer in the Sierra.* Boston: Houghton Mifflin, 1911.

Muir, John. *The Story of My Boyhood and Youth.* Boston: Houghton Mifflin, 1913.

O'Neill, William L. *A Democracy at War: America's Fight at Home and Abroad in World War II.* Cambridge, MA: Harvard University Press, 1998.

Pirsig, Robert M. *Zen and the Art of Motorcycle Maintenance.* New York: William Morrow and Company, 1974.

Porter, Beth. *Reduce, Reuse, Reimagine: Sorting Out the Recycling System.* Lanham, MD: Rowman & Littlefield, 2018.

Postma, Martine. *Weggooien? Mooi niet! (Toss it? I Don't Think So).* Amsterdam: Uitgeverij Genoeg, 2015.

Ray, Paul H., and Sherry Ruth Anderson. *The Cultural Creatives: How 50 Million People Are Changing the World.* New York: Harmony Books, 2000.

Schnase, Robert. *Five Practices of Fruitful Congregations.* Nashville: Abington Press, 2007.

Schor, Juliet B. *True Wealth: How and Why Millions of Americans Are Creating a*

Time-Rich, Ecologically Light, Small Scale, High Satisfaction Economy. New York: Penguin Books, 2011.

Schuyler, David. *Embattled River: The Hudson and Modern American Environmentalism.* Ithaca: Cornell University Press, 2018.

Slade, Giles. *Made to Break: Technology and Obsolescence in America.* Cambridge, MA: Harvard University Press, 2006.

Sloane, Eric. *Diary of an Early American Boy, 1805.* New York: Funk & Wagnalls, 1962.

Sloane, Eric. *Return to Taos: Eric Sloane's Sketchbook of Roadside Americana.* New York: Funk & Wagnalls, 1960.

Spelman, Elizabeth V. *Repair: The Impulse to Restore in a Fragile World.* Boston: Beacon Press, 2002.

Stewart, Alison. *Junk: Digging through America's Love Affair with Stuff.* Chicago: Chicago Review Press, 2016.

Strasser, Susan. *Waste and Want.* New York: Metropolitan Books, Henry Holt and Company, 1999.

Tocqueville, Alexis de. *Democracy in America.* Chicago: The University of Chicago Press, 2000. Translated and edited by Harvey C. Mansfield and Delba Winthrop.

Williams, Dar. *What I Found in a Thousand Towns: A Traveling Musician's Guide to Rebuilding America's Communities — One Coffee Shop, Dog Run, and Open-Mike Night at a Time.* New York: Basic Books, 2017.

Williams, Margery. *The Velveteen Rabbit.* London: George H. Doran, 1922.

Wilson, Katherine. *Tinkering: Australians Reinvent DIY Culture.* Clayton, Australia: Monash University Publishing, 2017.

Yarrow, Andrew L. *Thrift: The History of an American Cultural Movement.* Amherst: University of Massachusetts Press, 2014.

Magazine and Journal Articles

Alioto, Daisy. "Eileen Fisher's Westchester Factory Paves the Way to Sustainable Fashion. *Chronogram*, May 1, 2019. www.chronogram.com/hudsonvalley/eileen-fishers -westchester-factory-paves-the-way-to-sustainable-fashion/Content?oid=8261726 &storyPage=2.

Garthwaite, Betsy. "Restoring Clearwater." *Wooden Boat,* no. 253, Nov.–Dec. 2016.

Guldenbrein, Sarah. "Convivial Clothing: Engagement with Decommodified Fashion in Portland, Oregon." Thesis for MS degree in sociology, Portland State University, June 17, 2019, https://pdxscholar.library.pdx.edu/open_access_etds/5119/.

Pickworth, Amy, ed. "Repair." Special issue, *Manual: A Journal about Art and Its Making,* Issue 11 (Fall 2018). Providence: Rhode Island School of Design.

Sinclair, Jim. "Being Autistic Together." *Disability Studies Quarterly* 30, no. 1 (2010), http://dsq-sds.org/article/view/1075/1248.

South, Stanley. "Archeological Evidence of Pottery Repairing." South Carolina Institute of Archaeology and Anthropology, *The Conference on Historic Site Archaeology Papers 1967*, vol. 2, 1968, 62–71, PDF, https://scholarcommons.sc.edu/cgi/viewcontent .cgi?article=1180&context=sciaa_staffpub.

Stall-Meadows, Celia. "Weaving Sustainability into Family and Consumer Sciences Education." *Journal of Family and Consumer Sciences Education* 28, no. 1 (2010), https://natefacs.org/Pages/v28no1/v28no1Stall-Meadows.pdf.

Wiens, Kyle, and Gay Gordon-Byrne. "Why We Must Fight for the Right to Repair Our Electronics." IEEE Spectrum website. October 24, 2017. https://spectrum.ieee.org /green-tech/conservation/why-we-must-fight-for-the-right-to-repair-our-electronics.

Wilson, Louise. "Fixing the Future: A Study of the Repair Café Culture." Dissertation for BSc degree, Swansea University, 2018.

Film Resource

Bowermaster, Jon, executive producer. *Restoring the Clearwater*. Oceans 8 Films, 2018.

Online Resources

Aldo Leopold Foundation. aldoleopold.org.

AOGHS.org editors. "First American Oil Well." American Oil and Gas Historical Society website, March 24, 2013. aoghs.org/petroleum-pioneers/american-oil-history/.

Botsman, Rachel. "The Currency of the New Economy Is Trust." Filmed September 2012. TED Talk Global, 19:31, www.ted.com/talks/rachel_botsman_the_currency _of_the_new_economy_is_trust/up-next.

Federal Trade Commission. "Nixing the Fix: A Workshop on Repair Restrictions." July 16, 2019. www.ftc.gov/news-events/events-calendar/nixing-fix-workshop-repair -restrictions [description and full video].

IRP. *Re-defining Value: The Manufacturing Revolution. Remanufacturing, Refurbishment, Repair and Direct Reuse in the Circular Economy*. Nabil Nasr, Jennifer Russell, Stefan Bringezu, Stefanie Hellweg, Brian Hilton, Cory Kreiss, and Nadia von Gries. Nairobi, Kenya: International Resource Panel, United Nations Environment Programme, 2018. Available at www.resourcepanel.org/reports/re-defining -value-manufacturing-revolution.

McConnell, Austin. "Ink Cartridges Are a Scam." YouTube. March 15, 2018. www.you tube.com/watch?v=AHX6tHdQGiQ.

Motherboard. "How iFixit Became the World's Best iPhone Teardown Team." YouTube. February 15, 2018. www.youtube.com/watch?v=tx-9LkVIdz0.

"Poor Richard's Almanack." Ben Franklin Historical Society website. www.benjamin -franklin-history.org/poor-richards-almanac.

Portland Repair Finder. www.portlandrepairfinder.com.

UN Documents."Report of the World Commission on Environment and Development: Our Common Future."1987. http://www.un-documents.net/ocf-o2.htm#I.

World Economic Forum, the Ellen MacArthur Foundation, and McKinsey & Company. *Towards the Circular Economy*. Published annually, 2012–2014. vol. 1 (2012), *An Economic and Business Rationale for an Accelerated Transition*; vol. 2 (2013), *Opportunities for the Consumer Goods Sector*; Vol. 3 (2014), *Accelerating the Scale-up across Global Supply Chains;* and *Completing the Picture: How the Circular Economy Tackles Climate Change* (2019). All available at www.ellenmacarthur foundation.org/publications.

Illustration Sources

Illustrations

p. 6 "repair is/can" — Credit: Repair Matters. Founded by four women in Vancouver, Canada, in 2015. Cofounder Shea O'Neil says, "It's never a bad idea to try and fix something." Repairmatters.ca. Used by Permission.

p. 17 "Rethink Waste — 7Rs" — Credit: Ulster County Resource Recovery Agency, Kingston, New York. Image created by Angelina Peone and Melinda France. UCRRA.org. Used by Permission.

p. 65 "Owner vs. Consumer" — Credit: Image created by Genevieve DeGroot for Post-Landfill Action Network. Postlandfill.org. Used by Permission.

p. 69 "Circular Economy — 3 trash cans" — Credit: Image created by Leah Grubb, © 2019 The Final Co. LLC. Finalstraw.com. Used by Permission.

p. 71 "Circular Economy — squiggle" — Credit: Image created by Tom Harper for Rethink Global (UK). Rethinkglobal.info. Used by Permission.

p. 82 "How Well Something Works (After I Decide To Fix It)" — Credit: Image created by Randall Munroe, xkcd comics. Creative Commons license.

p. 99 "iFixit Repair Manifesto" — Credit: Image created for iFixit. Used by Permission.

p. 105 "Never Take Broken for an Answer" — Credit: Image created for iFixit. Used by Permission.

p. 107 "Nixing the Fix" — Credit: A Bureau of Consumer Protection staff artist's representation of Nixing the Fix. Courtesy Federal Trade Commission.

p. 128 "West Bloomington Illinois Tool Library logo" — Courtesy of the West Bloomington Revitalization Project. Used by permission. Thanks to Armando Baez.

p. 129 "Berkeley Public Library logo"— Courtesy of the Berkeley Public Library. Thanks to Aimee Reeder, Communications.

p. 129 "Denver Tool Library logo" — Courtesy of Denver Tool Library. Used by permission. Thanks to Sarah at Denver Tool Library.

p. 129 "HNL Tool Library logo" — Courtesy of the HNL (Honolulu) Tool Library. Used by permission. Thanks to the HNL Tool Library Team.

p. 129 "Station North Tool Library logo" — Courtesy of the Station North Tool Library, Baltimore. Used by permission. Thanks to Lynn McCann.

p. 130 "Chicago Tool Library logo" — Designer: Ryan Duggan. Courtesy of Chicago Tool Library. Used by permission. Thanks to Tessa Vierk.

Photographs

p. 9 "Simon Says" — Pictured: Elisa, Ray, and Bella. Taken at the at the Repair Cafe at Esopus Library, New York. Photo: John Wackman.

p. 15 "At the Repair Cafe electronics work table" — Pictured: Repair coach at work: Dan Casey. Left to right: Grant Brown, Henry Brown, Jeff Luoma, Marcy Cleveland, Nolan Brown. Taken at the Repair Cafe at the New Paltz United Methodist Church, New York. Photo: Diane Casey.

p. 33 "Rob Shaw and family at Repair Cafe digital work table" — Pictured left to right: Robert Shaw Jr., Zachary and Nathaniel Cardenas, and Raven Shaw. Taken at the Warwick Repair Cafe, Warwick Senior Center, New York. Photo: Elizabeth Knight.

p. 38 "Sarah's quilt" — Pictured: Sarah Perl. Taken at the Repair Cafe at the New Paltz United Methodist Church, New York. Photo: John Wackman.

p. 42 "Cyd and Adam" — Pictured: Cyd Charisse Villalba and Adam Factor. Taken at the Repair Cafe at the New Paltz United Methodist Church, New York. Photo: John Wackman. Note: this photo appeared in the *New York Times*, January 20, 2017.

p. 80 "4 Hands" — Taken at the Beacon Repair Cafe at Howland Cultural Center, Beacon, New York. Photo: John Wackman.

p. 90 "Oh Darn It!" — Photo: Vita Wells. Courtesy of the Culture of Repair Project. Cultureofrepair.org. Used by permission. Note: The flyer pictured is for a visible mending workshop given by Sally Walton at the Crown Pub in Hastings, on the south coast of England. Sally teaches wool darning and denim repairs, variations on Japanese sashiko — and wherever people's interests take her. Contact her at sallyswalton@gmail.com.

p. 94 "Erik and son with their sewing machine" — Pictured: Erik and his son with repair coach Ken Fix It. Taken at the Repair Cafe at Esopus Library, New York. Photo: John Wackman. Note: Erik wanted us to know that the sewing machine is his and his wife's — they both use it.

p. 114 "Bob Wilson at work" — Pictured: repair coach Bob Wilson. Taken at the Repair Cafe at the Hastings-on-Hudson Community Center, New York. Photo: John Wackman.

p. 139 "Boy with Dino at the Museum" — Pictured: Dean Ashton Sinkler. Taken at the Long Island Children's Museum, Garden City, New York. Photo: Melissa Iachetta.

p. 151 "Pramageddon" — Pictured: John Dawes and Ann Ledgerwood. Taken at the St. Enoch Centre in Glasgow, Scotland. Photo provided by Repair Cafe Glasgow.

p. 157 "Veronica with her doll Sonia" — Pictured: Veronica Pizzola and repair coach Felicia Casey. Taken at the Repair Cafe at the New Paltz United Methodist Church, New York. Photo: John Wackman. Note from Veronica: "My dad bought Sonia for me around 1951. She had a full head of hair in braids. Sonia is now in our guest room. She is dressed in my daughter Gina's first Christmas dress."

p. 162 "Deb and her granddaughter" — Pictured: Deb Cole and her granddaughter Shyanne McNair, with repair coach Antony Tseng. Taken at the Beacon Repair Cafe at Howland Cultural Center, Beacon, New York. Photo: John Wackman.

p. 182 "Boys watching their toys get repaired" — Pictured: Harvey and Ridley. Taken at the Repair Cafe at the New Paltz United Methodist Church, New York. Photo: John Wackman.

p. 188 "Kaleidoscopic Clock" — Pictured: Amelia, Stacy, Kaitlyn, Emily, repair coaches Frank Szenher and Dave West, Max Easton. Taken at the Repair Cafe at the New Paltz United Methodist Church, New York. Photo: John Wackman. Note: There is more to this clock than meets the eye. The action of the mechanism when it puts on its "show" is quite remarkable. This was truly a collaborative repair. Special thanks to Don Grice for combining two shots so that everyone's eyes are open.

p. 199 "Let There Be Light" — Pictured: repair coach Marisa Villareal. Taken at the Repair Cafe at the New Paltz United Methodist Church, New York. Photo: John Wackman.

p. 226 "Martine Postma" — Pictured: Martine Postma. Photo provided by Repair Café International Foundation.

p. 252 "Kids Take It Apart Table" — Pictured: Eli Harper, Jim Harper, Raymond Chang, and sons Easton and Wallace Chang. Photo: Lisa Tencza.

Special thanks to Jill Padua — Tusten, New York's Repair Cafe organizer — for her technical assistance.

Index

About the Authors

JOHN WACKMAN founded the first Repair Cafe in New York State and now describes his role as that of coordinator, communicator, and cheerleader for Repair Cafes in the Hudson Valley, Catskills, and Capital District of New York, as well as for the repair movement globally. He has participated in Repair Cafes in the Netherlands and co-presented with Martine Postma at the Drawdown Learn Conference at Omega Institute in Rhinebeck, New York. He has presented on community repair at the New York and New Jersey Library Associations' annual conferences and led a statewide webinar for the New York State Department of Environmental Conservation. He serves on the board of Sustainable Hudson Valley and is a commissioner for the City of Kingston Climate Smart Commission. John is a recipient of an Environmental Protection Agency Environmental Champion Award.

For nearly three decades, John wrote and produced programming for public television and national cable networks to encourage strength and creativity within communities. With Lightworks Producing Group in New York, he worked on many specials and series, and executive produced the civil rights documentaries *You Don't Have to Ride Jim Crow!* and *Here Am I, Send Me: The Journey of Jonathan Daniels.* For PBS, he created, with host Mary Ann Esposito, the cooking series *Ciao*

Italia, still in production and the longest-running cooking series on television.

ELIZABETH KNIGHT is the author of four books that have been featured in *New York* magazine, *USA Today*, the *Washington Times*, the *Chicago Sun-Times*, and *Woman's Day*, among other publications. A tea and entertaining expert and the former tea sommelier for the St. Regis Hotel, she was a frequent guest on over fifty nationwide radio and television programs, including WNBC's *Today in New York* and the Travel Channel. For more than twenty years, she managed marketing communications, trade advertising, sales promotion and special events, and visual merchandising for retail stores, wholesale showrooms, and trade shows. Clients included Royal Doulton china, American Express, and Bloomingdale's, among others.

More recently, she has become a sustainability activist and community organizer. In 2016, she started Orange County, New York's first Repair Cafe, which, four years on, serves people from as many as nineteen towns in two states. She and her team have received certificates of appreciation from county, town, and village officials. In celebration of Earth Day, Elizabeth founded an annual Too Good to Toss Community Swap, which is visited by hundreds of people who come to shop for free. In October 2018, she organized a pop-up Repair Cafe at the international ReuseConex convention in Cincinnati, Ohio, where Martine Postma, founder of Repair Café International, was the keynote speaker.